Macromedia
Fireworks MX 2004
ZERO TO HERO

Joyce J. Evans
Charles E. Brown

friendsof

DESIGNER TO DESIGNER™

an Apress® company

MACROMEDIA FIREWORKS MX 2004: ZERO TO HERO

Credits

At friends of ED, our mission is to unleash your digital creativity, providing technical know-how and inspiration in equal measure.

With our Zero to Hero series we've gone one better—we'll take you further, faster.

Zero to Hero is more than just a catchy slogan and an endless opportunity for gimmicks, puns, and graphical representations of phone booths, tights, and capes. It's a style of learning designed by friends of ED to reach beyond dry technical explanations and dusty old authors who wouldn't know good design if it slapped them round the face with a wet fish.

You can either first learn everything you need about Macromedia Fireworks or dive straight into the inspirational "Hero" chapters and refer back if you get stuck. And when you're done, you'll be ready to wear your underwear outside of your pants, metaphorically speaking of course.

We'll not only unlock the toolset for you, we'll also feed your imaginations—that's a promise.

So what are you waiting for?

Chapter Zero

Web Graphics and the Fireworks Interface   1

Table of Contents

Chapter Three

Object Properties 79

Chapter Four

Object Behavior: Interactivity 99

Table of Contents

Table of Contents

Chapter Eleven

Retouching and Enhancing Color 259

Table of Contents

Joyce J. Evans is a training veteran with over 10 years experience in educational teaching, tutorial development, and web design. She has been asked to speak at conferences such as Macromedia MAX 2003 and TODCON, and has authored books including *Macromedia Studio MX Bible*, *Dreamweaver MX Complete Course*, *Web Design Complete Course*, *Fireworks MX Zero to Hero*, and *Dreamweaver in 10 Steps or Less*.

Joyce is a Team Macromedia Volunteer and her work is also featured in the Macromedia Design/Developer center, the MX Developers Journal magazine, and the Macromedia Edge newsletter. Her personal web site is www.JoyceJEvans.com and she also runs Idea Design (www.je-ideadesign.com) with clients such as Century 21, a prominent college in Florida. She is also a subcontractor for a local service provider along with actively teaching new students on how to use the Macromedia Studio products.

Joyce lives with her husband, teenage son, dog, and cat in the Tampa Bay area in Florida. When Joyce isn't working, she can be found enjoying the many fruit trees and palms in her yard or at the beach.

Charles E. Brown is one of the most noted authors and teachers in the computer industry today. His first two books, *Beginner Dreamweaver MX* and *Fireworks MX Zero to Hero*, have received critical acclaim and are consistent bestsellers. In early 2004, Dr. Brown will be releasing books on VBA for Microsoft Access, and the new Microsoft FrontPage environment. He is also a Fireworks MX contributor for the MX Developer's Journal.

In addition to his busy writing schedule, he conducts frequent seminars for the PC Learning Center (www.pclearningcenter.com). His topics include Java Programming, using the Macromedia Studio MX environment, and the Microsoft Office environment. In 2004, he will also be involved in developing e-learning courses.

Charles is also a noted classical organist, pianist, and guitarist, and studied with such notables as Vladimir Horowitz, Virgil Fox, and Igor Stravinsky. It was because of his association with Stravinsky that he got to meet, and develop a friendship with, famed artist Pablo Picasso.

Charles can be contacted through his website at www.charlesebrown.net.

Web Graphics and the Fireworks Interface

In this chapter

Many computer books on the shelves perceive their readers as "dummies" or "idiots." But we know you're no fool. Sure, your computer might reduce you to feeling like a zero from time to time, but that's another matter. We're here to turn you into a Fireworks hero. By the time you finish this book, you'll be able to do just about anything you want with your web graphics.

In this chapter, we look at the stuff you need to know about Fireworks MX 2004 in order to make sense of this book. A couple of concepts might be a bit unfamiliar, but they'll soon be behind you so that you can skip ahead and jump in anywhere throughout the book.

We'll look at the following:

★ Understanding image file formats used on the web

   ★ Working with GIF, JPEG, and PNG file formats

   ★ Working with vector and bitmap image formats

★ Working in the Fireworks MX 2004 interface

   ★ Configuring the interface

   ★ Creating a new document

   ★ Understanding the context-sensitive Property inspector

   ★ Working with the Tools panel

   ★ Manipulating basic objects

How to use this book

This book is divided into three distinct sections to help get you working right away:

★ **Chapter Zero:** In this chapter, we cover all the basic concepts and tools that you need to get working with Fireworks.

★ **Chapters One through Eleven:** In these chapters, we've grouped everything you'll actually want to do in Fireworks. Although the chapters are arranged in order of increasing difficulty, they're also broken down into steps and examples that you can apply to your own work, dipping in wherever you choose.

★ **Hero Chapters:** It's all very well that you're able to use the software after you finish Chapters One through Eleven, but we've added some chapters to really get you thinking and working like the hero you undoubtedly are.

All the way through the book, you'll find every step clearly illustrated so that you can see exactly what's going on.

Styles

To make things a little clearer, we use a few special typefaces in the book:

★ If we have any specific files to mention, we'll write them like this: `thisphoto.png`.

★ Menu commands are written out using little menu arrows, for example: Modify ➤ Canvas ➤ Canvas Color….

★ When an important point is mentioned for the first time, we'll make it **obvious**.

★ Finally, really important points and special tips will appear in boxes like the one on the right.

Yes, this one!

Mac or PC?

Fireworks MX 2004 works on both Apple Mac OS X and Microsoft Windows–based machines. Very little distinguishes the two versions from each other, however keyboard shortcuts do differ slightly. So, if you have to press a different key on a different operating system, we'll let you know by writing both buttons on either side of a /, like this:

★ *CTRL/CMD+O* means that you should press *CTRL* and *O* at the same time on a PC, or *CMD* and *O* at the same time on a Mac.

Always hold the *SHIFT* or *CTRL/CMD* keys and tap the other specified letter of number key.

Download files

Although all the examples in the book are designed so that you can apply the techniques and effects to your own images, a chapter-by-chapter set of source files is available for download from www.friendsofed.com. You can use these files to work along with the images you see in the book.

Support

We at friends of ED pride ourselves on our book support. Although we're confident that every-thing within these pages is easy to follow and error-free, don't hesitate to get in touch with us on the message boards at www.friendsofed.com/forums.

Getting started

Fireworks MX 2004 is all about creating fantastic web graphics. Throughout this book, you'll learn how to get the most out of the program, and in no time at all you'll be producing clear and creative designs. But before we have you jumping in at the deep end, let's look at some of the basic concepts behind web graphics, and then fully explore the tools available in Fireworks.

We'll start by learning about the most common graphic file formats used on the web, before moving on to explore the Fireworks MX 2004 interface. Taking the time to understand the core concepts and interface elements at the heart of Fireworks will help you learn more effectively as you progress through the book.

Using images on the web

When we're talking about designing websites, the first thing that comes to our minds is graph-ics. The Internet is a highly visual medium with as much emphasis placed on pictures as words, so it's important that you understand the main image formats used on the web and consider how well Fireworks works with them. Hopefully, by the end of this chapter, you'll be able to make informed decisions on what graphic format is best suited for a specific purpose.

Web graphics can be split into two broad categories: **vectors** and **bitmaps**. The image infor-mation used to display vector graphics is held in mathematical equations, whereas bitmap images hold this data in grids filled with color dots, known as **pixels** (short for picture ele-ments). Each image type has its own advantages and disadvantages.

Vector images

Vector images are rendered (fancy word for created) through mathematical instructions about lines, shapes, and color fills. If you ever created a picture by connecting the numbered dots in a book as a child, you already have a rough idea of how this works. The mathematical equations create a series of points connected together by lines and curves. The points are called **vectors** and the connecting lines between them are called **paths**.

A great advantage of vector graphics is that no matter how much you enlarge or reduce their size, their image quality stays the same. This is because the mathematical equations that deter-mine the image's appearance are recalculated when the image is changed in order to adjust the image accordingly. So, it doesn't matter how far you zoom—the image's properties remain the same and you can't see any reduction in image quality (this is not the case for bitmaps, as you'll see in a moment).

Take the following example, for instance. On the left is the original image, in the center is an enlargement in a vector format, and at the right is an enlargement in a bitmap format (notice that the image quality has deteriorated):

Original image   Enlargement of vector image   Enlargement of bitmap image

Another advantage of vector graphics is that they're generally much smaller in file size than bitmaps because the information is stored in mathematical formulas rather than thousands of pixels. So why then are all graphic images not vectors? The answer is quite simple: complex images with large areas of color gradations can't be easily handled—imagine trying to break a photograph down into mathematical formulas. Currently, vectors are confined to relatively simple images and, because of this limitation, bitmap images are used widely.

Bitmap images

Bitmap images are defined using pixels (or dots of color) that make up the image, a bit like a mosaic. When you zoom into a bitmap, the pixel size increases and the image breaks up into blocks of color, producing a rough and blotchy looking (pixilated) image, or stepped, jagged edges. When you view such an image at a normal size, all the pixels blend together and you don't see them. However, imagine examining them under a magnifying glass—you start to see the individual dots and the blend is lost.

Although they don't maintain quality when enlarged, bitmaps are ideal for reproducing photo-realistic images. Because they are made up of hundreds of pixels, they can contain more subtle, realistic gradations of tone and color.

Bitmap images tend to have large file sizes and, in their pure state, were unpractical in the early days of the Internet. Back in the days of the 26k modem connections, images took such a long time to download that the process was impractical. As a result, different methods of **compression** were developed that didn't cause significant loss in image quality yet reduced the file size to enable faster download times.

GIF (Graphic Interchange Format)

The GIF file format was developed by CompuServe and uses **lossless** compression, a type of image compression that stores color and shape information exactly as it is, without losing any image information. The benefit of using lossless compression is that the image will store and display without any degradation.

GIF is the ideal format for images composed primarily of lines and solid blocks of color because the format is limited to a maximum of 256 colors. This is fine if the image doesn't contain any extreme gradations of color like you may find in a photograph. Reducing the millions of colors in a rich photograph down to a maximum of 256 would seriously affect the image quality.

In the following illustration, the left image is the original photo and the picture on the right is a GIF with 256 colors. Notice the blotchiness of the black fur, the loss of the original eye color, and the jagged quality of the clouds in the sky.

original   GIF format

Remember, a GIF image is limited to a 256-color palette. However, if the image contains a color that isn't part of this palette, a process called **dithering** is used. This is where color pixels are mixed to create the illusion of a color that isn't part of the palette. GIFs simply can't re-create the kind of subtlety present in the original image. If you want to display rich, detailed photographs on the web, JPEGs are the format to use (we'll look at these in a moment).

GIFs also provide useful transparency and animation features (transparency is covered later in this chapter and Chapter Six is entirely dedicated to animation).

JPEG (Joint Photographic Experts Group)

JPEG (pronounced "*jay-peg*") is another compression format. Although JPEGs can't support transparency or animation, they do use a 16 million color palette. This massive amount of available colors makes them the best choice for photographs and other images with continuous tone or color gradations.

Unlike GIFs, JPEGs use **lossy** compression to help manage file size. Lossy compression means that some information from the original image is sacrificed to reduce the file size. A drawback of this, however, is that the attempt to "smooth out" colors often results in blotchiness. Another disadvantage is that every time you edit and save a JPEG, you incur an additional amount of data loss, which degrades your image. If at all possible, never JPEG a JPEG—edit the source image and re-export it (exporting is covered in Chapter Five).

For photographs, the color differences and removal of data are hardly noticeable; there's so much information to start with that losing a small amount doesn't really matter. However, you'll see noticeable changes when you're working with text and line art images, as these don't start with such a large amount of information. Also, if you see any degradation at all, it's usually around hard edges. The best format to use for these kinds of images is the GIF with its lossless compression, which allows color blocks to be saved smooth and unchanged.

Frequently though, web graphics contain both photographic images and text. Fortunately, you can use a selective JPEG, and apply different levels of compression to different areas of the same image.

In Chapter Five, you'll see how Fireworks can optimize JPEG files to achieve the lowest possible file size while maintaining the highest possible quality.

PNG (Portable Network Graphics)

PNG is an extensible file format for the lossless, portable, and well-compressed storage of bitmap images. It's a relatively new format that provides a patent-free replacement for GIF and JPEG formats. There are two levels of PNG:

★ **PNG8** supports the 8-bit (256) color palette and compresses images in a similar way to the GIF format, compressing blocks of solid color while preserving hard edges and maintaining a small file size. This makes it well suited to line art images, text, and logos.

★ **PNG24** supports the 24-bit (16 million) color palette. Like the JPEG format, PNG24 is well suited to images that contain complex gradations of color but, like a GIF, it also preserves sharp detail and hard edges. However, because it is lossless, the file size can be larger than a JPEG. PNG24 can be used for line and text art; it supports indexed-color, grayscale, and true-color images; and it also has an optional alpha channel for transparency.

As you can see, PNG can handle everything that GIF and JPEG can handle but with a few extra benefits. Unlike GIFs, PNG can handle up to 256 levels of transparency. This opens a whole new world of possibilities. So, if PNG is so good, why not use it for everything? Modern browsers are starting to provide *some* PNG support but it's still not 100 percent and PNG files haven't been widely adopted.

Also, it's important to note that the PNG file format used for web graphics is not the same as the Fireworks PNG, the native file format in Fireworks. This is a PNG32 format that, as of now, is virtually unsupported by browsers.

> *You can find out more about the varying levels of PNG support in different browsers at* www.libpng.org/pub/png/pngstatus.html#browsers.

Fireworks PNG format

Fireworks uses its own version of PNG as its native file format, which isn't meant to be used anywhere other than within Fireworks (except for other Macromedia products like Flash) because it stores **meta information** (internal programming necessary for the operation of the document) particular to Fireworks. When you finish editing an image, you need to optimize and export the file to a web-friendly format (optimizing and exporting images is covered in detail in Chapter Five).

You can **import** and **export** documents in a variety of graphic file formats including GIF, JPEG, PNG, TIFF, PICT, SWF, BMP, Lotus Domino Designer, Adobe Illustrator, and WBMP (for portable devices); you can also use Adobe Photoshop documents.

However, when you **save** a file in Fireworks MX 2004, unless you specify differently, it will always be in **PNG** format (with a .png extension) regardless of whether the file was originally in another graphic format. Fireworks MX 2004 now allows you to also save the file back to its original format without exporting it again.

A final point to note about PNGs is that you can import them directly into Flash, completely intact, and with all the transparency and vector characteristics intact.

> *You can of course export the image to your desired format, such as GIF or JPEG for use on the web, but it's best to always save your work file version (PNG) in case you need to work with the original image again.*

That completes a brief introduction to the various web graphic file formats. Here's a table that you may find useful as a reference when selecting your desired file formats in the future.

Graphic file type	Advantages	Disadvantages
GIF	Supports animation Widespread browser support Transparency Sharp vector images	Uses 256-color palette, so is unreliable for photographic images
JPEG	Maintains richness and color gradation in photographs and movie stills	Doesn't maintain quality when working with line art, text, or where sharp color contrast is needed
PNG	Good for text, line art, and general web graphics Patent-free and a good replacement for anything that is a non-animated GIF	Less reliable for displaying photographs Historical lack of browser support

Fireworks MX 2004 interface

Enough with the theory! Let's get started on the road to becoming a hero by starting the program and opening a new blank document to work on.

Creating a new document

When you first open Fireworks, you're greeted with an opening screen from which you can either start a new document or open one you have recently worked on. This screen, with a few minor variations, is seen in all the Macromedia MX 2004 programs.

This screen also shows an option for obtaining **Extensions**, which allows you to add functionality to the program (discussed in detail in Chapter Eleven). You can also check out the new features and/or use the Learning Fireworks MX 2004 tutorial. If you don't want to see this opening screen in the future, check the Don't show again option in the lower-left corner.

You can start a new document in one of three ways:

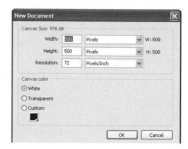

★ Select Create New Fireworks File from the opening screen.

★ Select File ➤ New from the main menu bar located along the top of the interface.

★ Use the keyboard shortcut CTRL/CMD+N.

Whichever method you choose, the New Document dialog box appears, where you define the size of the new image (known as the **canvas**) and the background color.

Clicking OK with the settings shown here creates a 500×500-pixel canvas with a white background color, set to a resolution of 72 **pixels per inch** (or **ppi**).

So what does a resolution of 72 pixels per inch actually mean? As discussed earlier, a pixel is one of the many colored tiny squares that make up a digital image. Imagine you had an image of a postage stamp that's 1 inch wide and 1 inch high. At 72 ppi, your stamp would be 72 pixels wide and 72 pixels high, containing a total of 5,184 pixels (72×72). The higher the amount of pixels an image contains, the higher the resolution. So, if your 1-inch stamp contained 300 ppi, it would have a much higher resolution than your 72 ppi stamp did. Because Fireworks is mainly used for producing web graphics, the default resolution is 72 ppi—computer monitors typically have a resolution of 72 ppi (or 96 ppi maximum in some cases).

You'll notice that the Width, Height, and Resolution attributes are each accompanied by a drop-down menu where you can change the units of measurements to inches, centimeters, or pixels. Likewise, you can change the resolution from pixels per inch to pixels per cen-

> *Make sure you use higher resolutions when printing. Typically, to print a high quality photograph, you need to use 300 ppi or higher. Also, when resolution for print is being discussed, ppi is sometimes referred to as **dpi** (dots per inch).*

timeter. When you're creating images for the web, it's better to specify the dimensions of your document in pixels in case you want to enter the values by hand into HTML code.

You can also either create a transparent background for your canvas or specify your own canvas color. If you plan to export the image as a GIF and are going to use it as an overlay above other images, you'll want to change the background to Transparent. However, if you need to select a background color from another source, you should use Fireworks (and in all the MX 2004 products) great **Color Chooser** feature.

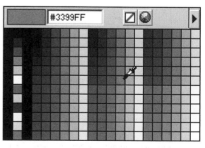

Select Custom in the New Document dialog box and click in the color box. The color palette opens up.

The **Eyedropper** tool replaces the mouse cursor. It uses a technique called **sampling** where you place the eyedropper over any other color source, not just the color palette here, and it'll "capture" that color and display the hexadecimal code for it. If you program or need very precise color matches, this takes a lot of the guesswork out of the process.

> *Web graphics use a color system called* **RGB** *where all colors are a mixture of red, green, and blue, and are formed by varying the intensity of each of these three colors. The 6-character code represents 3 pairs of numbers with each set representing red, green, and blue, respectively. In the box at the top of the color palette, the first 33 represents the amount of red, 99 represents the amount of green, and FF represents the amount of blue. In the hexadecimal system 16 numbers are used. 0–9 are the first 10 numbers, while the letters A–F represent the next 6 numbers.*

For now, continue with the default settings and click OK to start your blank document. You're now in the Fireworks interface.

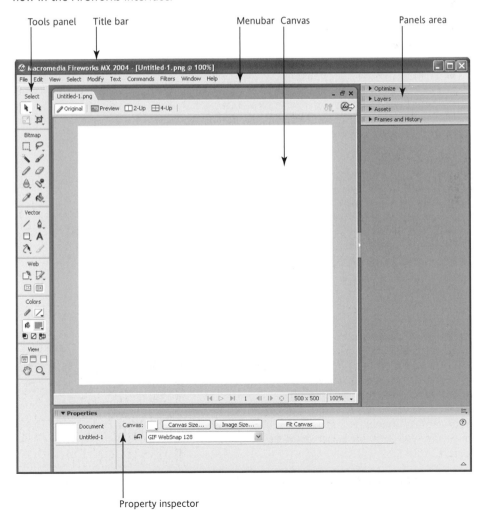

Tools panel   Title bar   Menubar Canvas   Panels area

Property inspector

Title bar

In addition to the obvious fact that you're working in Fireworks MX 2004, the title bar tells you the name of the image you're working with, the component of that image currently selected, and the zoom factor. In addition, as you work, you'll notice that an asterisk appears at the end of the title bar's text; this tells you that the image has been modified since you last saved it.

Panels

Panels are a way of grouping common tools together in order to make them easier to find and use. Some related panels are then grouped further into **Panel groups**, such as the **Assets** panel. The Styles, URL, Library, and Shapes panels are all grouped together here.

You can configure panels anyway you like in order to help make your job easier. Let's see how to adjust them to accommodate your own style of work.

Configuring the interface

You should see the panels located along the right side of the interface. To open or close them, simply click the expander arrow or panel name at the top left of each panel. When you close the panels, they stack very neatly on top of each other.

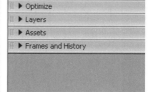

You can actually do this to all panels, except for the Tools panel on the left side of the screen.

If you take a closer look, you'll see some small dots to the left of the panel name. These are **grippers** (or drag handles). If you move your mouse over a gripper, your cursor changes to a four-headed arrow. You can drag the panels around the interface, placing them anywhere you wish.

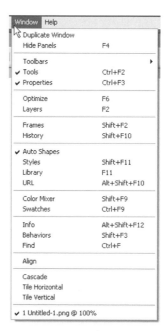

If you remove the panel from its home on the right side of the screen and then move it back, you'll notice that when you return it a blue line appears. This indicates where the panel will snap back to if you release the mouse button. Once you release the panel and let it snap back into place, the panel becomes **docked**. If it's dropped somewhere outside of its home, the panel is described as **floating**. It's usually easier to dock a panel by dropping it into the gray area of the Panels section.

If you're uncertain as to where a panel is located, just select Window in the menu bar located along the top. All the individual panels and their respective keyboard shortcuts are listed here.

Now look at the main toolbar at the top of the interface. It contains several useful options that will no doubt be familiar to you from other applications you've used.

Choose Window ➤ Toolbars ➤ Main, and you'll notice a toolbar appear below the main menu options. It contains familiar commands such as Open, Save, Print, Cut, Copy, and Paste.

> You can choose to hide all the panels within the Fireworks interface by pressing the TAB key or F4.

Keyboard shortcuts

In the same way that you can press the New button in the main toolbar instead of choosing the File ➤ New menu option, you can also use keyboard shortcuts to speed up your productivity. The keyboard shortcuts are fully customizable and you can view and edit them by choosing the Edit ➤ Keyboard Shortcuts… menu option. This opens the Keyboard Shortcuts dialog box, where you simply select the key you'd prefer to use as the shortcut and click OK.

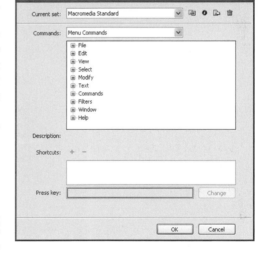

The context-sensitive Property inspector

The **Property inspector** is so important that it has its own location along the bottom of the interface. You use it to manipulate all of your project's content from one central area, and you'll be using it extensively throughout this book. By default, it's located at the bottom of the Fireworks interface. If you can't see it, you can open it by choosing Window ➤ Properties (*CTRL/CMD+F3*).

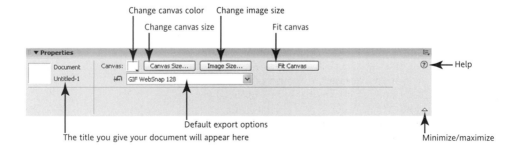

The Property inspector is populated with the properties of whatever Fireworks element you currently have selected. If you select a tool, the Property inspector shows this to you and lets you alter its properties. If you select a graphic, you get a set of properties belonging to that graphic, and so on. This is why the Property inspector is described as **context sensitive**.

Because you don't have any content on the canvas yet, the Property inspector simply shows the global properties of the document. Let's see how you can alter these properties to change the name, size, and color of your canvas (there's no point in getting involved with the default export options until there is something to export, so we'll save these for Chapter Five).

Renaming a document

To change the name of an unsaved document, you actually have to save it first. Choose File ➤ Save (*CTRL/CMD+S*), or press the Save button on the main toolbar. Because this is the first time you're saving this document, the Save As dialog box appears.

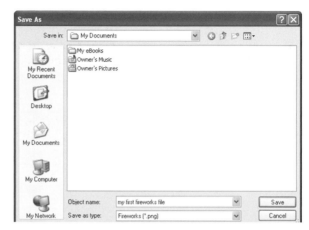

Choose a location to save your file to, enter a file name, and click Save.

The new file name then appears in the Property inspector and on the tab located at the upper-left corner of the document.

Changing the size of a document

If you look at the Property inspector, you'll see that you can also use its buttons to change either the canvas or image size. Click the Image Size button to open the Image Size dialog box:

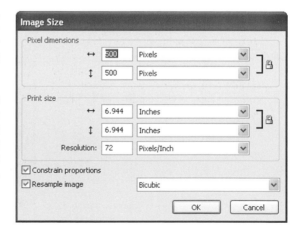

★ Pixel dimensions: These options let you choose whether to view your document's measurements in pixels or percent (meaning you can resize your document in terms of a percentage of its original size).

★ Print size: These width and height options allow you to switch from centimeters, inches, or percent, and you can change your resolution between pixels per inch to pixels per centimeter. These two sets of measurements are basically just different ways of accomplishing the same thing. Whatever resizing you choose to do here affects your entire image.

★ Resample image: This process adds and deletes pixels as you resize the image. However, if you uncheck it, it also turns off the Pixel dimensions feature. If you resized your image with Resample image checked, the pixels would be spread further apart and the resolution would decrease. By using this option, the resolution remains the same.

★ Constrain proportions: Whenever you resize your image, you can choose whether or not the horizontal and vertical dimensions remain in proportion to each other.

To see an example of how to change the canvas, open anchor.png from the download files for this chapter. It's a plain blue canvas with two images on it.

Now click the Canvas Size button in the Property inspector. You change the size of the canvas by entering new values in the width and height fields at the top of the dialog box, but *where on the canvas* are you adding and deleting pixels? Well, luckily, you can specify this yourself by pressing one of the Anchor buttons. The center button, for example, adds pixels evenly to all sides of the canvas.

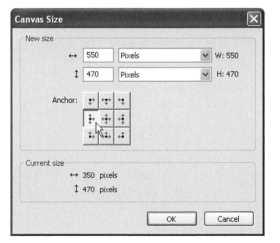

Here though, I've forced Fireworks to add the new pixels to the right hand edge of the canvas by selecting the center-left Anchor button.

If you make your canvas too small, it'll crop your images. However, you may encounter situations where you want to trim the canvas to make your images fit the canvas exactly. To do this, select Modify ➤ Canvas ➤ Trim Canvas. Your canvas is then nicely resized to the content present.

Changing the canvas color

Your document's canvas color is something you ought to consider when planning your piece of work, particularly if you want it to match the color of a web page. You can change it simply by clicking the Canvas color box in the Property inspector (visible only if nothing is selected) and choosing a color from the pop-up color picker. You can also use the Eyedropper tool to perfectly match your colors.

You have a number of different options you can use when selecting colors for graphics. These are discussed in detail in Chapter Three.

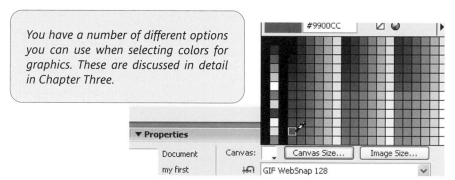

The Tools panel

The Tools panel is located along the left side of the interface by default. This is where most of the drawing tools are located. Notice that it's subdivided into six sections: Select, Bitmap, Vector, Web, Colors, and View. You'll learn what each of these sections are used for as you progress through the book.

Exporting your first web graphic

Let's say you were just hired to design a basic web page to advertise a devilishly handsome, young (kind of) classical guitarist.

1. Open guitarist1.png from the download files.

2. If the image is a little large, you can zoom out by pressing *CTRL/CMD+−* (that's the minus key, and you can zoom back in using *CTRL/CMD++*). A zoom factor of between 30 and 40 percent should work fine. Notice that the factor is also shown in the title bar.

Notice that there's a lot of wasted white space around the picture; you'll want to get rid of it. You can select the portion of the image you want to delete using the Crop tool.

3. Hold your mouse button down over the Crop tool icon and a submenu opens. Just drag your mouse over the Crop tool and release it. (Alternatively, you can press the shortcut key C, which toggles between the two tools in the submenu.)

Your mouse pointer should now change to the Crop tool icon.

4. Holding the mouse button down, draw a box around the area of the image you want to keep. In this case, draw it within some of the grey area because you're going to discard that background in a bit anyway.

5. Double click inside the bounding box to confirm the crop. Firework keeps whatever was inside the box and deletes the rest of the image you no longer need.

   Now you're ready to do some real magic. You're going to eliminate the grey background from this photo.

6. Select the Magic Wand tool from the Tools panel. In the Property inspector, set Tolerance to 32, select Feather from the Edge drop-down menu, and set the amount of Feather to 2.

7. Click anywhere on the gray background of the image. A **selection** is made around the whole background, indicated by the "marching ants." Press the *DELETE* key to remove the background.

8. Choose Select ➤ Deselect to remove the selection from the image.

   Now it's time to consider the web page that you want to put this web graphic on.

9. Start by clicking the Preview button located on the top left of the canvas so that you can go into Preview view.

10. Open the Optimize panel by selecting it in the Panels area (or use Window ➤ Optimize or press *F6*). As mentioned earlier, only GIF and PNG graphic formats support transparency (specifically, PNG 8-bit). Because PNG is not widely used, let's use GIF. Use the Optimize panel to change the file type to GIF. When you do, the panel shows the transparency tools.

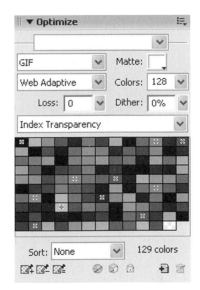

The panel shows the colors that are being used (currently set to 128). The squares marked with a small diamond are the colors that are considered web safe. This means that most web browsers see them the same way. (Color palettes are discussed in detail in Chapter Three.)

11. Because you want to eliminate the background colors that aren't present in the image you'll use Index Transparency. Select it from the Transparency drop-down menu.

12. At this point, it's important to decide the background color of the web page on which this graphic will be placed. You should set the Matte color box, at the top right of the Optimize panel, to be the same color as this web page. (If you don't already have a web page in mind to put it on, just make a note of this color, as you'll need it for the next step.)

However, there's a problem. Parts of the graphic also appear to now be transparent as well as the background. Not to worry though—at the bottom of the Optimize panel you'll find three tools to assist you in creating and modifying the transparency. The + and − tools are obvious from their tooltips, and the third tool allows only one color to be selected as the transparency, discarding any other colors.

Select transparent color
Remove color from transparency
Add color to transparency

13. Select the Remove color from transparency tool and then click the area of the graphic that you *don't* want to be transparent. Here, this is the small area of pixels on the forehead.

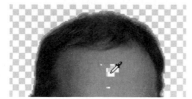 

Your image graphic should now be sharp with the web page background color (the color you selected in the Matte color box earlier) visible around the edge of the graphic and the perimeter of the image. This ensures that the graphic will blend in smoothly with the web page background color without any stray pixels of gray around the border (sometimes referred to as a "halo" effect).

> *If you still have areas of transparent pixels in your graphic, you need to reselect the Remove color from transparency tool and go back to select these areas of stray transparent pixels.*

Before you export the image, let's do some resizing.

14. Choose Modify ➤ Canvas ➤ Image Size. Reduce the width to 250 pixels and click OK.

You're now ready to **export** your image as a GIF file.

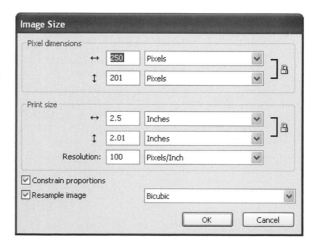

15. Choose File ➤ Export Preview….

You can do the same things here that you can in the Preview view. Many graphic artists like to use this for a final check before exporting (and you'll be using it in depth later in the book).

16. If everything looks in order, click the Export... button. Call your image `guitarist1export` and Fireworks will add the `.gif` extension.

17. Close the image. You'll be prompted to save the image. Wait!!! Didn't you just save it? Remember, you exported it as a GIF file; however, Fireworks' working format is PNG so it's asking you to save the working copy here. It's a good idea to do this in case you need to do additional editing later on.

18. For additional practice, open the `guitarist2.png` image from the download files. As you did in the last exercise, crop it, resize it, and export it as a GIF file called `guitarist2export`. Don't worry about making this image transparent. When you've finished, save the working PNG file.

Assembling the graphics

Now you're going to assemble and build the finished graphic.

1. Create a new 500×500 pixel canvas with a resolution of about 72 pixels. Make the canvas background color the same as you chose for the Matte color in the previous exercise.

   Now import the two images you created.

If you're new to creating transparencies, as you did with the first image, the darker the background, the more you'll see any spots you might have missed.

2. Select File ➤ Import… and browse to the `guitarist1export.gif` you made previously. Click the Open button to import the image.

3. To finish the import, click anywhere on the canvas, and then use the Pointer tool to position the graphic wherever you like on the canvas.

   Notice how the transparency works—the background color shows through the transparent areas of the graphic around the head and shoulders.

4. Repeat the previous steps to import and position `guitarist2export.gif`.

5. If there's a lot of extraneous space on the canvas that you want to get rid of you can always use the Crop tool or use the Modify ➤ Canvas ➤ Trim Canvas menu option.

   You can now save this image for inclusion in a website later on. As you can see, there's a bit of modular construction here. You created individual components and assembled them into a larger graphic.

6. Save this graphic as `guitaristgraphic.png`.

Using the Property inspector to manipulate basic objects

All you're going to do here is add a simple shape to the canvas to see how its properties are documented within the Property inspector. You'll then use the Property inspector to manipulate the object's appearance.

1. Create a new document that's 468 pixels wide and 60 pixels high with a plain white canvas. These are the standard dimensions for the banner ads you see on the web.

2. If they aren't open already, open up both the Property inspector (Window ➤ Properties) and the Tools panel (Window ➤ Tools).

3. Now click the Canvas color box in the Property inspector and change the canvas color to light blue.

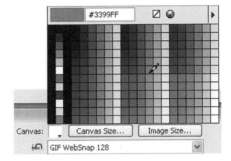

Once you've selected your color, you'll see that it's documented in the small window at the left side of the Property inspector: This window highlights any object you've selected inside your document. Currently, the object you've selected is your canvas.

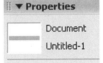

Now let's add some content to the canvas.

4. Select the Text tool from the Tools panel or use the keyboard shortcut *T*.

Notice that the Property inspector has changed to reflect the fact that you're now using the Text tool. It displays all the text-related properties, some of which will no doubt be familiar to you from word processing applications.

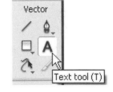

Don't worry about what all these properties do for now—you'll be looking at the Text tool and working with text later in the book. For now, let's add some plain text to the web banner.

5. Once the Text tool is selected, move your cursor to the canvas and the arrow changes to the text cursor. Click your mouse near the middle of the canvas and a text box appears.

6. Type any text you like into the text box.

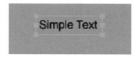

7. Like most programs you've probably worked with, you need to select the text before you change it. You can do this in several ways:

★ Click and drag your mouse across the text to highlight it.

★ Select the text box using the Pointer tool.

★ Press *CTRL/CMD+A*.

8. Next, go back to the Property inspector and click the chevron next to the font size field. A slider appears. Move the font size slider up to 40 (alternatively, you can type *40* directly in the font size field) and press *ENTER*.

9. Finally, apply an italic format to the text by clicking the Italic button, and stretch the horizontal scale up to 140 percent.

10. Now move back to the Tools panel, and select the **Pointer** tool. This is the main tool you use in Fireworks to select and move your objects. Notice, however, that the submenu shows another option, the **Select Behind** tool.

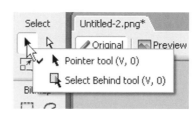

The Select Behind tool works in a similar way to the Pointer tool except that it applies to objects behind other objects. For example, if you had an image behind the text on your banner that you wanted to highlight, you could use the Select Behind tool to get directly to it, rather than having to move the text out of the way first.

> *All buttons in the Tools panel with a chevron in the bottom right corner contain multiple tools.*

11. For now, move the Pointer tool over your text and click and drag it to the center of your banner.

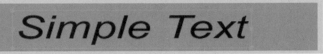

OK, it's a little (well, a lot) on the simple side, but you've created it using some of the simple tools you've learned so far. For practice, you could try opening up the `guitaristgraphic.png` file you created earlier and adding some text to the canvas. Try experimenting with different fonts and styles.

Summary

You've covered a lot of ground in this chapter. You've learned about graphic and file formats, and when different types are appropriate; you know how to find your way around the Fireworks interface; you've started using the most important panel in the program, the Property inspector; and you've even exported and assembled multiple graphic images, one with a transparent background.

And the best part is that now that you've covered the basics, things can start getting more interesting. In the next chapter, you're going to look at all the available tools in Fireworks MX 2004.

One

Creating Content:
Fireworks Tools

In this chapter

In this chapter, you're going to build on Chapter Zero by taking a detailed look at the various tools and developing a better understanding of the relationship between these tools and the Property inspector. As you'll see, the Property inspector increases the potential functionality of each tool.

We'll look at the following:

★ Exploring the Tools panel
  ★ Working with Vector tools
  ★ Working with Bitmap tools
★ Learning to use Canvas tools
  ★ Making selections
  ★ Retouching bitmap images

What is an object?

Anyone who has had even a superficial relationship with computers has come across the word **object**. You see it whether you're just using a word processing program or whether you're working with high-level programming languages. Although the definition or the word changes a bit with context, an object is anything that is self-contained, can be reproduced as many times as necessary, and can be changed without adversely affecting other objects. In Fireworks, an object is either a vector image or bitmap image.

Here's an example: in Fireworks, you can draw a simple rectangle and color it red. This would be an object. You can then make as many copies of this rectangle (called **instances**) as you want. Finally, you can change the color of one instance without changing the color of the other instances or the original object. Many times you combine, or aggregate, objects to create even larger objects.

You must understand objects in order to maximize the capabilities of Fireworks MX 2004. Because of objects, you can create something once and use it many times. Each time you use it, you can modify its **properties**. With this concept in mind, let's take a detailed look at how to use the Fireworks tools.

The Tools panel

It's worth spending a few moments examining how Fireworks tools are arranged and what tools are available to you. Of course, as you progress through the book, you'll be using these tools in a variety of settings and refining the knowledge you gain here.

As mentioned in Chapter Zero, all of Fireworks' tools are logically grouped together into panels. Most of the drawing tools are located on the **Tools panel** at the left side of the interface. The panel has six sections, three of which we'll look at in the first part of this chapter.

★ The Select section holds all the tools you need to select and move the various objects in your image, and also those that help you scale and crop objects.

★ The Bitmap section contains the tools you needed to create and edit bitmap objects. The tools in the Select section are used for selecting and manipulating *objects*—the Bitmap tools enable you to select and manipulate groups of *pixels* within the objects to perform operations on them.

★ The Vector section contains the tools for creating and working with vector objects, including a variety of line, curve, and regular shape tools, plus the Text tool, which you used at the end of Chapter Zero.

★ The Web section contains the tools you need to perform operations associated with web page design. As an example, you may want to select a portion of an image map and connect it to a hyperlink (this is known as creating a hotspot and is covered in detail in Chapter Four).

★ The Colors section is used to control the color of the stroke (line) or fill (the area inside an outline) of an object. This is detailed in the second section of this chapter.

★ The View section contains tools you can use to zoom in and out of your image, and move around the canvas. You may find these useful when you're working on complex images or images with very small detailed sections.

You'll probably notice that not all tools are available at the same time. Fireworks recognizes the objects you select and then decides which tools are applicable. Those tools that aren't applicable are grayed out.

So, let's get you to work. Rather than working systematically from the top of the panel, start with the Vector section and get something interesting onto your canvas. You'll then move to the Bitmap section, and then return to look at the more advanced vector tools. You'll finish off by looking at the remaining selection tools. Don't worry about trying to memorize all the information in the coming sections—you'll become more familiar with each tool as you work with it throughout the rest of the book. You can always come back to this chapter and use it as a reference later on.

Drawing basic vector shapes

The number of available vector shapes has greatly expanded with the addition of **Auto Shapes** in Fireworks MX 2004. As well as the regular Rectangle, Ellipse, and Polygon tools, you can use a whole host of new vector shapes.

1. Create a new canvas that's 500×500 pixels with a resolution of 72 ppi and a white canvas color.

2. Start with a simple rectangle by selecting the Rectangle tool.

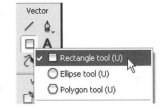

3. You can tell that the Rectangle tool is selected because the Property inspector now says Rectangle tool at the left.

Whenever you draw an object, you have two colors to consider: the fill and the stroke. The **fill** is the color of the object itself, and it is represented in the Property inspector by the paint can icon. The **stroke** is the outline around the object, represented by the pencil icon. In the preceding screenshot, the fill is set to a light gray and the stroke color box has a red line going through it. This red line means that no stroke is currently set.

4. Click the fill color box to the right of the paint can icon and select white. Open the stroke color box just to the right of the pencil icon and select black.

5. Draw the rectangle on the canvas by positioning your mouse where you want the upper-left corner to be and, while holding down the mouse button, drag to where you want the lower-right corner to be.

6. Let go of the mouse and the rectangle shape appears with the four sides highlighted. Don't worry too much about the size or position for now.

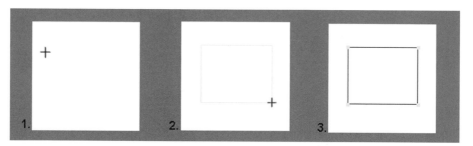

Notice that each of the four corners has a small square on it. These are called transform handles (in Microsoft products, they're called graphic handles or, in some cases, simply handles) and are used to resize and reshape the object.

If you draw your rectangle and can only see four small squares, or nodes, rather than clearly defined lines, it's likely that the stroke is turned off. Just open the stroke color box and select a color.

7. In order to use these transform handles, you first need to change to the Pointer tool. Next, select one of the four transform handles, hold down the mouse button, and drag the handle to change the size of the rectangle.

Now let's try something a little different.

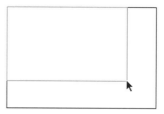

8. Select the Subselection tool, located just to the right of the Pointer tool.

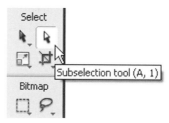

9. Click once inside the rectangle. Your transform handles should become clear. As your mouse cursor approaches one of the handles, the tail should disappear.

10. Click a corner and you should see the following dialog box. Just click OK.

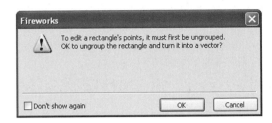

11. This ungroups the transform handles and allows you to manipulate each one individually. Give it a try—manipulate each corner.

Alternative strokes

As mentioned earlier, you can control the colors within the object (fill), as well as the color around the object (stroke) but you're not limited to just the color. You can change the size, texture, pattern, and edge too.

1. With your rectangle from the previous exercise still selected, look at the stroke options in the Property inspector.

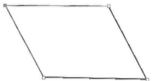

You can adjust the stroke thickness using the slider to the right of the stroke color box. For instance, try changing the stroke size to 5 pixels (either by moving the slider or typing 5 directly into the field). Here are the results:

Experiment with a few different thicknesses.

Also notice the Edge field. The higher the number here, the more blurring occurs around the edges, resulting in a softer effect. Try setting this to 100, and compare the results with what you get when you set it to 0. Although the results aren't dramatic now, they will be in a few moments.

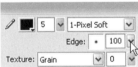

2. Take a look at the Stroke category drop-down menu, just to the right of the stroke color box, and as an example, select Charcoal ➤ Pastel.

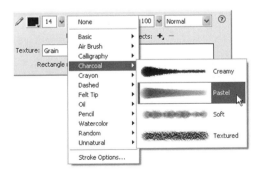

Notice that all of the other stroke settings on the Property inspector have now changed. It's worth spending some time trying different options available here and then, when you've got it selected, editing the color, edge, or thickness of the stroke. The possible combinations are endless.

Another interesting option in the Property inspector is the ability to apply **textures** to strokes (and fills also).

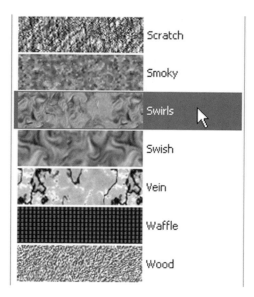

3. Try applying the Swirls texture to your rectangle—you may see a little change. However, right next to the Textures dropdown menu, is a percentage slider to control the amount of texture showing in the stroke. Here is what happens when you move it right up to 100%:

4. Another handy feature is if you select Stroke Options… from the Stroke category dropdown menu. This opens this useful panel:

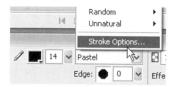

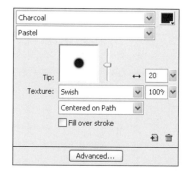

This panel provides many of the same features as the Property inspector, but it does offer one additional feature. Once all your settings are complete and you have the desired effect, you can click the plus symbol (+) located in the lower right corner and save the setting with a name of your choosing.

The name is saved under the menu classification you had at the time that you went to save it. So, if you're working with Charcoal at the time you go to save, your customized setting is saved under Charcoal in the Stroke category menu.

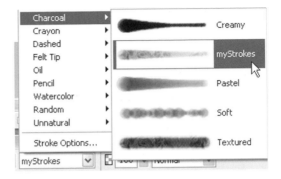

1

Fine tuning the object's size and position

Using the transform handles is a quick and easy way to resize the object. However, in many cases, you need to be a bit more precise with the process. This is possible by typing numerical values directly into the four fields on the left side of the Property inspector.

★ The W field is the width of the object measured in pixels.

★ The H field is the height of the object measured in pixels.

★ The X field is the object's horizontal position, measured in pixels from the left edge of the canvas.

★ The Y field is the object's vertical position, measured in pixels from the top of the canvas.

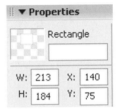

With these four fields, you can precisely resize and position an object right down to the exact pixel. However, you can use yet another tool to fine-tune your object's position and size . . .

Scale tool

This tool is located directly beneath the Pointer tool in the Tools panel.

When you select this tool, your object is surrounded by an additional box with additional transform handles in the center of each side.

The corner handles resize the object proportionately and the center handles of each side change the proportion of the object by stretching just that side.

In addition, you can see a strange transform handle in the middle of the object. This allows you to rotate the object using that handle as the **pivot point**. If you place your mouse cursor outside of the object, it changes to rotating pointer.

If you hold down the mouse button, you can now rotate the object. If you need to change this pivot point, select the center handle and drag it to a new location (including, believe it or not, a point outside of the object itself).

Try dragging your pivot point around and rotating your object.

As you can now see, the Scale tool and the Property inspector can really help you fine-tune the size and position properties of your objects.

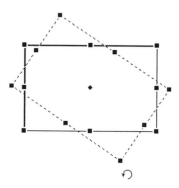

Rounding rectangles

Many times you may want to soften your rectangles by rounding their corners. You can do this easily by typing values directly into the Property inspector. Let's set your Rectangle roundness to a factor of 50. Of course, the higher the number is, the more pronounced is the roundness.

Skew tool

A variation of scaling an object is **skewing** an object. When you skew an object, you change the proportions of the object on just one of its sides using the **Skew tool**. When you drag the transform handles now, you'll see something like this:

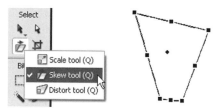

Distort tool

There is one additional variation of scaling called the **Distort tool**. This gives each of the transform handles a life of its own in much the same way that the Subselection tool does (which one you use is a matter of personal preference; however, you may find this tool a bit easier to use). As a result, you can move one graphic handle and change the proportion of only that handle.

 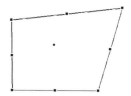

Repeatedly pressing Q cycles you through these three tools. You can look in the Property inspector to see which tool you are currently using.

Drawing tips

Part of a good web design requires drawing. Here are some suggestions for maximizing the use of the drawing, and related, tools.

When you draw something, you are creating an object. The results may not always be perfect. You can delete an object by selecting it with the Pointer tool and pressing the *DELETE* button on your keyboard.

In some cases, you may want to draw a perfect square. You can easily accomplish this with the Rectangle tool by holding down the *SHIFT* key in addition to the mouse button when you draw the rectangle. This constrains the rectangle to a perfect square.

Be aware of a good habit you should get into early on. You'll probably be using Fireworks to assist in web page design, and many web pages work in a programming environment, such as JavaScript. As an example, you may want a rectangle that contains some text to turn on or off in response to a particular event. For this reason, a good designer gives each object a unique name. You can use the **object name** field in the Property inspector to do just that.

Because many programming languages are case sensitive, some naming standards have been adopted by the industry.

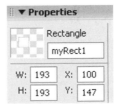

★ Use all lowercase letters except for a mid-word capitalization. For example, the name "My Work" would be entered as myWork.

★ Start the name with a letter instead of a number.

★ No spaces—where a space is needed use the underscore character.

Ellipse tool

The Ellipse tool is similar to the Rectangle tool. Just as you can use the *SHIFT* key to force the Rectangle tool to draw a perfect square, you can also use the *SHIFT* key to force the Ellipse tool to draw a perfect circle.

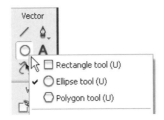

In addition, you can use the *ALT* key to begin drawing a circle at a center point rather than the upper-left corner (you can do the same thing with a rectangle but it's more common to do this with an ellipse).

Now that you've gotten your toes a bit wet by doing some relatively simple object manipulations, it's time to move a little deeper into the graphics pool.

Polygon tool

The **Polygon tool** allows you to create more complex shapes. Once you select it, you need to give the Property inspector some information before you can begin drawing. Select the Polygon tool and turn your attention to the right side of the Property inspector.

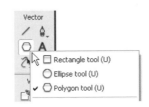

You can specify how many sides you want the polygon to have and what the angles should be. In most cases, however, you may want to leave the Angle field set to Auto. When you do this, Fireworks decides the best angles for the shape and size used. In this example, you're going to draw a five-sided polygon with automatic angles.

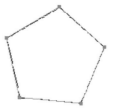

Once this is set, you can then draw the polygon as you did the rectangle and the ellipse.

Notice that the Property inspector also has a Shape drop-down menu. This gives you the option of drawing your polygon as a star. The Sides represent the points of the star. This example shows a seven-point star with the angles automatically calculated:

Note that a polygon is automatically drawn *from its center outward* unlike rectangles and ellipses, and that the number of sides for a polygon can't be changed once it has been drawn. Also, when drawing out your polygon or star, holding the *SHIFT* key limits the rotation of the shape to increments of 45 degrees.

> *Pressing CTRL/CMD while the Shape tool is selected switches you temporarily to the Pointer tool. Releasing CTRL/CMD returns you to the Shape tool.*

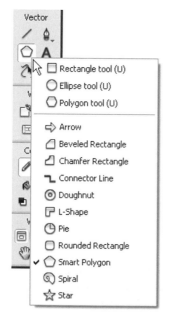

Auto Shapes

Fireworks MX 2004 introduces a new tool (or, more properly, a new group of tools) called **Auto Shapes**. These are predefined vector shapes that allow you to change many of the properties visually.

Smart Polygon

1. As a contrast to what you've just done, select Smart Polygon and draw a polygon as you did with the rectangle and ellipse (or simply click in the document and a predefined size will be placed):

Let's assume that you now want to change this to a seven-sided polygon. You'll notice that four diamonds are located around the object. These are called **control points** and, they not only help you set the properties visually, but provide tooltip instructions on how to use them.

2. Click the control point located at the lower-left corner of the object.

The tooltip tells you that this control point controls the number of sides. It also says that *ALT/OPT*+drag will split the polygon.

3. Experimentation shows that dragging the control point clockwise adds more sides. Give it a try.

4. You can use the *ALT/OPT* key to add spokes to your polygon. By using the *ALT/OPT* key and dragging counterclockwise, you can remove the spokes.

5. Using the center control point, you can draw an inner polygon and by clicking the center point once again, you can remove the inner polygon.

6. Point to the control point located at the top of the object. You can use this control point to scale and rotate your shape.

This is a good time to take a few minutes and experiment with the other Auto Shapes. As you'll see, the concepts are exactly the same as those you just used for the Smart Polygon. By now, you should be starting to have a good idea of how these drawing tools work. Let's refine this knowledge by looking at the other vector tools.

Line tool

The Line tool, as you would expect, draws straight lines.

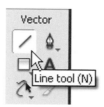

1. Select the Line tool and choose a place on the canvas for one of its endpoints.

2. Now click, hold, and drag the mouse to the point where you want the other endpoint of the line to be.

3. If you like the outline currently displayed, let the mouse go, and the line appears with its ends highlighted.

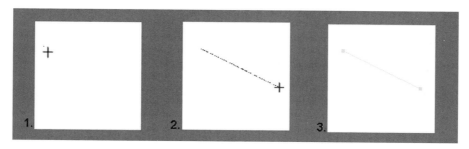

4. If you're not happy with the line as you've drawn it, press the *DELETE* key while the line is highlighted to remove it from the canvas.

When drawing lines, it's useful to note the following:

★ Holding down *SHIFT* means you can only create vertical and horizontal lines, or lines at 45 degrees to the horizontal.

★ Pressing *CTRL/CMD* temporarily brings up the Eyedropper tool with which you can choose the color of your line. Releasing *CTRL/CMD* returns you to the Line tool.

Just like the other objects you've worked with, you can use the Property inspector to adjust properties such as height, width, position, color, and line thickness.

Text tool

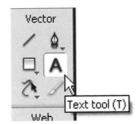

As you saw in Chapter Zero, you can use the Text tool to generate a piece of text with the font and typographic options applied as required.

1. To place a piece of text on the canvas, first select the Text tool.

2. Choose a place on the canvas to be the center point of your text, and click.

3. Type in your text. If you want to change its format, highlight it and change the appropriate properties in the Property inspector.

4. If the text isn't exactly where you want it, press and hold down the *CTRL/CMD* key or select the Pointer tool. You can drag the text wherever you like on the canvas and then release *CTRL/CMD* when you're finished.

5. To finish editing the text, deselect the highlighted box containing the text by pressing *CTRL/CMD+D* or by selecting another tool.

You'll recognize most of the options available in the Property inspector from word processing programs. However, some properties are unique to text and worth taking a few minutes to examine.

Kerning

Kerning controls the horizontal spacing *between* letters. You can set this value yourself manually or let Fireworks handle this automatically.

1. If you want to manually set it, first turn off Auto kern in the Property inspector.

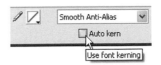

2. Either click between the two letters you want to change, or highlight the block of text.

3. Enter the amount of spacing you want (as a percentage) in the Kerning field. As an example, change the kerning to 10%. There should be now greater space between the letters.

Welcome To Fireworks MX 2004

You can visually change the level of kerning by pressing *Ctrl/Cmd* and using the left or right arrow keys to adjust it in 1-percent increments. Holding *Shift+Ctrl/Cmd* adjusts it in 10-percent increments.

Horizontal scale

Try not to get kerning mixed up with the **horizontal scale** feature.

This feature changes the width of the selected characters rather than the space between them. The default setting is 100%. However, if you increase it to 120%, you'll see something like this:

Welcome To Fireworks MX 2004

Leading

Leading controls the amount of vertical spacing between the lines of a paragraph and is measured as either a percentage or as a number of pixels. You can set this before or after you type the text.

First though, what is a paragraph? A paragraph is formed when you press *Enter* to start a new line of text. You can also start a new line without starting a new paragraph by pressing the *Shift+Enter* key.

1. As an example, type out the two-paragraph text block shown in the following illustration. Use *Shift+Enter* to create a new line for each paragraph (note that unlike a word processor, no word wrap occurs here). Press the *Enter* key twice between paragraphs.

This is an example of using some of
the text tools in Fireworks MX 2004

This is a second paragraph using
Fireworks MX 2004

2. Use the Pointer tool to select the whole text block and change the leading to 120%.

This is an example of using some of
the text tools in Fireworks MX 2004

This is a second paragraph using
Fireworks MX 2004

Both paragraphs were affected.

3. Set the leading back to 100% and highlight the first paragraph. Change the leading to 120% again.

This is an example of using some of
the text tools in Fireworks MX 2004

This is a second paragraph using
Fireworks MX 2004

Only this paragraph is affected.

Like kerning, you can use the arrow keys to adjust the spacing visually. *CTRL/CMD+* the up or down arrow keys change the spacing in increments of one unit (percent or pixels, depending on what you have set in the Property inspector). Adding the *SHIFT* key to the combination allows you to change the spacing in increments of 10 units.

Text orientation

The text orientation controls enable you to set the direction of your text in four different ways:

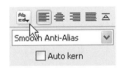
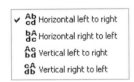

The first option is normal text that runs horizontally from left to right.

*This is a test of the Fireworks MX 2004
Text Orientation Feature*

The second option reverses the text horizontally:

> *4002 XM skroweriF eht fo tset a si sihT*
> *erutaeF noitatneirO txeT*

The third and fourth text orientation options run the text vertically, from left to right, and right to left respectively.

```
V F        F V
e i        i e
r r        r r
t e        e t
i w        w i
c o        o c
a r        r a
l k        k l
  s        s
T            T
e M        M e
x X        X x
t            t
  2        2
I 0        0 I
n 0        0 n
  4        4
```

Text alignment

The first four of these buttons should be familiar from word processing. They align the text to the left, center, and right of the text block or justify the text across the whole width of the text block. The last button at the far right may be new. It's the stretch alignment button, and it stretches a line of text to fill up the size of the text box.

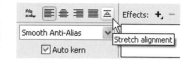

As an example, here's a normal left-aligned piece of text:

> *This is a test of the Fireworks MX 2004*
> *Text Alignment Buttons*

After clicking the stretch alignment option in the Property inspector, the bottom line of text stretches to fill up the available space in the text box:

> *This is a test of the Fireworks MX 2004*
> *Text Alignment Buttons*

Indenting text

You can use the indent control to indent the first line of a paragraph. Use the slider to adjust the amount of indentation or type a value directly into the field.

Paragraph spacing

The upper field allows you to define the amount of spacing before a paragraph, while the lower field controls spacing after a paragraph.

Baseline shift

If you don't see this in the Property inspector, make sure your text itself is highlighted (not just the text box selected). You can use this feature to adjust text above or below the baseline. You could use this for either superscript or subscript characters—positive values produce superscript and negative values produce subscript.

If you think you now know everything you need to know about text, you're in for a surprise. You can do lot more with text; Chapter Eight is entirely dedicated to creating visual effects using text.

Knife tool

As mentioned in Chapter Zero, Fireworks stores every vector shape as a set of points on the canvas joined by lines. The lines that join the points are called **paths** and you can bisect a path at any point you like using the Knife tool. If you use the knife to cut a line, the result is two lines.

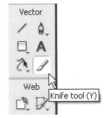

1. To bisect a path, first select the path you want to cut.

2. Select the Knife tool (*Y*).

3. Drag the pointer across the path so that it intersects at the point at which you want to cut the path, and let the mouse go. Alternatively, you can click directly on the point on the path where you want to cut.

   The path(s) and the new endpoints are highlighted.

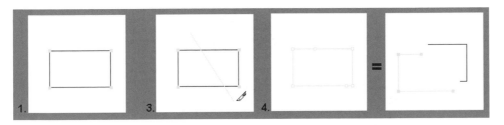

When using the Knife tool, it's useful to note the following:

★ Holding *SHIFT* while dragging the Knife tool across a path limits the angle the line takes to a multiple of 45 degrees.

★ Holding *CTRL/CMD* down temporarily changes the Knife tool to the Pointer tool, allowing you to change the path you are cutting. Releasing *CTRL/CMD* returns you to the Knife tool.

You're not restricted to cutting one path at a time. It's perfectly legitimate to select, for example, three rectangles and cut them along the same line all at once.

You're now well on the road to being a vector shape hero, but there are still more advanced vector drawing and selection tools, which we'll come back to later in the chapter.

Now its time to turn your attention to the other half of the graphics family: **bitmap tools**. It's important to note that you can't use bitmap tools to modify vector objects, and vice versa. In fact, Fireworks has separate bitmap and vector modes, depending on what graphic you're currently working with, and it switches between the two modes automatically.

A visual border around a bitmap image is turned off by default. If you prefer, you can choose to see this border when working with bitmaps. Choose Edit ➤ Preferences ➤ Editing and check Turn off "hide edges" in the Bitmap options area of the Preferences dialog box.

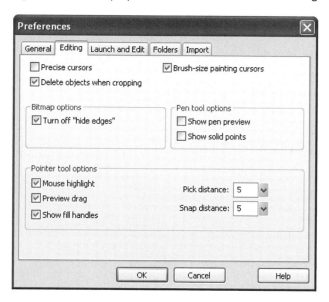

Many designers still prefer to leave this feature turned on in order to distinguish easily between bitmap and vector objects.

Bitmap tools

The Tools panel contains eight basic bitmap tools. Two create new bitmap objects, three enable you to select groups of pixels within existing bitmaps in order to edit just these pixels, and the remaining three help you to retouch your graphics. Let's start with the creative set.

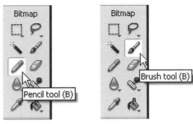

Pencil and Brush tools

Both the Pencil and Brush tools allow you to draw freehand on the canvas, creating and adding new bitmap objects to the current layer of the graphic. However, the Pencil tool can only draw one-pixel-wide lines (either freehand lines or constrained straight lines). The Brush tool enables you to adjust the thickness of the line in much the same way as you would select the thickness of a brush to paint with. The Brush tool also has various brushes that respond well to a pressure-sensitive pad.

1. To draw a bitmap line, first select the Pencil or Brush tool (pressing *B* toggles between the Pencil and Brush tools).

2. Click and drag the mouse to draw the line; release it to stop drawing.

Once you've finished using the tools, all the lines you created with them are grouped together as a single bitmap object (as long as you haven't switched to another tool while drawing). This object can then be moved with the Pointer tool as required.

The differences between these two tools are exemplified through the different options each offers. The Pencil tool restricts you to drawing a line (or stroke) one pixel wide, just like a real pencil. However, you can change a few settings in the Property inspector before you start.

Working along the Property inspector from left to right, you can

★ Change the stroke color and pattern of the line.

★ Smooth the edges of the lines you draw (Anti-aliased).

★ Switch the color of the line from the stroke color to the fill color if you start drawing from a point on the line that's in the current stroke color (Auto erase).

★ Restrict yourself to drawing a line only on existing bitmap objects. This mode won't let you draw in the transparent area of a bitmap file (Preserve transparency).

★ Set the stroke's level of opacity.

★ Change the blend mode.

Like in real life, you'll find a lot more brushes to choose from than pencils. Gone are the pencil's Anti-aliased and Auto erase options and, instead, you can completely customize the style of the brush you want to use.

You saw these features earlier when we discussed strokes. However, let's review. Clockwise from the top left, the options in the third panel enable you to

★ Change the stroke color, the tip size, and the type of brush you want to use (the Stroke category).

★ Change the Edge (the softness) of the brush.

★ Change the Texture of the canvas onto which the brush is drawn and the strength of that texture.

When you're using the Brush or Pencil tool, it's also useful to note the following:

★ Holding *Shift* while drawing a line limits the angle the line takes to multiples of 45 degrees.

★ Holding *Ctrl/Cmd* while drawing lines temporarily switches you to the Pointer tool so that you can move the current bitmap object as required on the canvas. Releasing it switches you back to the tool you were using previously.

★ Holding *Alt/Opt* while drawing lines temporarily switches you to the Eyedropper tool so that you can choose the color for the next line to be drawn. Releasing it switches you back to the tool you were just using.

Pixel selection tools

A great deal of work with bitmaps begins when you select pixels within a **marquee** and then modify them in some way—by adding a special effect, erasing it, changing the color, and so on. The question here is how to create that marquee. You have the **Marquee**, **Lasso**, and **Magic Wand** tools. Each enables you to create a marquee in a slightly different way.

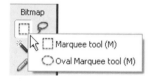

Marquee tools

Of the three, the default **Marquee** tool is the easiest to use because it works exactly the same way as the Rectangle tool, only in this case, you draw a marquee (also known as a selection) rather than a vector object. Similarly, the **Oval Marquee** tool works in exactly the same way as the Ellipse tool, but it creates an elliptical marquee rather than a rounded shape. The key point is that the Marquee tools allow you to create marquees with a regular shape.

1. Open alhambra.png from the download files for this chapter.

2. Select the Marquee tool (*M* toggles between the two Marquee tools).

3. Draw a rectangular marquee around the center area of the picture.

4. Select the Pointer tool and click and drag the selected area.

Instead of moving the selected area, you could just as easily deleted it. Or, if you want, you could cut or copy and paste it within another image or object. You have many possibilities here.

You can modify both the Marquee and Oval Marquee tools with the same keys as their respective vector shapes:

★ Pressing *SHIFT* ensures that the marquee is constrained to a perfect square or circle.

★ Pressing *ALT/OPT* allows the marquee to be drawn from its center point rather than from corner to corner.

How many times have you seen a humorous photo with someone's face superimposed on another photograph? The technique used is what you're using now.

The Property inspector offers some additional options for the Marquee tool:

Once the marquee has been drawn, the width and height of the marquee and its coordinates (the location on the canvas where 0,0 is the top-left corner) are displayed at the left of the Property inspector. However, before it's created, you have three options in the Style drop-down menu to choose from that determine how the marquee is to be drawn:

★ Normal draws the marquee as usual.

★ Fixed Ratio sets the width to height ratio of the marquee. For example, to mimic the SHIFT key's role in maintaining proportion, the ratio would be 1:1.

★ Fixed Size sets the exact size of the marquee. Clicking the bitmap then establishes where the top-left corner of the marquee should be located.

There are three options that affect the Edge of the marquee: a Hard (jagged) edge, an Anti-aliased (smooth) edge, or an edge with a feathered border of a given width. You can use a feathered edge to blend the area smoothly into another image.

Lasso tools

The Lasso tool is the freehand version of the Marquee tool, much like the Pencil tool. You can draw a completely irregular shaped marquee mirroring, for example, the shape of someone's head.

1. To create a marquee with the Lasso tool, first select the Lasso tool (L).

2. Hold the mouse down while drawing out the shape of your marquee.

3. A marquee must be a complete (closed) shape. To close the marquee, draw the cursor back to roughly the original start point (a small square will appear next to the cursor when you're close enough). Alternatively, release the mouse button and Fireworks will draw a straight line between the two endpoints of your path.

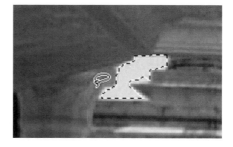

You may have noticed that this tool has a counterpart: the Polygon Lasso tool. Unlike the Polygon tool, you're not limited to drawing any regular-sided polygon, but in contrast to the freeform Lasso tool, here you click the mouse to indicate a corner, or **key point**, of the marquee. You then go on to click the next key point. As you do, you should see a line stretching from point to point. By clicking one key point after another, you can map the entire outline of your marquee with your cursor. To complete your marquee, simply click the start point again. Meanwhile, Fireworks joins each point to the next one with a straight line.

At any time while you're defining the edges of your marquee with this tool, pressing SHIFT will force the angle of that particular edge to a multiple of 45 degrees. The Lasso tools have the same options in the Property inspector as the Marquee tool, with the exception of the Style property, which is specific to the Marquee tool.

Magic Wand tool

Last but not least, the Magic Wand tool approaches pixel selection in a completely different way than the Marquee and Lasso tools.

Instead of defining the shape of the marquee, you specify a color in the bitmap by clicking a pixel. The Magic Wand then creates a marquee surrounding that pixel and any other pixels next to it that are of a similar color. What "similar" actually means is determined by the Tolerance setting in the Property inspector.

A low Tolerance setting means that colors must be very close to the original selected pixel for them to be selected. Conversely, a high value means that a very wide range of colors is included in the marquee. Do remember, though, that a marquee will define only one contiguous area of color. The Magic Wand tool won't pick out every instance of the selected color on the graphic.

So, to create a marquee with the Magic Wand, here's what you do:

1. Select the Magic Wand tool.

2. Change the Tolerance value for the tool in the Property inspector.

3. Click the colored area you wish to select.

Let's try it out.

1. Open a fresh copy of alhambra.png from the download files.

Notice the shadings of stone in both the background structure and the columns in the foreground.

2. Select the Magic Wand tool and set Tolerance to 25 in the Property inspector.

3. Click somewhere on the stone in the background of the image.

As you can see, with a low Tolerance of 25, the marquee doesn't even reach across the top of the arch.

4. Press the *ESCAPE* key. Change the Tolerance to 50, and click the same spot in the image.

Notice that a larger continuous area is now selected. It has expanded into a much larger range of shades and colors.

Quick tricks for all pixel selection tools

You've already seen the keyboard shortcuts for the Marquee tools as you create a marquee, but you can use a few more immediately after a marquee has been created.

★ Press and hold *SHIFT* to create and add a new marquee that overlaps the current selection. Where the two marquees intersect, they merge to become one. The cursor becomes a cross with a small plus sign (+) to the bottom right.

★ Press and hold *ALT/OPT* to define an area to remove from the current selection. The area where your new marquee intersects with the old one is removed from the original. The cursor becomes a cross with a small minus sign (–) to the bottom right.

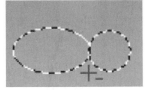

★ You can move a marquee created with any of the tools by moving the cursor onto the marquee without switching to the Pointer tool. The cursor becomes an arrow with a tiny marquee to the right of it. You can now drag the marquee to wherever you like on the screen.

★ You can move a marquee and its contents by moving the cursor onto the marquee and pressing *CTRL/CMD*. The cursor becomes an arrow with a pair of scissors to the right of it. Click and drag to move the marquee and its contents about the canvas. This has the same effect as selecting the Pointer tool first and then moving the cursor to the marquee.

★ Press *ESCAPE* at any time when using a pixel selection tool to remove all marquees and switch to the Pointer tool.

Eraser tool

As its name suggests, the Eraser tool enables you to erase the contents of a bitmap to reveal any graphics beneath (or the canvas background). Much like with the Brush tool, you have plenty of different erasers to choose from, varying in size, shape, and effectiveness.

1. Select the Eraser tool (*E*).

2. Choose the type of eraser by setting the properties in the Property inspector.

3. Move the cursor over your bitmap. It changes into either an outline of the eraser you're using or a "no-go" icon, indicating that the cursor is still over a vector object rather than a bitmap.

4. Click and drag over the parts of the graphic you wish to erase. Press and hold *SHIFT* if you want to erase in a horizontal or vertical line.

The Eraser seems quite an unsubtle tool at first until you start altering its properties.

Using the Property inspector you can

★ Set the Shape of the Eraser as round or square.

★ Set its width to a value between 1 and 100.

★ Set the Edge (softness) of the Eraser between 0 (very hard) and 100 (very feathered).

★ Set the opacity. At 100 percent, the Eraser completely rubs out any pixels it touches, but if it is set to 0 percent and it has no effect at all. Values between produce a pseudo-fade between your bitmap and whatever lies beneath it.

As a little experiment, try erasing portions of the Alhambra picture and changing the settings in the Property inspector to see how they work.

Bitmap retouching tools

The remaining tools in the bitmap section of the Tools panel are there to help you retouch a bitmap graphic you've created or imported into Fireworks. Retouching can involve cloning pixels, changing colors, changing the focus of the pixels, and darkening or lightening the image.

Let's start with the Rubber Stamp tool.

Rubber Stamp tool

You've already seen how to select areas of pixels for further use, and you could, for example, copy and paste them onto another area of the canvas. Another way to duplicate pixels is by **cloning** them with the Rubber Stamp tool. With this tool, you can clone much more precisely than with the copy/paste method.

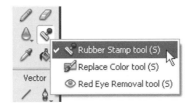

1. Open a fresh copy of alhambra.png again.

2. Select the Rubber Stamp tool (*S*).

3. In the Property inspector make sure Source aligned is checked and Use entire document is unchecked.

4. Click one of the stone columns in the foreground. Your mouse pointer should turn into a crosshair (known as **sampling pointer**), which indicates that this is the source to clone.

5. Point to the stone ceiling. Your mouse pointer is a circle, the destination marker. Hold down the mouse and drag it around like you did with the Eraser and Brush tools. Notice that the sampling pointer moves in tandem with the destination marker, capturing the source pixels. You should see the stone column being reproduced on the ceiling. You can use this, sometimes, to create reflection effects.

6. Release the mouse button when you've finished.

   If you want to reposition your crosshair (and change the source area of the graphic you're cloning), press and hold the *ALT/OPT* key and click the new source.

7. Look in the Property inspector again. Size and Edge work in the same way as they do for the Eraser tool. Likewise, the opacity and blend mode options work as normal. The two new options, Source aligned and Use entire document, affect how the stamp actually works in the following ways:

   ★ You may have noticed that once you finish cloning an area of pixels, the target crosshair continues to mimic the motion of the target cursor. By unchecking Source aligned, the source crosshair remains fixed.

   ★ You may have noticed that once you finish cloning an area of pixels, the target crosshair continues to mimic the motion of the target cursor. By unchecking Source aligned, the source crosshair remains fixed.

   ★ By default, the Rubber Stamp only clones pixels from the currently active object. To clone from all the elements in your graphic, check Use entire document.

   ★ The blend mode affects how the cloned pixels interact with the new background.

Let's move on and look at the two other tools associated with the Rubber Stamp tool.

Replace Color tool

Like the Rubber Stamp tool, this tool allows you to select a source and then brush it to a new location. Let's take a quick look at an example. This also gives you a chance to see the Eyedropper tool in action.

1. If necessary, bring up a fresh copy of alhambra.png.

2. Select the Replace Color tool (you can toggle to it using the *S* key) and then look in the Property inspector.

You can select the color you want to capture (change). As you may recall from Chapter Zero, color is described as a hexadecimal value representing intensities of red, green, and blue. However, it would be very difficult to find the exact value of the color you want to capture in the object, which is where the Eyedropper tool helps out.

3. Assume you want to change a particular shade on the stone columns to a light tan. Click in the Change color box to open the color palette and you'll see the eyedropper appear. Move the eyedropper to the color you want to capture.

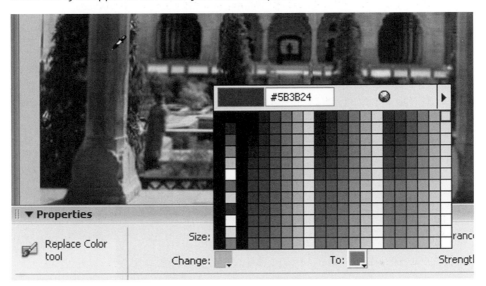

4. In the preceding example, the hexadecimal code of the color directly beneath the eyedropper is #5B3B24. Click the mouse to capture (or sample) the color.

5. Using the To color palette in the Property inspector either:

★ Capture a color in the image.

★ Select a color from the palette picture.

★ Type a hexadecimal number directly into the field at the top of the color palette. I've chosen a light color #CCFF99.

6. Like the Rubber Stamp tool, brush the other column on the right of the foreground. Wherever the color #5B3B24 is found, it's replaced by #CCFF99.

You'll notice that it doesn't change the color as much as it *tints* it. If you want to change the color entirely, check Colorize in the Property inspector. The Strength modifier determines how intense the replacement color will be. You've already seen the other options in the Property inspector with previous tools. Tolerance determines the range of colors captured (up to 255) and you can control the size and shape of the brush.

Red Eye Removal tool

This tool does exactly what it says, removing shades of red and replacing them with shades of gray or black.

1. Locate a photo that needs some red eye retouching.

2. Select the Red Eye Removal tool and place your cursor over the eye. Adjust the Size setting in the Property inspector until the circular cursor is just slightly larger than the eye you want to retouch.

3. Click to darken the red hues in the eye.

Unfortunately, the options for this tool are pretty limited (you're out of luck if your friends in the photo have blue, green, or brown eyes):

★ Size determines the tip size of the tool.

★ Choose between a square or circular brush Shape.

★ Use Tolerance to specify the range of hues to replace with the tool. You can set it between 0 and 255 where 0 will only replace pure red and 255 will replace all hues containing red.

★ Strength controls how dark the replacement gray color is.

Blur tools

The Blur tool, along with its companions, constitutes the basic deform and retouch operations you can perform on a bitmap.

So they appear in the Tools panel, you can

★ **Blur** elements of an object.

★ **Sharpen** or emphasize the edges of colored areas in an object to correct, for example, an out of focus scan.

- ★ Brighten an area of the graphic (**Dodge**).
- ★ Darken an area of the graphic (**Burn**).
- ★ **Smudge** the colors of a graphic by blending them together.

The five tools split into two pairs and a single. The couples compliment each other by performing opposite actions. The aims of Blur and Sharpen, for example, are to emphasize an area of the graphic where the focus is sharp and draw attention away from where the focus is blurred. Indeed both tools can and should be approached in exactly the same way. Let's try a quick example.

1. If necessary, open a fresh version of alhambra.png.

2. Select the Blur tool.

3. Set Intensity to 100 in the Property inspector. This determines the degree to which the graphic is blurred or sharpened. At minimum (0), no blurring occurs. At maximum (100), a few sweeps of the mouse blur a graphic very quickly.

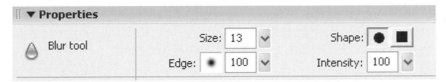

4. Brush over the background building so that it is blurred out and the emphasis is on the foreground.

While using the Blur or Sharpen tools, it's useful to note that

- ★ Pressing *ALT/OPT* at any time toggles between the Sharpen and Blur tools.
- ★ Pressing *ESCAPE* returns you to the Pointer tool.

The second pair of retouch tools is Dodge and Burn. Photography developers used these techniques to brighten and darken areas of a photograph by adding light to (or removing light from) the negative as the photo was developed. Indeed, the settings for these tools still reflect these origins.

Exposure mirrors the Intensity level of the Blur and Sharpen tools, the difference is that here you're defining how intense the bright\dark light is when you sweep it over the graphic—0 is off, and 100 means maximum effect. The options in the Range drop-down menu define to what degree the dodge\burn will affect certain areas of your graphic:

★ Shadows targets the darker areas of the graphic.

★ Midtones targets areas of medium brightness.

★ Highlights targets the bright areas of the graphic.

Note that just because the tool is set to Highlights, it doesn't mean that it won't affect dark areas; it just won't affect them as much as if the Range was set to Shadows.

5. Bring the Alhambra picture back up and select the Dodge tool. Use it to brush the left stone column.

6. Now select the Burn tool and brush the right column.

By doing this, you change the perspective of light across the image.

Again, pressing *ALT/OPT* at any time while using Dodge or Burn toggles between the tools. Likewise, pressing *ESCAPE* finishes your editing of the graphic and returns you to the Pointer tool with the current bitmap selected as an object.

Last but not least, is every five-year-old's favorite art activity—smudging pictures. And it's just as much fun in Fireworks as it is with poster paints and a finger.

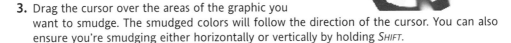

To smudge a graphic, follow these steps:

1. Select the Smudge tool (remember *R* toggles through the Blur tools).

2. Set the size and shape of the "finger" you'll smudge the graphic with. The cursor reflects your choice.

3. Drag the cursor over the areas of the graphic you want to smudge. The smudged colors will follow the direction of the cursor. You can also ensure you're smudging either horizontally or vertically by holding *SHIFT*.

The Property inspector displays some options unique to the Smudge tool.

You can choose whether or not your "smudger" already has some color on its finger by checking or unchecking Smudge color and choosing a particular color. Notice that you can also select a smudge color on the Property inspector.

You can specify how intense the smudges are on the picture by changing the value of the Pressure setting. A maximum value of 100 means that your finger is pushing down very hard on the canvas, causing a great deal of smudging. Conversely, a low-pressure value results in almost no smudging at all. You can also choose whether to smudge the colors belonging to just the active bitmap object in the graphic by unchecking Use entire document, or to smudge everything by checking it. Of all the tools in the Fireworks Tools panel, these are the hardest to describe in words. The best way to understand what they do is to draw some simple brush strokes on the canvas and then experiment with these tools.

The two tools at the bottom of the bitmap section are the Eyedropper and Paint Bucket tools. The reason they're separated from the rest of the bitmap tools is because they can be used for both bitmaps and vectors. You'll be working with these tools when you examine color in depth in the next chapter.

Advanced vector tools

With all the bitmap tools out of the way, let's go back and look at the pair of vector tools that haven't been covered yet: the Pen and Freeform tools. These deal specifically with the creation of irregular-shaped vector objects. They're not more advanced because their operation is tricky, but because the concept behind them is more complex.

Pen tool

Fireworks is excellent at drawing vector shapes with straight edges because the rules for drawing the object are simple—Fireworks just needs to know the coordinates for the corners of the object and the order in which they should be plotted—then it simply plots them, drawing straight lines between these corners. Likewise, an ellipse is easy because its edge follows a very simple formula given its center point, height, and width.

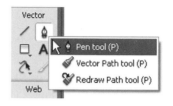

Drawing a squiggle, however, is not straightforward because the equations to define it are very complex—at least it would be if not for a certain mathematician named Pierre Bezier. The difference between a **Bezier** curve and a normal curve is that the latter is made up purely of points, whereas Bezier curves are made up of points and two additional pieces of information: **direction** and **speed**.

The Pen tool is specifically used for creating irregular vector shapes and changing the direction and speed of the Bezier curves that describe these shapes. Let's take an example and see how this translates visually.

1. Select the Pen tool. The cursor changes to a pen nib.

2. Plot the corner points of your shape one at a time by clicking the canvas. When each new point is chosen, Fireworks joins it to the previous point wit a straight line.

3. If you want to leave the object as an open shape, double-click the last point. If you want to close the shape, either change tools, or click back on the first point you created.

To add in the curves, you need to alter the direction and speed of the line into one of the corner points.

4. To do so, click and hold onto one of the corner points and drag in the general direction you want the curve to go. You'll see a line start to appear as you drag with three points marked, one at each end, and another at the center (sometimes referred to as a "bowtie" line). As you change the bowtie line around the point, you'll see the outline of the shape change in real time on screen. Let go of the mouse when you're happy with the current outline of the shape.

5. Continue editing the curves on the shape until you've finished.

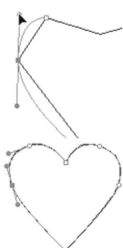

In this example, you've drawn a shape in two stages—you started with the outline and then applied the curves—but, as you experiment, you'll realize that you can just create curved edges from the outset.

If you need to edit your shape beyond defining a new curve around a point, you have the following options:

★ To remove a point, move the Pen cursor to the offending point, where the cursor should inherit a minus sign (–), and click it. Fireworks recalculates the shape automatically.

★ To add a new point on the shape's edge, move the cursor to the relevant place on the edge, and it inherits a plus sign (+). Click to add the new point to the shape.

★ To move a point about the screen, hold down *CTRL/CMD* and Fireworks temporarily switches to the Subselection tool, allowing you to select and move the point (you could also select the Subselection tool from the Tools panel). Releasing *CTRL/CMD* returns you to the Pen tool.

From Fireworks' point of view, all you're doing with the Pen tool is creating a new vector path on the canvas and the properties reflect it, matching those for the Line tool that you saw earlier.

Vector Path tool

You may be forgiven for initially mistaking the **Vector Path** tool for the Brush tool, as it has the same properties to alter in the Property inspector, uses the same keyboard combinations, and effectively creates the same thing—a freeform line of color. However, like the Pen tool, it also stores the line drawn as a series of Bezier curves, which you can edit as you would a line.

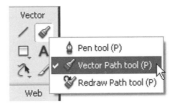

Redraw Path tool

The Redraw Path tool allows you to extend or redraw a path from one of the defined points on that path. It also allows you to change the qualities of the path. To accomplish this, follow these steps:

1. Select the Redraw Path tool.

2. Select the properties for the brush you're redrawing the path with. You'll find that the Property inspector contains the same options as it does for the bitmap Brush tool. Although this may seem strange, remember this: redrawing a path doesn't just mean changing a direction. It also could mean changing a property.

3. Move the cursor to the point on the path where you want to redraw the line from.

4. Click and drag where you need to redraw the path to. The cursor changes to a brush icon with a plus sign (+) next to it and the current path will remain in outline.

Note that if you start redrawing the path from a point that is not an endpoint, you'll end up removing a piece of the original path. This piece is indicated in red.

Chapter One

Freeform tool

The Freeform tool allows you to bend the path of the object.

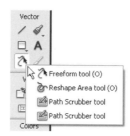

1. Select the vector object that you want to deform.

2. Select the Freeform tool. The cursor changes to an arrow with a small **s** beside it.

   You can either "pull" the shape into a new one or "push" into an edge (from inside or outside the shape) with a circular block of a specified size.

3. Hold the mouse button down and either pull, or push, the path into the shape that you want.

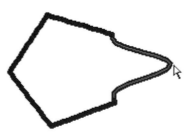

4. Using the Property inspector, try adjusting the sizes of the area being reshaped.

Reshape Area tool

Whereas the Freeform tool allows you to "attack" an edge, pushing it or pulling it in different areas, with the Reshape Area tool, you can distort all the paths within the range of the tool. It's easier to see this than describe it:

1. Choose the Reshape Area tool. The cursor becomes an arrow with an **o** beside it.

2. Move the cursor over the paths you wish to alter, and they are highlighted.

3. Click and drag the cursor in the direction you want to reshape the paths. The cursor becomes two concentric circles. The tool at full strength affects the paths inside the inner circle. The sections of path between the two circles are affected slightly less.

4. Release the mouse to stop redrawing.

As with the Freeform tool, the size of the area being reshaped can be altered while you're editing, but the ratio between the size of the two circles will remain constant.

This has the same effect as changing the Size value in the Property inspector. The other option, Strength, changes the size of the inner circle as a percentage of the outer circle.

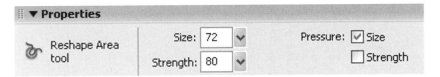

Path Scrubber tools

Last but not least are the Path Scrubber tools, which you use in conjunction with the **Edit Stroke** dialog box to change not the vector path itself, but the stroke it makes. Using this tool, you can change the stroke size, angle, ink amount, scatter, hue, lightness, and saturation, using pressure and speed (as set in the Property inspector) to indicate how much they should be changed.

The key to this tool, however, is that the stroke for the path must be pressure sensitive, a characteristic you set as follows:

1. Select the Line tool. Make sure the size of the stroke is fairly wide (25 or more).

2. In the Property inspector, choose Stroke Options... from the Stroke category drop-down menu.

3. Now click the Advanced button to bring up the Edit Stroke dialog box.

   The Sensitivity tab lets you specify how various aspects of the stroke change over the length of the path and by what factors. The two of interest here are Pressure and Speed. These mimic the idea that when you draw or write, the pressure you put on pen against paper and the speed with which you write alter the amount of ink placed on the paper over time.

4. Select the Sensitivity tab and alter the values for Pressure and Speed for a couple of stroke properties. The window at the bottom previews the resulting stroke. Click OK to confirm the settings.

5. Back on the canvas, draw a line.

   It may not look like the stroke on this line is any different from that on another line you drew, but you can use the path scrubbers to change this.

6. Select the Path Scrubber (Subtractive) tool from the Tools panel (the tool icon has a little minus sign [–]).

7. In the Property inspector choose whether the scrubber will reduce the Pressure, Speed, or both on the stroke, and by what Rate (low values are very slow and high are very quick).

8. Now drag the scrubber cursor over areas of the new pressure-sensitive line. You'll see the stroke reduce away in these areas.

Should you choose to, you can reverse these effects using the Path Scrubber (Additive) tool. The Path Scrubbers require a fair amount of experimentation to get comfortable with, but they can be used to give an authentic hand-drawn look to vector objects.

Cropping objects

As you saw in Chapter Zero, with the Crop tool you can quickly crop your work area, redefining the size of the canvas by cutting off some of the extraneous edges. Here's a quick reminder of how it works.

1. Select the Crop tool (*C*).

2. Click and drag a rectangle out over the current canvas. The outline of the rectangle represents the new canvas and the contents within it.

3. If you're happy with it, press *ENTER/RETURN* (or double-click within the crop area).

4. If you need to adjust the outline of the rectangle, drag the transform handles to adjust its size. You can also move the whole crop box to a new location.

Areas of bitmap objects outside the crop window will be deleted automatically. If part of a vector object is outside of the crop window, the whole object is retained so that if you wish to pull it into the new resized canvas, it's still available.

Lurking under the Crop tool is the Export Area tool, which works similarly to the Crop tool but, rather than cropping the canvas, it copies the specified area into a temporary file, ready for exporting into a different format (exporting is covered in detail in Chapter Five).

Summary

We'll, you've covered a lot of ground in this chapter. Just think back through what you've done. You're now a competent Fireworker! You know what each Fireworks tool does and how to use it. In addition, you have all the basic information you need to work effectively with Fireworks. In the next chapter, you'll add to this knowledge by learning how to use color in Fireworks and the important considerations you need to take into account about color when you're designing graphics for the web.

Two

Working with Color

In this chapter

You know how to create and work with basic shapes in Fireworks, but what about colors? At one time, designers were restricted to the 256 "web-safe" colors that were known to work in all existing browsers. Today, with more sophisticated graphic technology capable of reproducing millions of colors, this is less of an issue. However, it's important to remember that because not all visitors to your website are technologically up to date, you may still sometimes need to restrict yourself to these colors. In this chapter, you'll learn about the following:

★ Using colors and color modes

★ Working with gradients

★ Exploring custom styles

Typically, the first place to select a stroke or a fill color is the Colors section of the Tools panel.

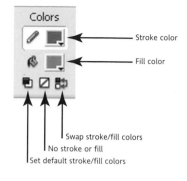

Stroke color

Fill color

Swap stroke/fill colors
No stroke or fill
Set default stroke/fill colors

There are several ways to change the stroke and fill colors, but the most direct is to select the object, click the stroke or fill color box, and choose a new color from the pop-up color palette that appears. Regardless of where or how you choose a new color, if you want it to be the new stroke color, you need to make sure that the pencil icon is selected first. The process is the same for changing the fill color—except that you need to select the paint bucket icon first. Also, you can select objects on the canvas and change their stroke and fill colors in the Property inspector.

If you skip ahead to the section on the Eyedropper tool and the Color Mixer, you'll be able to appreciate these rules much quicker. For now though, let's take a step back and see what it takes for Fireworks to make and distinguish colors.

Understanding color modes

If you've ever written your own HTML page, you know that browsers define colors as a mix of red, green, and blue. If you've been unlucky, you probably also know that different browsers may display the same color differently. Sometimes, what looks like a beautiful shade of fuchsia on your monitor can become a hideous shade of mustard in someone else's browser. You can't ensure that everyone browsing the web uses the same equipment so that they see your work as you do, but you can use Fireworks to make sure that your work uses a web-safe color palette (more on this later).

The red, green, and blue (RGB) model is just one of five color modes that Fireworks supports, all of which are available in the Color Mixer, located on the Colors panel (Window ➤ Color Mixer/*SHIFT+F9*). You can find the modes in the Color Mixer's options menu (click the icon at the top right of the panel).

The color modes are

★ **RGB:** This mode defines colors as a ratio of red, green, and blue, mirroring the way that monitors display color. The combination of the levels of the red, green, and blue, specified as a value between 0 (no color) and 255 (pure color) makes up the color of the pixel on the screen. So, for example, pure red has a value of 255, 0, 0, pure blue is 0, 0, 255, pure black is 0, 0, 0, and pure white is 255, 255, 255.

★ **Hexadecimal:** In this color mode you specify colors as a combination of red, green, and blue, but the RGB values are now in hexadecimal, varying between 00 and FF. This mirrors the way you define colors in an HTML page.

★ **CMY (Cyan Magenta Yellow):** Used mostly in full-color printing, CMY defines individual colors as a combination of cyan, magenta, and yellow. Again, values are between 0 (no color) and 255 (pure color). So, for example, pure magenta has a value of 0, 255, 0. In the reverse of the RGB model, however, pure black is 255, 255, 255, and pure white is 0, 0, 0.

> *This model is also called CMYK, where K stands for a Key color, usually black. Again, this would be given a value between 0 and 255.*

★ **HSB (Hue Saturation Brightness):** This is probably the hardest model to describe in words, but the easiest to appreciate graphically. HSB defines colors in the same way that humans perceive color. In this model, each color is defined as a combination of the pure color in question (the **hue**), the relative **brightness** of that color from black (no brightness) to white (full brightness), and the **saturation** of the hue from gray tone (no saturation) to pure, vivid color (high saturation).

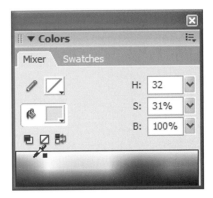 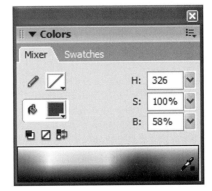

In the left screenshot shown here, the selected color is toward the top left of the color bar. The color has a low hue value, as it's very near the beginning of the bar. It's at full brightness and, because it's approaching the top of the color bar (and the color white), it's a little washed out, so it has a fairly low saturation level. In the right screenshot, there's a much higher hue value and full saturation, although this time the color is not as bright because it's chosen from the lower half of the color bar. You could say that the color bar acts as a combination of hue and saturation, with zero hue and zero saturation at the top-left corner, and both at maximum value at the bottom right. The vertical axis of the bar determines how bright your color is.

★ **Grayscale:** You can work in black and white, defining all possible colors as a percentage of black, where pure black is 100 percent and pure white 0 percent.

Experiment with switching between the modes. You'll notice that because the correct color mode values for the currently selected color are displayed in the fields at the right of the Color Mixer, this is a handy way to translate values between models should you need to make a note of them.

Understanding color palettes

Whichever color mode you choose to use when picking colors for your graphics, it's only by adding them to the graphic's **color palette** that you can actually use them. The model you use presents the colors at your disposal, but the color palette restricts the number of colors you can use at one time, usually down to 256 in the case of PNG or GIF files (imagine if you were able to use as many colors as you liked—you'd have a beautiful looking graphic, but it would take an enormous file size to hold all that color information).

You have a choice of predefined palettes to use for your creations in the Optimize panel (Windows ➤ Optimize/*F6*). The second drop-down list on the left contains the list of palettes.

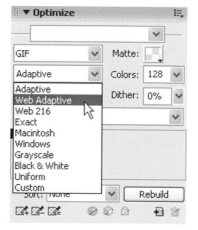

Here's a quick rundown of the different palettes:

★ **Adaptive:** Rather than a predefined set of colors, the Adaptive palette contains all the colors being used in the current graphic. However, it is limited to 256 colors.

★ **Web Adaptive:** The single difference between this and the Adaptive palette is its prerogative to convert any color in the palette that's close to one of the 216 web-safe colors to that web-safe color. Web-safe colors are the colors most likely to be reproduced consistently by all browsers on any operating system or machine. For more information on web-safe colors, take a look at www.webdevelopersjournal.com/articles/websafe1/websafe_colors.html.

★ **Web 216:** This palette contains only the 216 web-safe colors.

★ **Exact:** This contains a maximum of 256 exact colors used in the image. If the number of colors increases beyond 256, the palette switches to Adaptive.

★ **Macintosh and Windows:** These palettes are copies of the 256 color system palettes as defined by the Macintosh and Windows operating systems, respectively.

★ **Grayscale:** This contains the 256 different shades of gray that you saw in the grayscale color mode. Note that choosing this palette won't immediately change the image to black and white. This only happens when you export the image.

★ **Black and White:** A two-color palette containing only pure black and pure white.

★ **Uniform:** This palette contains 256 colors and attempts to store the colors in the graphic as a mathematical relationship between their RGB values.

★ **Custom:** A Custom palette is one that has been modified or imported from a palette (ACT) or GIF file stored externally of Fireworks. Custom palettes are discussed later.

Note that while you're working on a graphic in Fireworks, it can have as many colors as you like. Changing the color palette in the Optimize panel only affects the colors in the image once it has been exported. You'll see exactly what this means when we discuss the export process in Chapter Five.

Choosing a color to work with

When traditional artists need a color to add to their masterpiece, they're limited to the colors on their easel, or a mixture of them. Should they need to re-create a color already on the canvas, only their skill in color mixing can help them. By comparison, digital artists are spoiled. You have a canvas of over 16 million colors to work with, each of which you can re-create with total accuracy if needed.

Eyedropper tool

The Eyedropper tool is almost universal in paint packages today. It's this tool that lets you pick a color from the canvas and reuse it. This removes the guesswork from choosing colors.

1. Open `color.png` from the download files and you'll see that it contains six blocks with different fill colors and styles.

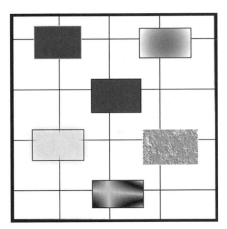

2. Select the Eyedropper tool from the Tools panel (or press *I*), and you'll see that the cursor changes to an eyedropper.

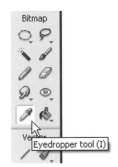

3. Drag the cursor over a graphic and click it. You'll see that the stroke or fill color (depending upon which is selected in the Colors section of the Tools panel) changes to the new selected color.

4. Try choosing some other colors for your stroke and fill and notice that your eyedropper cursor changes slightly. When you select a stroke, a squiggly line appears beside the eyedropper and when you select a fill, a small square appears.

The Eyedropper tool can analyze an object and change the stroke color to that of the object's outline or the fill color to match the object's fill color. Conveniently, if the object has a gradient or textured fill, the eyedropper copies the fill style too.

5. Check this feature out by selecting the Eyedropper tool again, and holding down *CTRL/CMD*. The cursor changes back to a standard cursor. Now move the cursor over `color.png` and you'll see that each object is highlighted as the cursor passes over it, letting you know which object will be sampled.

6. Still holding *CTRL/CMD*, click the bottom gray and black rectangle. The stroke color changes to black and the fill color now mimics the black and gray gradient fill.

Colors panel

The Eyedropper tool takes care of re-creating colors already in your graphic, but how do you pick a color you haven't used yet? You use the Colors panel in this case. As you saw earlier, you can choose from the full 16 million colors in the Color Mixer, or you have a straightforward choice of the web-safe colors to choose from in the Swatches panel.

Swatches panel

If it's not already visible, open the Swatches panel (Window ➤ Swatches or *CTRL/CMD+F9*). By default, the 216 web-safe colors are displayed as color cubes. Selecting a color is as simple as moving the cursor (which changes to an eyedropper again) over the color you want and clicking it. As before, if there's a squiggly line next to your cursor, you're selecting the stroke color. If there's a square beside it, you're selecting the fill color.

If you're not happy with the color cubes' arrangement, you can rearrange them as a set of continuous tones or sort them by color using the options menu. Alternatively, you can choose to view a set of completely different swatches, comprising the Windows System colors, Macintosh System colors, or Grayscale tones.

Color Mixer

The other tab in the Colors panel is the Color Mixer, which you saw earlier when you looked at the different color modes. There are three parts to the Color Mixer:

★ At the top left, you can specify whether you're choosing the stroke color or the fill color.

★ At the top right are the color values for the selected color. You can type in the color values directly to define the color you want or click the down arrow to the right of the value to use the slider instead. With the Color Mixer's option menu you can specify your preferred working color mode.

★ At the bottom of the Color Mixer is the familiar color bar. Essentially, it's just a Swatches panel containing many more colors than you really ever use. By default, it shows all 16 million colors available under the RGB system. However, if you *SHIFT*+click the bar, it toggles through the 216-color web-safe palette, the grayscale palette, and the original color bar.

The Color Mixer is very handy for picking a single custom color, but if you change the color again, the original isn't readily available. If you're going to work with several custom colors, you'll need to use the **Color Picker**.

Color Picker

With the system Color Picker, you can select any of the 16 million colors available and store them as **custom colors** so that they're easily retrievable for future use.

1. Click the fill or stroke or color box, which brings up a swatch palette.

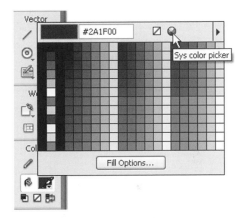

2. Click the color wheel above the palette to open the system Color Picker.

Like the Color Mixer, the Color Picker has three distinct areas:

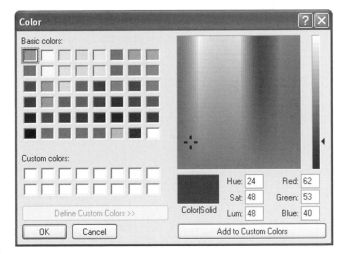

* ★ The top-left corner contains 48 distinct web-safe colors to choose from.

* ★ The bottom-left corner contains 16 bays containing the custom colors you've defined for use with your graphics. These custom colors are stored here until Fireworks itself is closed, at which point they're erased.

* ★ At the right side, you can define a custom color either graphically or by entering the specific RGB or HSB colors. The slider bar on the far right lets you pick the brightness for your color. The color shown here is the color selected. This is a great way to pick a lighter or darker version of the same color. Once you've chosen your color, simply hit the Add to Custom Colors button.

Organizing your colors

The Color Picker is great when you're trying out new colors in your graphics, but it only stores the custom colors until you shut down Fireworks, at which point they're lost. It's also two clicks away rather than one, and it rapidly gets frustrating clicking that color wheel to open the Color Picker. Fortunately, you can remedy this by tuning the Swatches panel to suit your own needs. Not only can you add your own custom colors to the palette, replacing those you don't use, but you can also export your custom palette out to a file for reuse later.

Customizing and saving the Swatches panel

1. Open `color.png` from the download files (if it isn't already open) and ensure the Swatches panel is visible (Window ➤ Swatches or *Ctrl/Cmd+F9*).

2. Select the Eyedropper tool and click to sample the pink area of the graphic. The stroke or fill color box (depending on which you have selected) turns pink.

   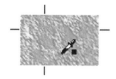

3. To add this pink to the Swatches panel, hold down the *Shift* key and move the cursor over the Swatches panel. The cursor changes to the paint bucket icon.

4. Click a swatch to change it to the pink you sampled.

   In addition to changing the color on the palette, you can also delete some of the colors you're not using.

   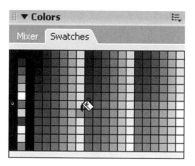

5. Move the cursor over a swatch in the Swatches panel and press the *Ctrl/Cmd* key. The cursor turns into a scissors icon.

6. Still holding *Ctrl/Cmd*, click the swatch. The remaining colors scroll round to fill in the gap, leaving the bottom row to display the empty swatches.

   If you want to start from scratch, you can delete all the colors from the Swatches panel by selecting Clear Swatches from the Colors panel option menu. Also, if you want to return to the default set of swatches, choose Color Cubes or one of the other palette options from the same options menu.

   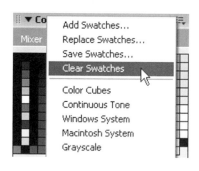

   The reward for organizing your colors comes in being able to save your custom palette for reuse later.

7. To save your custom palette, select Save Swatches... from the Colors panel options menu.

8. A normal Save dialog box appears. Choose a directory to save the palette in and save it as `myPalette.act`.

   With your palette saved on file, the next time you open Fireworks, you can replace the whole default Swatches panel with your own.

9. Choose Replace Swatches... from the options menu or add your custom colors to the palette already in place with Add Swatches....

Note that you can replace or add color swatches to the palette by sampling the 256 colors in a GIF file and adding them all to the palette. Try choosing a GIF rather than an ACT file when you want to add or replace your swatches to see this.

2

Finding and replacing colors

A powerful feature is the ability to find and replace colors. To do this, select Edit ➤ Find.

The first field sets the scope of the search and replace. In this case, you're telling the second field to Find Color. You then use the color palette (or the Eyedropper tool) to set the Find color and the Change to color. You can apply it to fills and strokes, all properties, just fills or just strokes, or effects. You can also issue a Replace All command or decide each occurrence manually.

More fun with fills

Up to this point in the book, you've been working with solid colors. That is, every object you've created has been filled with a single, solid color. With better control of the available colors, let's start using Fireworks to create some cool eye-catching fill effects. The first multicolored trick to learn is how to create and manipulate **gradients**.

Using gradient fills

A gradient is a set of two or more colors that blend together in a variety of designs or categories. All of the gradient presets are in the **Fill Options** dialog box. To open it, click the fill color swatch in the Tools panel and click the Fill Options button in the resulting palette.

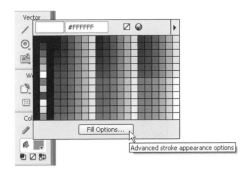

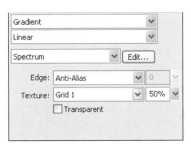

The Fill category drop-down menu at the top of the dialog box allows you to specify what type of fill you want to use, and the one immediately beneath it contains a list of style categories. The Edit button to the right of the list brings up the Gradient tool, where you can define your own gradient color schemes.

1. Open a new 500×500 pixels canvas with a white background.

2. Draw a rectangle on the canvas with a white fill and a black stroke. The size doesn't matter, but make the stroke size 5 pixels so that it stands out.

3. In the Property inspector, set the Fill category to Gradient ➤ Ellipse.

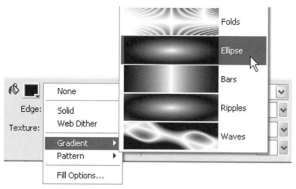

Your image should look something like the one shown here. Notice that the gradient doesn't entirely fill up the interior of the rectangle.

4. Select the Pointer tool and click the gradient.

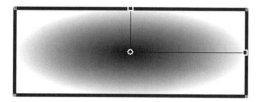

You can make three adjustments to the gradient here:

★ Grab the center circle to move the center point of the gradient.

★ Use the top, or smaller, square to change the skew and height of the gradient.

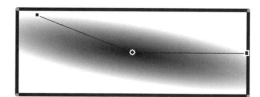

★ Use the horizontal, or larger, square to change the skew and width of the gradient.

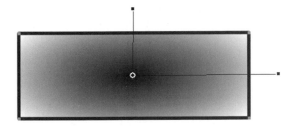

In addition to changing the height, width, and fill, you can change the color scheme of the gradient.

5. Click the fill color box in the Property inspector.

   By far, the easiest way to change your gradient colors is to use one of the many Preset schemes that come with Fireworks.

6. As an example, select Spectrum from the Preset drop-down menu.

   There are six color boxes underneath the color bar at the top of the dialog box, known as the *Color Ramp*. Each of these boxes can be moved, deleted, or edited. You can also add more boxes.

7. Click the second color box from the left. You can easily change the color of the color box here with the familiar Color Picker.

8. Each color box can easily be moved. As an experiment, working from the left, try dragging the second box over between swatches five and six. Take what was swatch five (now four) and make it swatch two. You should now see the colors reversed in your gradient. Experiment a bit and try rearranging your colors.

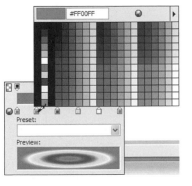

Notice that when the cursor is between color boxes it has a small **+** next to it. This means you can now add additional color boxes by just clicking where you want them beneath the color ramp. Then, once in place, they can be handled like any of the other existing color boxes.

9. To remove a swatch, simply drag it off of the panel.

The slider controls along the top of the color ramp handle the opacity (or transparency) of the color.

10. Click the opacity control at the top right. From its position, it is handling the outer red ring. Change the Opacity slider to 50 percent.

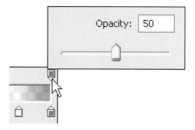

Again, like the color boxes, you can add more opacity boxes as needed. They can be moved and deleted just like regular color boxes.

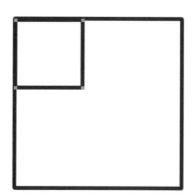

Let's try another little exercise to show a unique use for gradients.

More complex gradient fills

1. Close any work you have open (you won't be revisiting the previous exercise).

2. Open a new 500×500 canvas with a white background.

3. Draw a 250×250 rectangle with a white fill and a black stroke. Set the stroke size to 5 pixels.

4. Draw another rectangle in the upper-left corner of the rectangle. Make it 100×100 with the same stroke and fill properties as the larger rectangle.

5. With the inner rectangle selected, choose Edit ➤ Duplicate and move the copy to the upper-right corner.

6. Repeat the process until there's a vector rectangle in each corner.

   There are two tools to fill in selected vector shapes. You've seen the Paint Bucket tool, but another handy tool is the Gradient tool. You can toggle between these two tools with the G key.

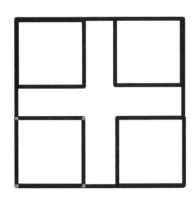

7. Choose the Gradient tool from the Tools panel.

8. Set the Gradient category to Ripples and use the color scheme of your choice.

9. Select all four inner rectangles and click in the center of your graphic with the Gradient tool.

Fireworks distributes the gradient over each of the vector objects selected. You can rotate and stretch the gradient using the handles as normal.

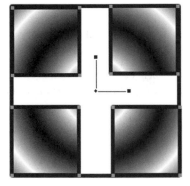

Summary

Now that you've learned all about colors, gradients, and how to control your object's appearance, let's move on to learn more about objects and how to work with them effectively in the Fireworks interface.

Three

Object Properties

In this chapter

Everything that you create in Fireworks is an **object**. These are self-contained units that can be used again and again, as needed, and all objects must have the following three characteristics:

★ **Properties:** Such as shape, color, and size.

★ **Behavior**: Such as linking to another web page and swapping images.

★ **Identity**: The name you assign to the object.

In this chapter, you'll learn about properties and identity (behavior is discussed in Chapter 4) including the following:

★ Learning about object properties

★ Dealing with layers

★ Manipulating and organizing objects

    ★ Learning to use rulers, guides, and grids

    ★ Ordering objects

    ★ Grouping objects

★ Modifying objects

★ Using masks and blending modes

★ Creating, editing, exporting, and importing symbols

Let's begin our discussion of objects by drawing a simple circle. Make it any size and color that you want.

These properties should seem familiar to those you were introduced to in Chapter Two when you learned about the vector tools. Of course, although your circle is an object, it's also still a vector shape, and so it retains the properties of the tool that created it. What is lacking, however, from your circle as an object is a name (in programming parlance, this is known as the **object identity**).

You can name your object by simply typing the name into the field at the left side of the Property inspector.

Often, and especially if you're creating web content, your work needs to interact with programming from other sources. Many of the newer programming environments are highly case-sensitive so, as a result, it's important that you employ the naming conventions that are recognized and used throughout the industry. Even if you don't intend for your objects to be referenced externally, it's worth using the following standard naming conventions because they make your projects clearer and easier to follow:

★ Object names should be lowercase.

★ The name should have no spaces.

★ If your name contains two words, you should differentiate them using mid-word capitalization, such as myCircle, for example.

When you create your object something else happens. Open the Layers panel (Window ➤ Layers or press *F2*). Your circle now appears on Layer 1.

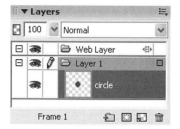

Layers

The concept of layers is an important and integral part of designing graphics in Fireworks. In many ways, it's a very old concept. Imagine you have a complex graphic that contains many objects. Would it be easier to draw the complex graphic on a single sheet, or to draw each object on a separate transparency, and then assemble these transparencies so that the viewer sees the final composite? If you selected the latter option, you're close to understanding the many benefits of layers. If you selected the former, let's spend the rest of the chapter changing your mind!

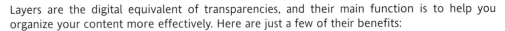

Layers are the digital equivalent of transparencies, and their main function is to help you organize your content more effectively. Here are just a few of their benefits:

★ Organize graphic components more effectively by placing separate objects in their own layer, giving each of them a unique label.

★ Group related objects together so that your complex graphic acts as a single image rather than a collection of individual objects.

★ Freely arrange your objects or groups across the canvas as needed.

★ Share objects on one layer across frames for animations.

★ Export objects that reside on a separate layer as CSS Layers.

By default, every new document you create in Fireworks opens with two default layers:

★ **Web Layer:** Contains all the web elements of a layer, such as hotspots and slices. These elements often have programming behaviors attached to them (behaviors are covered in the next chapter).

★ **Layer 1:** For the first objects you create, such as the circle you created earlier. If you create a button made up of a basic shape and a hotspot, then the shape object appears in this layer, whereas the hotspot resides in the Web Layer. You can add more of these layers as you need them.

Discussions of objects and layers are tightly intertwined with each other. For example, try drawing a second object on your screen that contrasts in shape and color with the circle. When you create a new object, Fireworks automatically puts it on Layer 1. Very tidy indeed!

Unless you tell it differently, Fireworks places all of your objects on Layer 1. With the exception of rectangles, Auto Shapes, and text, Fireworks assigns the object the default name Path. A path is the line between two vector points. As already discussed, this name is unusable. For instance, assume you have some JavaScript code that needs to call the object. If you have four objects all named Path, how will the JavaScript know which one to call? Therefore you should give each object a unique name.

For now, take a closer look at your objects and layers.

Notice that each object in the Layers panel is represented by a **thumbnail** image. When you select the different objects on your canvas, the corresponding thumbnail in the Layers panel is highlighted. It works the other way around too: you can select an object on the canvas by clicking its thumbnail in the Layers panel.

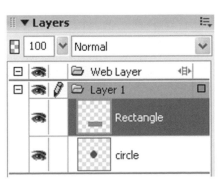

You can change the size of these thumbnails by selecting Thumbnail Options… from the Layers panel options menu to open the Thumbnail Options dialog box. Simply select the size option that is most comfortable for your working style, and click OK.

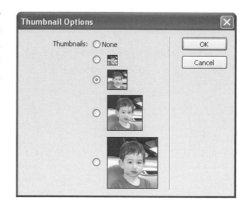

Manipulating objects

Objects can be selected with the Pointer tool either via the Layers panel or directly on the canvas but, once selected, what can you do with them?

You can use the Property inspector to change an object's properties such as color, texture, and opacity, and you can also add effects, resize, and move an object around the canvas. Let's look at moving an object using the Property inspector now. Although clicking and dragging is the easiest way to move an object, if you need to position your objects precisely, you can use the Property inspector to set specific x and y coordinates (in pixels).

For reference, an x,y coordinate of 0,0 is the upper-left corner of the canvas. You can move an object in two other ways:

★ Select the object and use the arrow keys to move it one pixel at a time (as you move the object with the arrows, watch the coordinates on the Property inspector clock up and down).

★ Hold down the *SHIFT* key and use the arrow keys again to move the object by 10 pixels at a time.

You can also configure your canvas to make it easier to accurately position your objects using **rulers**, **guides**, and **grids**.

Rulers

Switch on the rulers with View ➤ Rulers (*CTRL+ALT/OPT+R*).

As you can see, your canvas is bordered by a vertical and a horizontal ruler. The measurements are in pixels.

If you look in the upper-left corner of the rulers, you'll see the **zero point crosshairs**.

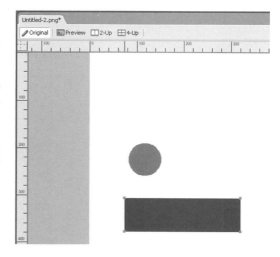

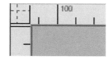

By clicking and dragging them onto the canvas, you force the rulers to reposition the point 0,0.

Repositioning the point 0,0 like this can be very useful if you want to use the Property inspector to reposition your objects at the coordinates 0,0 but don't want 0,0 to be the top-left corner of your canvas.

To reset your rulers back to their default position at the top-left of the canvas, simply double-click the zero point crosshairs.

Guides

Guides are nonprintable lines that you can place on your canvas to help position objects and can only be used with rulers turned on. To turn the guides on, select View ➤ Guides ➤ Show Guides (*CTRL/CMD+;*).

Once guides are turned on, drag them onto the canvas by placing your mouse pointer inside one of the rulers and clicking and dragging out on to the canvas. Double-click a guide to set an exact position in pixels.

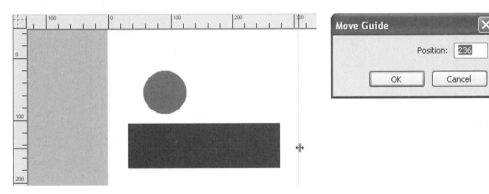

You can then use the guides to help position your objects on the canvas. To be really precise, drag out multiple guides from each ruler.

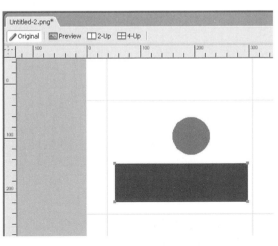

Once the guides are in place, you can lock them with View ➤ Guides ➤ Lock Guides (*CTRL/CMD+ALT/OPT+;*) so you don't accidentally move them while working.

You can also edit the properties of the guides in the Guides dialog box (View ➤ Guides ➤ Edit Guides…). You can adjust the guides' color (you wouldn't want to use the default green if your canvas background was the same green, for example), and you also have the options of showing and locking them again here.

The most useful option here is Snap to guides. This forces the object to lock onto the nearest guide when you drag it, which can save a lot of time fiddling about trying to position your objects correctly.

A variation on guides is the **grid**.

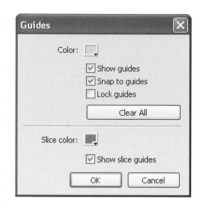

Grids

Turn on the grid with View ➤ Grid ➤ Show Grid (*CTRL/CMD+ALT/OPT+G*). You don't need to have rulers on to see your grid, but you can use both at the same time.

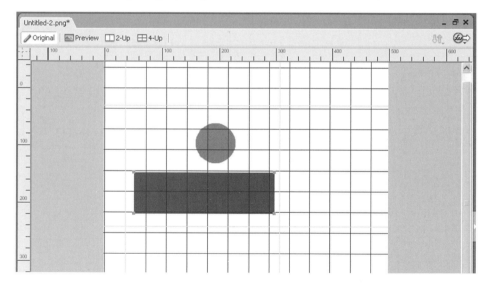

Like the guides, you can also edit the grid (View ➤ Grid ➤ Edit Grid…).

It's a similar setup to the Guides dialog box, but here you can set the horizontal and vertical spacing of the grid lines. Also, interestingly, if you check Snap to Grid, the object snaps to the grid, even if the grid is not visible.

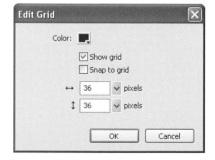

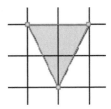

As well as aiding in positioning objects, the grid is also very useful when you're creating objects. For example, you can use grid lines to help create accurate geometric shapes with the Pen tool. When you're clicking with the Pen tool to determine the points of the shape, click grid lines to precisely place them. Guides can also be used to similar effect.

Ordering objects

The canvas in Fireworks acts as a three dimensional space. For example, if you place your objects in the same space, they appear as if on top of one another. Here, the circle is on the bottom, the rectangle is in the middle, and the triangle is on the top. This order is mirrored in the Layers panel.

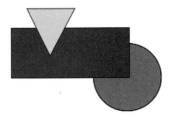
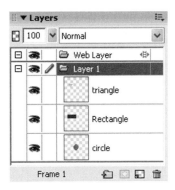

The order of the objects is exactly the same and is imposed when you create the objects: the first object you create is the bottom layer, the next goes on top, and the next on top of that. You can change the stacking order of the objects by selecting the object in the Layers panel, and dragging it up or down to the new position you want. Notice that when you do this, the order of the objects changes on the canvas.

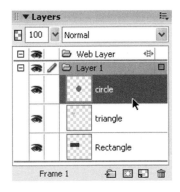
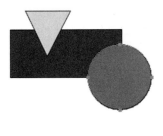

You can also change the order of objects in a layer by selecting the object you want to move, choosing Modify ➤ Arrange, and then choosing from the following:

★ **Bring to Front:** Moves the object to the top of the stack.

★ **Bring Forward:** Promotes the object one level.

★ **Send Backward:** Demotes the object one level.

★ **Send to Back:** Moves the object to the bottom of the stack.

Rearranging objects on the canvas

If you've been trying out the examples in this chapter so far, you may already have a Fireworks project open with a circle, rectangle, and triangle all on Layer 1. If not, follow these steps:

1. Use the vector shape tools to create a circle and rectangle on the canvas. Use the Property inspector to give them different colors and object names (refer back to Chapter One for a reminder of how to use the vector shape tools, if necessary).

2. Next, turn the grid on (View ➤ Grid ➤ Show Grid) and use the Pen tool to draw a triangle, using the grid lines as a guide. When you're done, use the Property inspector to give your triangle a name and a color (again, refer back to Chapter One for a reminder of how to use the Pen tool).

3. Turn the grid off again. You should now have three shapes on your canvas, all represented in Layer 1:

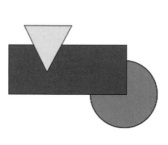
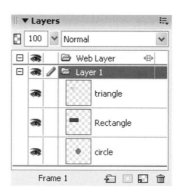

4. Click the first button at the lower right of the Layers panel to create a new layer, which is called Layer 2 by default.

5. Click the thumbnail of your triangle object in the Layers panel, drag it up, and drop it on Layer 2.

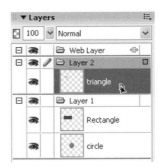

6. Create one more layer, and then place your circle object on it. You should now have three layers, each containing one of your objects.

7. Double click one of your layer names. This brings up a dialog box in which you can rename your layer.

8. Give each of your layers an appropriate name, and then save your project as objects.png.

Take a look at the eye icon on each layer in the Layers panel. This is the **show/hide** button.

The Share across frames *option lets you share the layer across multiple frames, which actually means that when you update the layer, all the corresponding frames are updated. Frames are discussed in Chapter Six.*

If you click it, it will turn the object off and on. Because of this, you can

★ Control visibility

★ Prevent accidental editing

Use this button to isolate certain objects temporarily without interference from others. Notice that each object has a show/hide button as does each layer.

You can also lock a layer to prevent accidental changes on it. To do this, click the pencil icon between the show/hide button and the layer name. It changes to a padlock icon, indicating that it's locked.

Aligning objects together

Now, assuming all of your layers are unlocked and visible, turn your attention to **aligning** your objects with the Align panel (Windows ➤ Align).

There are two types of alignment: aligning objects to each other or to the canvas. You use the same controls for both with one difference—the To Canvas button. When this is depressed, selected objects align to the canvas. When not depressed, they're aligned to each other.

1. Arrange your objects as shown here and select all three objects.

2. Click the Align top edge button in the Align panel.

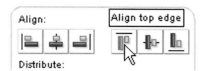

Fireworks finds the uppermost object (the circle) and aligns the other two objects to the circle's top edge.

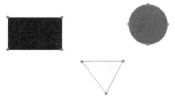

3. Try switching the To Canvas button on and then pressing the Align vertical center button. Your objects are now centered between the top and bottom of the canvas.

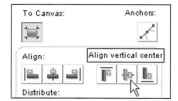

4. Your instincts are probably telling you to try Align Horizontal Center now. However, with three objects selected, this is what you will get:

All three objects tried to align against the center of the canvas.

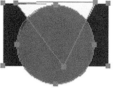

One of the most useful features is to use the Align panel to evenly space objects apart, such as when you're creating buttons. You just select all the objects you want to space evenly and then select one of the two Space buttons.

Space:

Grouping objects

Imagine you'd just created a great-looking graphic consisting of six very carefully placed objects, but you need to move the whole thing to another location. You don't want to move one object at a time and repeat the placement process. What you want to do is **group** the objects as they are and move them as a single unit.

Grouping makes multiple objects act as one. When a set of objects is grouped, whatever you do to one object happens to the others. For example, if you group your rectangle and triangle together, and change the color of one of them, then the other makes the same color transformation.

To group objects, first select the objects you want to group. You can either

★ Use the Pointer tool and draw an invisible rectangle around the shapes (all the objects within the rectangle will be selected).

or

★ Hold down *SHIFT* and click each of the objects you want to select. Note, however, that if any layers are locked, you won't be able to select the objects on those layers.

Once you've selected your objects, choose Modify ➤ Group (*CTRL/CMD+G*); an implied rectangle appears around the selected objects, with the familiar handles at each corner.

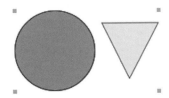

When you group objects together that exist on different layers, Fireworks groups them together on a single layer and indicates that your selected objects are now a group. In essence, by grouping objects together, you create a new object, which can have its own name, own layer, and its own life.

To ungroup your objects, select Modify ➤ Ungroup (*CTRL/CMD+SHIFT+G*).

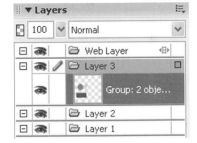

Copying an object

Although the easiest way to copy an object is to use the standard technique of copy and paste, here are additional options:

★ Select your object, press *ALT/OPT*, and then click and drag out a copy of your object.

★ Use Edit ➤ Duplicate to reproduce the object slightly offset from the original.

★ Use a slight variation of Edit ➤ Duplicate, Edit ➤ Clone. This places the new object directly over the original.

★ Select your object in the Layers panel, then drag the layer down and drop it on the New / Duplicate Layer button. You should now see a copy of the object in a new layer all of its own.

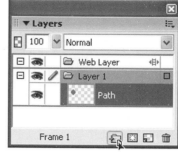

Now that you're familiar with using multiple layers, let's take a look at one of the most impressive Fireworks capabilities that makes use of multiple layers: **masks**.

Using masks

A mask is used either to hide or reveal portions of a layer. Masks can be very useful when you're creating image compositions like the following:

1. Start a new 300×300 canvas and import cat.png from the download files for this chapter (File ➤ Import).

2. Position the right-angle mouse pointer in the upper-left corner of the canvas, and click to place the image. The image is larger than your canvas, but this is okay, as you'll only need the cat's head. Use the Pointer tool to position the cat as shown in the illustration.

3. Use the Ellipse tool to draw a circle around the head of the cat.

4. Use the Property inspector to ensure that the fill color is white and solid, set the Edge to Feather, and the amount to 30.

Remember that when you use the Ellipse tool, you can hold down the SHIFT key to maintain a perfect circle and you can reposition the circle while drawing it by holding down the SPACE BAR.

Your cat should look something like this:

Now your cat image has the most important part blocked out. This might not immediately sound like a good thing—but it is. What you've done here is defined the shape of your mask.

5. Take a look at your ellipse in the Layers panel. Rename it maskArea and rename your original bitmap image originalImage.

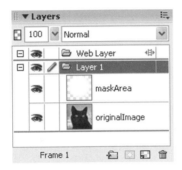

6. In order to create the mask, you need to select the defined area and the graphic you're masking. Because only two of these components exist on the canvas, it's easy. Choose Select ➤ Select All.

Both the mask area and the original image are now selected, and you can verify this in the Layers panel. Both layers should be highlighted. You're ready to create the mask.

7. Select Modify ➤ Mask ➤ Group as mask.

And voila! You can see how the area you defined was actually the shape of the mask, which now reveals the cat's face and conceals the rest of the bitmap.

You can experiment with the opacity and Effects menu in the Property inspector to enhance your graphic even more.

8. To temporarily disable the mask, select Modify ➤ Mask ➤ Disable Mask—and to re-enable it, choose Modify ➤ Mask ➤ Enable Mask.

Blending modes

Blending modes determine how the pixels of one layer or object interact, or blend, with the pixels of another below it. When you're considering blending modes, you need to take four main factors into account:

★ **Opacity:** Also known as transparency.

★ **Blending color:** The color that you want to blend into. It may be easier to think of this as the foreground color.

★ **Base color:** The color you are blending from (the color underneath the blending color). Again, it's easier to think of this as the background color.

★ **Result Color:** The new color created from the blend.

Colors are made of three components—red, green, and blue (RGB)—where each is assigned a numerical value between 0 and 255 for its intensity. For reference, pure white means the intensity of all three colors is 255 and for black the intensity of all three colors is 0.

Now, this may seem like a contradiction to what we said in Chapter Two. If, in the hexadecimal system, the largest number is FF, how does that translate to 255? Let's do a bit of reasoning.

Hexadecimal (or hex for short) means that the number is based on a value of 16. In your system, there are 16 possible numbers. The first 10 numbers are 0–9, and the next 6 numbers are represented by, respectively, A–F, with F representing 15. Each color is represented by a two-digit decimal number, which you read from right to left. FF would be

F = 15×1 = 15

F = 15×16 = 240

Total number = 255

As another example, suppose you have a hex color intensity of 93:

3 = 3×1 = 3

9 = 9×16 = 144

Total number = 147

Blending modes mathematically play with these numbers between layers.

1. Begin by creating a new 300×300 canvas with a white background.

2. Create two circles on two separate layers. Layer 1 should contain a yellow circle and Layer 2 a blue circle. Make the circles overlap each other.

Look at the two drop-downs at the top of the Layers panel. The left field displays the layer's **opacity** and the right menu displays the **blending mode**, set to Normal by default.

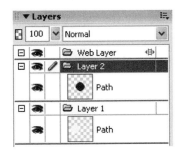

So what does "Normal" mean when you're blending? In the simplest terms, it means one color of 100 percent opacity will completely cover the other. In this example, the blue circle completely covers the yellow circle on the layer beneath.

3. Select Layer 2 and change the opacity to 50 percent. The blue circle becomes more transparent. Where the circles overlap, you can see through to the yellow circle below.

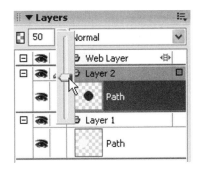

Try a few different opacity percentages and then set it back to 100 percent.

4. When you are blending, you usually select the foreground, or blend, color. Make sure the blue circle is selected, and that its opacity is back at 100 percent, and then change the blending mode from Normal to Multiply.

Notice that the intersection of the two circles is nearly black. Mathematically, Fireworks multiplied the RGB values of the blend layer by the RGB values of the base layer and then calculated them in terms of percentages of 255. Still want to learn the math involved? Okay...

$$Resulting\ Color = \frac{1}{255}(Foreground \times Background)$$

Because, mathematically, the resulting color will be a smaller number, it will tend to move toward a very dark result.

5. Try playing with the opacity setting now. You'll get some interesting results. After you've finished with this, set it back to 100 percent.

6. Change the blending mode from Multiply to Screen. Your blue circle should have turned almost white.

This mode first inverts the foreground (or blend) color before multiplying it by the base (or background) color.

Let's take a look at the Darken and Lighten blend modes. Darken compares the blend and base layers and uses the darkest of the two. Translated to a formula, it would be

> *Result Color = min{Background Color, Foreground Color}*

The Lighten mode, as you may have guessed, does the opposite. It uses the color with the largest value.

7. Try the Difference mode now. This mode subtracts the darker color from the lighter one.

Unfortunately, the resulting arithmetic is a bit more involved. If you look at it closely, you could end up with negative color values. So, you need to add one more step: if the resulting color is a negative value, the negative sign is converted into a positive sign. In mathematics, this is called the absolute value.

The remaining blending modes alter the balance between the hue (colors), saturation (intensity), and luminosity (brightness) of each layer:

★ **Hue:** The actual shade of color. This blending mode takes the actual color of the foreground and blends it with the luminosity and saturation of the background color.

★ **Saturation:** The pureness of the color with respect to white. For instance, if you blend white with red, red's saturation decreases and moves toward pink. Without white, the saturation is 100 percent. This blend mode takes the saturation of the foreground color and blends it with the luminosity and hue of the background color.

★ **Color:** The result of blending the hue and saturation of the foreground color and the luminosity of the background.

★ **Luminosity:** The brightness. This is calculated by blending the luminosity of the foreground color with the hue and saturation in the background.

★ **Tint:** Used to add gray to the background color.

★ **Invert:** Reverses the background color.

★ **Erase:** Erases the background color.

Symbols

As you've seen, as soon as you create a shape or component, you create an object. But, say you need the same object ten times in this project or, better still, in five other separate projects. It's hardly time-effective to build this object from scratch each time.

A **symbol** is simply an object saved for future use. Symbols are saved to a **library** that's attached to the document you're working on. They can also be saved for use in other documents. By storing symbols in this way, you can build up huge libraries of components that you can use anytime and anywhere.

You use the symbol in the library to create **instances**, or copies, to use in your project, reusing symbols as many times as you want. When you use a version of a symbol on the canvas, you're creating an **instance** of that symbol. Then, when you edit the master symbol, all the instances of that symbol on the canvas change automatically to reflect that edit. For example, if you have ten instances of a button symbol on the canvas, and you change the color of the original symbol, all ten instances on the canvas undergo the same color change. Likewise, you can change the **properties** of individual instances without affecting the symbol or other instances on the canvas.

As you'll see in Chapter Five, using symbols wisely can also help keep file sizes down. If you have ten identical instances, they're treated as a single object (the symbol in the library) and then duplicated ten times. (However, if you change the properties of these instances you don't get this benefit.)

Let's see how to create a symbol.

Creating a symbol

1. Start by creating an object on the canvas. Draw a circle and place some text on it.

   My Symbol

   At the moment, these are two separate objects, a circle and some text.

2. Select both of these objects and go to Modify ➤ Symbol ➤ Convert to Symbol… (*F8*) to open the **Symbol Properties** dialog box:

   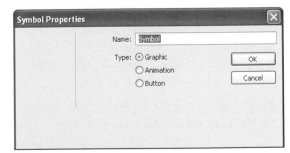

   As you can see, symbols come in three flavors:

   ★ A **graphic** is a static object.
   ★ An **animation** is a series of frames that create the illusion of motion.
   ★ A button is a navigation tool with built-in actions or behaviors.

3. For the time being, we're just interested in creating a static symbol, so leave Graphic checked and type "mySymbol" in the Name field. Once you've named your symbol, press OK.

> *You could have also created the symbol from scratch by selecting* Edit ➤ Insert ➤ New Symbol... *and then drawing the shape. You can also copy and paste, import, or drag an object from one document into the Symbol Editor.*

When you pressed OK to create the symbol, several things happened. First of all, the two object graphics were converted into a single grouped symbol. You can see an instance of this symbol on your canvas, indicated by the small arrow at the lower-left corner.

The second change can be seen in the Library panel (Window ➤ Library or *F11*). The Library displays all the symbols you've created in your project, as well as a thumbnail of each of them. This is where the actual symbol is stored.

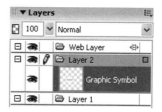

Finally, if you look at the Layers panel, you'll see that your two objects have become a single symbol, and Fireworks labels it so.

As you saw at the beginning of the symbols section, an instance is a copy of a symbol from the Library. Each instance can be given a unique name on the canvas, using the same techniques you learned when naming objects. You already have an instance on your canvas—it's the original object from which you created the symbol.

4. Using the Property inspector, give your instance the name "instance1".

5. Click the symbol in the Library (either the thumbnail or the name) and drag another instance of the symbol out onto your canvas.

6. Name this second instance "instance2", and save your project as symbols.png.

Now that you have a symbol and two instances of it, let's move on to look at how to edit them.

Editing a symbol

To edit a symbol, you need to use the **Symbol Editor**. You can open it by double clicking any instance on the canvas or the symbol name or image in the Library. This opens a new canvas identified by the tab as a symbol and its name.

Once in the Symbol Editor, you can edit just as you would any other object on the canvas. The symbol is automatically ungrouped ready for editing so that, in this example, you can change the properties of the text and the circle, treating them as two different objects.

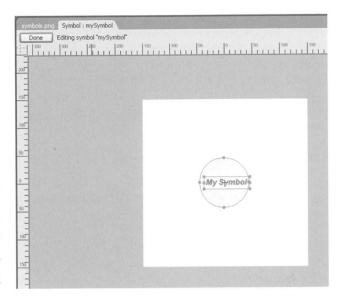

Try changing the color of the circle. When finished, press the Done button at the upper-left corner of the Symbol Editor. Both instances on your canvas should now have changed to reflect the new color property of the circle.

You do have some ability to alter the properties of individual instances without affecting the others by selecting an instance and using the Property inspector. You can change the size or add an effect, for example. However, more extensive property changes need to be done in the Symbol Editor.

Exporting and importing symbols

Initially, symbols are attached to the document you create them in. However, you can make them available in other documents. To do this, you first need to **export** the symbols to a common library and then import them into the new document you want to use them in. Let's try this out with the symbol you created a moment ago.

1. If it's not already, open symbols.png (available in the download files) and then open the Library (Window ➤ Library or *F11*).

2. Select Export Symbols... from the Library options menu to open up the **Export Symbols** dialog box, where you can choose which symbols you want to export.

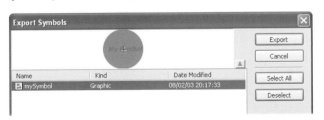

3. Because you only have this one symbol, press the Export button and, in the next dialog box, give your symbol a name and choose somewhere to save it. After you save it, your symbol will be saved to an external PNG file.

4. Now start a new document, go to the Library options menu again, and select Import Symbols…. Use the following dialog box to locate your symbol.

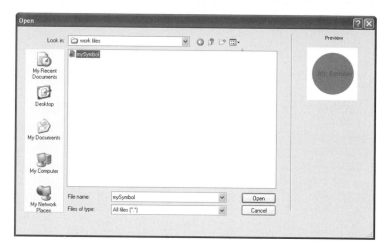

When you select the symbol you want to import, you should see a preview of it at the right of the dialog box.

5. Press Open. This brings up the **Import Symbols** dialog box where you can pick and choose exactly which individual symbols you want to import.

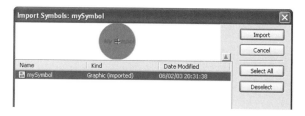

6. In this case, you only have one symbol, so select this one and click Import.

Your symbol should now appear in the Library of your new document and there you can use it as you wish.

Summary

In this chapter, you've examined objects and their properties and looked at how to manipulate objects by moving, grouping, ordering, and copying them. Using masks and blending modes has also been discussed.

The concept of using symbols and libraries may seem unfamiliar at first, but once you get a grip on the fact that a symbol is simply an object that has been saved for future use and that the Library is where it's stored, you'll soon be creating, editing, and reusing symbols without a second thought.

In the next chapter, you'll build on your knowledge of objects to look at adding behaviors and functionality to objects in order to create **interactivity**.

Four

Object Behavior: Interactivity

In this chapter

You're going to learn more about objects, specifically the methods of adding interactivity to them so that they respond to user input such as mouse clicks or rollovers. We'll also introduce button symbols as a means of easily creating and reusing interactive images. You'll become familiar with the following:

★ Exploring **behaviors**

★ Creating **hotspots** and **slices** to add interactivity

★ Working with **rollovers** and disjoint rollovers

★ Building a navigation bar

★ Creating simple **pop-up menus**

Behaviors

You know that an object is a self-contained component that can be reused anywhere you want and that it has three characteristics: identity, properties, and behavior. Without behaviors, your object will just sit there and look pretty—it won't actually do anything. For instance, you may want to create a behavior that makes the object change color when the mouse moves over it (called a rollover) or have the object contain information to take the user to another location within your website (linking). In some instances, you may want to add both of these behaviors to the same object.

In very basic terms, in order to have a behavior, you need programming code with instructions for that behavior. Usually, this is HTML combined with JavaScript that's attached to the object and defines what the object will do. If the words "programming code" send you screaming to the hills, don't worry! Fireworks does most of the work for you.

In very nontechnical terms, this is the sequence a behavior takes:

1. An event occurs (a mouse moves over an object, the mouse is clicked, etc.).

2. The programming code attached to the object "sees" this event and triggers an action by calling up different programming code.

3. This code carries out the actions it is designed to perform.

Fireworks is the ultimate tool for easily applying behaviors and image-related code and script to your web pages without requiring you to have any programming experience.

Objects with HTML or JavaScript attached to them are called web objects, and they reside in their own layer in the Layers panel: the Web Layer. Fireworks creates this layer automatically; in other words, you don't need to create it.

Before you start trying out these behaviors, let's briefly discuss frames (discussed in much greater detail in Chapter 6 on animation).

A note about frames

You tend to think of frames in terms of film or animation—a series of pictures that are flashed before you at a high speed in order to create the feeling of motion. The same is true for a rollover. You store different images in different frames. In the case of animation, you play back a sequence of frames at a high speed, just like a conventional animation. In the case of rollover effects, however, Fireworks creates JavaScript code that calls up a different frame in response to a particular event. Frames can also be used as storage for different design compositions of the same object.

Fireworks has a Frames panel, which you'll be working with a lot (Window ➤ Frames or Shift+F2).

If you're still a little unclear about all of this, don't worry; you'll soon get some practical experience to see how it all works.

Buttons are interface elements that enable you to navigate through web pages and sites. They typically have up to four different states, each appearing in response to the user's mouse.

★ **Up state:** How the button initially appears. This is sometimes referred to as the "at rest" or "default" state.

★ **Over state:** This is how the button appears when the user's mouse moves over the image; it's often characterized by a change in color. It's also sometimes referred to as the "hover" state.

★ **Down state:** This state is used to indicate that the button has been pressed or a link has been selected. It's often characterized by another change in color and shape to make the button appear as if it's been pressed into the page.

★ **Over while down state:** This is a continuation of the down state. Even though the button remains in a down state when you arrive at the destination, you may want to still include a rollover effect as a visual indicator of some sort.

You can edit all of these states in Fireworks. Let's make a button to see exactly how.

How to create a button

To make a button, you need to use the Button Editor to design each of the button's four states.

1. Start a new 500×500 pixels canvas, at 72 dpi resolution, with a white background.

2. Choose Edit ➤ Insert ➤ New Button to open up the Button Editor.

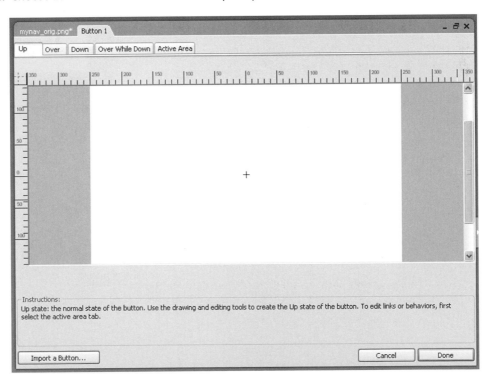

Notice that as soon as you enter the Button Editor, four new frames are created in the Frames panel, one for each of the four states.

Next, you're going to use a combination of drawing tools and text tools to create a button.

3. Ensure the Up state tab is selected at the top of the Button Editor, and select the Rectangle tool with no stroke and a fill color of your choice. Draw a rectangle in the center of the Button Editor (use the crosshair or the Align panel to center the shape). The rectangle should be 120×50 pixels.

4. Next, create a bevel effect on the rectangle by first selecting the rectangle and then selecting Effects: the plus sign (+) in the Property inspector. A list of Live Effects appears. Select Bevel and Emboss ➤ Inner Bevel from this menu.

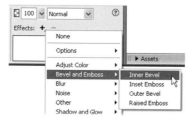

5. Once you've selected Inner Bevel, a small configuration box pops up where you decide how the Live Effect appears. For this example, set the inner bevel to Flat, with a width of 10. The other settings control the amount of contrast, softness, and angles. Experiment a little with the settings. Press ENTER to select the changes.

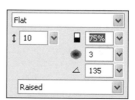

6. Next, select the Text tool. Make the text white and bold with a size of 25 pixels, and type the text "Home" over the button. To ensure that your text is always going to be centered, using the Pointer tool, extend the sides of the text box so that it encompasses the face of the button and then, using the Property inspector, press the center alignment button. Your button should look like the one shown here on the right.

7. Select the Over tab in the Button Editor. Notice that when you do, a Copy Up Graphic button appears at the bottom right of the Button Editor. Click this button to transfer the image you created in the Up tab to the same location on the canvas in the Over tab. This saves you the tricky job of having to line up your Over text with your Up text.

8. Select the rectangle part of your button and change the fill to a lighter color. This tells the user that the button is active and can be pressed.

9. Move on to the Down tab. If you're going to include this button as part of a navigation bar and want the button to stay pressed down when the visitor arrives at the destination page, check Include nav bar Down state.

10. On the Down tab, click the Copy Over Graphic button to transfer your graphic from the Over state. Make sure the rectangle of the button is selected, go into the Property inspector, and double click the Inner Bevel effect you created earlier. This brings up the configuration box again. Change your bottom button preset option from Raised to Inverted.

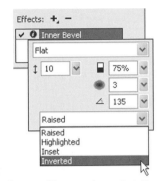

Now let's move on to the Over While Down state, which can be a little tricky. Remember when you checked Include nav bar Down state? This means that when you go to the web page associated with a button, the button stays down, indicating the page you're on. However, there should also be a rollover effect to show that the mouse is over it. Here you can apply a rollover effect to the button, even though it is already in the Down state.

11. Select the rectangle in your button and change the fill color slightly.

12. Finally, click the Active Area tab in the Button Editor.

When you create a button, Fireworks creates something called a **slice**. This is needed for interactivity. You use slices to carve an image up into smaller separate images or to define separate objects. Each of these smaller images becomes a web object and its own behavior can be added to it. The slice you can see on the Active Area tab is large enough to encompass the button and all of its states, but you can adjust its size if you want. As an example, you may want to create an area larger or smaller than the button object. By doing this, you change where the mouse pointer actually "sees" the button. Most of the time, you won't need to change this.

13. For now, just click Done in your Button Editor. This returns you back to the canvas, which now displays your button with the slice guides.

14. Click the Preview button located in the upper-left corner of the canvas to try out your button's states.

Button library

If you're not the next Picasso, or you simply need to produce buttons quickly, you can use many different prebuilt buttons stored in the Button library (Edit ➤ Libraries ➤ Buttons).

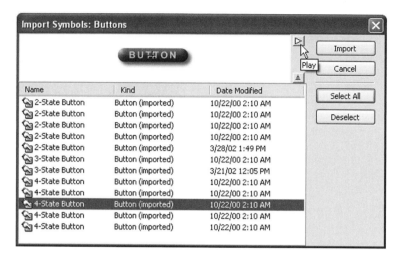

You can select buttons from the list in the lower portion of the window and see them in the preview pane at the top. If you click the Play button, you can preview all four button states in sequence.

Once you've chosen a button you'd like to use, press the Import button to import it into your canvas. Your button is now on the canvas. Double click it to open the Button Editor, and you can modify the button in the same way as you would modify a button you've created yourself.

As well as this library, you can download buttons from the free button resources that are available on the web. www.macromedia.com/devnet/mx/fireworks is a good place to start.

Hotspots

A hotspot is a layer that lies on top of an image onto which you can add all sorts of web instructions (usually a web link, but occasionally also JavaScript). By attaching hotspots to images, you can create **image maps**.

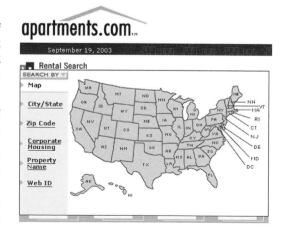

Image maps are used to define areas of an image that link to different places, meaning that your single picture can contain a number of links. If you've done any amount of browsing on the web, you've probably come across one of these, although you may not have realized it. As an example on the web, take a look at www.apartments.com.

On this map of the USA, each state has been partitioned off into hotspot areas. This means that when you click a particular state, it triggers a unique URL (Uniform Resource Locator, used to reference the global address of a document or resource on the web) and also displays the full name of the state in the Alt/tooltip text.

Behind the scenes, an image map is simply an instruction to the browser that marks out certain areas as having certain properties.

How to create hotspots

1. First of all, you need a graphic. Open car1.png (included in the download files). OK, so it might not be the sportiest car you've ever seen, but it's all you need to learn how to create hotspots!

2. Select the Rectangle Hotspot tool. You use the Rectangle and Circle Hotspot tools in exactly the same way as the Rectangle and Ellipse vector tools, but instead of creating graphic shapes, you create hotspot areas. The Polygon Hotspot tool is used to closely select irregular shapes by clicking joining points.

3. Draw a rectangle over the windshield using the Rectangle Hotspot tool. Make it roughly the same size and shape as the graphic.

   Don't worry if your hotspot rectangle covers the actual wind-shield graphic. This will only be true for editing. When you come to use the image in a web browser, the hotspot rectangle will be invisible.

   You can show or hide hotspots by toggling the buttons shown here (or toggling the keystroke 2).

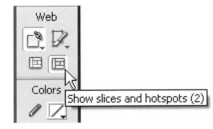

You can use this process to create circular or polygon-shaped hotspots as well. The only thing to point out here is that when you're using the Polygon Hotspot tool, just click to place vector points, which Fireworks connects with straight lines as you go. To close the polygon shape, simply click the first vector point you created. The fill defines the hotspot area whether the path is open or closed.

At the outset of this chapter, you learned that web objects such as hotspots are created in the Web Layer. If you take a look at the Layers panel now, you'll notice that the layer containing the hotspot has been automatically created. Like other layers, it's a good idea to name it appropriately.

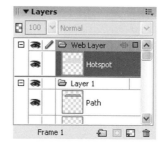

4. Now, with the hotspot still selected, take a look at the Property inspector.

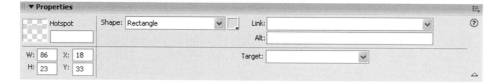

Here you can name your component, specify its size and position its coordinates, and change its color. You'll also see a few new features. The Shape drop-down menu simply describes which of the Hotspot shape tools you're using (Rectangle, Circle, or Polygon). If you like, you can change this property to apply to a hotspot you have already created on the canvas. At the right side of the Property inspector, you have the Link, Alt, and Target fields. These are the juiciest bits.

The Link drop-down menu holds the URL you want your hotspot to link to and handily records any previously referenced URLs, saving you from retyping them if you want to use them again. There are two types of URLs used on the web: **absolute** and **relative**. To link to a page that isn't part of your website, you must use an absolute URL. These are complete URLs that include the http:// prefix. An absolute URL for the friends of ED website would be http://www.friendsofed.com. Relative URLs are relative to the absolute URL, meaning that the document the URL is linking to is on the same website. An example of a relative URL for the friends of ED home page would be /books/1590593065/index.html.

5. For your hotspot link information, type http://www.friendsofed.com (or add your own site information) in the Link drop-down menu. Notice that you need to add the http:// part to your link because you're using an absolute URL.

The Alt field contains any descriptive text you want to appear when the mouse moves over a slice area. This can provide extra information for the user, and in the event that the image itself doesn't display, at least you have the text option available.

6. Type "Windshield Information" in the Alt field.

Target defines where the URL in the Link menu will be opened. You can specify one of five different reserved targets for your link from the drop-down menu:

★ blank loads the document in a new browser window.

★ parent loads the document in the parent frame or the window of the frame that contains the link (if the frame containing the link is not nested, the linked document loads into the full browser window).

★ none and _self load the linked document in the same frame or window as the document containing the link. This is the default option.

★ top loads the linked document in the full browser window, removing all frames.

If your web page uses HTML frames, you can specifically type in a frame name instead of choosing a target from the drop-down menu. This means that your link will open in that specific frame. If you're not using HTML frames (or have no idea what they are), don't worry, the presets are fine for your needs here.

7. Choose _blank from the Target drop-down menu to open your link in a new window.

8. As mentioned earlier, it's always a good idea to properly label your work, so type "windshield" in the Hotspot field. Take a look at the Layers panel; the name should have changed correspondingly.

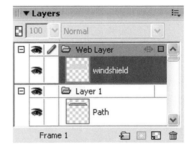

You can use one other technique to create hotspots. Let's look at this now.

9. Using *SHIFT*+click, select the two headlights.

10. Select Edit ➤ Insert ➤ Hotspot. Because you have multiple objects selected, you should see this prompt:

If you select Single, Fireworks will automatically draw a single rectangular path surrounding the two headlights and all graphics in-between. This whole area would be treated as one hotspot. If you select Multiple, the two headlights will remain selected separately but with the same behavior.

11. Select Multiple, and use the Property inspector to give the headlights a name, a link of your choice, and alternative text. Notice that Fireworks automatically recognized the shape of the object and selected the proper hotspot shape.

12. Press *F12* or select File ➤ Preview in Browser. Place your mouse pointer over the windshield or headlights. You should see your Alt text appear and, when you click, you should be taken to the link you specified.

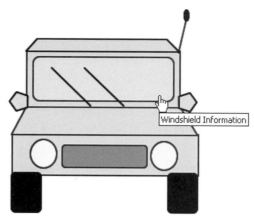

Now that you've seen how easy it is to create hotspots in an image, try using the hotspot tools to link various portions of the car image to your favorite websites. Test your links with your web browser.

If you're at all familiar with HTML and web page creation, or even if you're not, the code Fireworks generates for your web page is fairly easy to follow. You can see this code by selecting View ➤ Source in your browser or by clicking the Code view button in Dreamweaver for your document:

```
<img name="car1_final" src="car1_final.gif" width="244" height="260" border="0"
usemap="#m_car1_final" alt="">

<map name="m_car1_final">

<area shape="poly"
coords="28,185,29,178,33,172,38,168,45,167,52,168,57,172,61,178,62,185,61,192,
57,198,52,202,45,203,38,202,33,198,29,192,28,185,28,185"
href="http://www.friendsofed.com/catalogue.html" title="See the whole
friends of ED catalog" alt="See the whole friends of ED catalog" >

<area shape="poly"
coords="182,187,183,180,187,174,192,170,199,169,206,170,211,174,215,180,216,187
,215,194,211,200,206,204,199,205,192,204,187,200,183,194,182,187,182,187"
href="http://www.friendsofed.com/forums" title="Go to friends of ED forums"
alt="Go to friends of ED forums" >

<area shape="poly" coords="30,61,212,61,212,119,30,119,30,61"
href="http://www.friendsofed.com" target="_blank" title="Windshield
Information"
alt="Windshield Information" >

</map>
```

Fireworks simply puts the image in place (img src), and then creates a "map". Next, it uses all those complex numbers you just saw to set coordinates for where your hotspots are, and then it lists the information you want to associate with them (links, Alt text, etc.).

We'll cover the HTML that Fireworks generates in later chapters, but for now, you just need to understand what image maps and hotpots are if you see them in the flesh, so to speak.

URL library

If you're working on a website project with multiple pages, you'll have to enter many different URLs several times to make the site fully navigable—a time-consuming task. Fortunately, you can create a **URL Library** to contain your most commonly used URLs.

1. To add a URL to the library, first choose Window ➤ URL to open the Assets panel in URL mode.

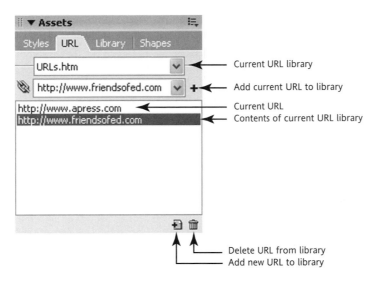

Current URL library
Add current URL to library
Current URL
Contents of current URL library

Delete URL from library
Add new URL to library

2. Now simply type the URL in the Add current URL to library field and then click the + button to add the URL to the library. Alternatively, you can click the Add new URL to library button at the bottom right of the URL panel to open the New URL dialog box.

3. Type in the new URL and click OK. To remove the URL, select the link in the lower pane and click the trash can icon in the URL panel.

4. To add a URL to an object, simply select the object on the canvas and then select the URL in the library. The link will now be added to the library. Notice that the Link drop-down menu in the Property inspector and the drop-down menu in the URL library contain the same information. After adding a URL to an object, you could also add it to the library by selecting it from the list and clicking the + button.

5. To edit an existing URL, select the URL you wish to edit, and then choose Edit URL from the URL panel options menu. If you wish all instances of the URL in the document to be changed, select Change All Occurrences in Document.

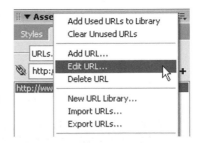

You can also create a brand new URL library by selecting New URL Library from the options menu.

Editing hotspots

You can reshape and resize your hotspots as you can any other vector image by using the same tools. Like vectors, you can resize, move, reshape, and so on with the Pointer, Subselection, and Transform tools as normal, and you can also scale or rotate selected hotspots using the Numeric Transform function (Modify ➤ Transform ➤ Numeric Transform…).

Image maps vs. navigation bars

At this point, you may be thinking about just getting rid of your text navigation bars and using image maps and hotspots instead. Not so fast! Some things you might want to consider first are listed here:

★ Images take longer to download then text.

★ It may not be entirely clear to users that they have to click on each portion of the picture.

★ Image maps are not reactive to mouse actions other than being clickable. For example, when you move your mouse over a hotspot, it won't change color.

★ Web search engines send out spiders to analyze and classify sites. When they do this, the spiders look for text. If your site navigation just contains image maps, they may not find the text that you want them to have.

★ Image maps add more code to your page making the file size larger.

Most web designers use a combination of image maps and navigation bars. Use your image maps judiciously! Later you'll learn how to create image-based navigation bars, which, in many ways, represent the best of both worlds. To create these, however, you first need to learn how to create slices.

Slices

As you saw when creating the button earlier, you need slices to add interactivity. The slice around the button was the area that "listened" to the user's mouse rolling over or clicking the button. Slices have three main advantages:

★ **Optimizing:** Slicing an image enables you to optimize each slice using the most appropriate file format and compression settings. This can improve the quality of the image being sliced and make it download quicker (as you'll see in the next chapter).

★ **Interactivity:** You can use slices to create rollovers to add interactivity to your site.

★ **Updating parts of a web page:** When you slice a web page correctly, changing a section of it becomes very simple. For example, your website might have a "Book of the Month" section. Using slicing techniques, you can make it easy to update this section without editing any of the other sections.

Fireworks enables you to create entire interfaces, which you can then import into Dreamweaver or FrontPage. Such interfaces can easily be edited and modified back in Fireworks. You can also set slices to contain HTML rather than images to allow for the textual content of your site.

Let's begin by creating some basic slices so that you can see what they do and how they work. As you'll quickly learn, the techniques used to create slices are nearly identical to those used to create hotspots, but the potential for creativity is much larger.

How to create slices

1. Use a combination of vector drawing tools and the Text tool to create the navigation bar shown here. (Or you can start with slices_start.png in the download files. If you do use the source file, look at the layers to see how they were created.)

If you prefer, create your own simple interface. Just make sure there are three rectangular buttons.

2. Select the Slice tool (K), located right next to the Hotspot tool.

The default Slice tool creates rectangular shapes, but as you can see, you can also use a Polygon Slice tool, which allows you to use vector points to handle irregular shapes. Note that although you can create irregular shaped slices, the final exported JPEG or GIF image will still be a rectangle.

3. Draw a rectangle over the Books section of the bar, just like you did with the Hotspot tool earlier.

> *If you used the Button Editor to create the buttons, then the slices will have been added automatically. Don't add another slice in that case.*

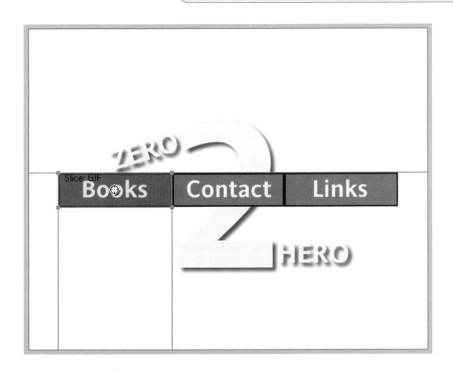

Notice the lines that appear at the edges of the slice. These are called the slice guides. You can grab and move these guides using the Pointer tool to fine-tune the size and position of the slice. These red lines are also used by Fireworks to automatically slice the areas within the red lines when exporting, if you so choose.

4. As you draw your slice object, if you keep the mouse button depressed and press the spacebar, you can actually drag the slice to another location on the canvas.

   Also notice the words Slice.gif inside your slice. This indicates that when this file gets saved, this portion of the image will be saved as a completely separate GIF file.

5. Now go to the Property inspector and fill in the rest of the fields as you did for the hotspot. Create a link to a website of your choice and add some Alt text.

Notice that Fireworks gave the slice a default name. This is because it's essential for each slice to be named. Because the slices will become part of a table, the default name consists of the file name with the table position added. You may find this name a bit cumbersome to work with and find it easier to give the slice the same name as the button graphic text.

6. For this reason, name the slice "books" in the Property inspector (follow the case conventions discussed throughout the book). The image name inside the slice now changes to books.gif.

7. Repeat steps 3 and 4 for the Contact portion of the image. Be sure not to leave any gaps between this slice rectangle and the one you created for the Books slice. If there are any gaps, HTML will automatically convert them into additional cells, which could throw off your ability to smoothly rebuild your images in a table and will leave gaps between slices. This is purely a feature of HTML. Give this slice the link: mailto:(your email address).

8. Repeat the same steps 3 and 4 for the Links portion.

9. Save your work and leave it open—you'll be building on it later in the chapter.

Previewing your work

Now comes the part where you preview your work in a browser.

Go to File ➤ Preview in Browser. You have the option of viewing the file in either your primary or secondary browser. You can also define the location, if necessary, of these browser files, which varies with your computer and operating system.

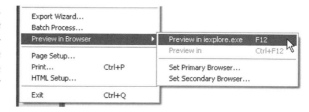

Provided everything is set up properly, click the browser you want to preview your work in. As you roll the mouse over each image, you should see the corresponding tooltip text, and the link you created should appear in the status bar. Try clicking the images to test your links.

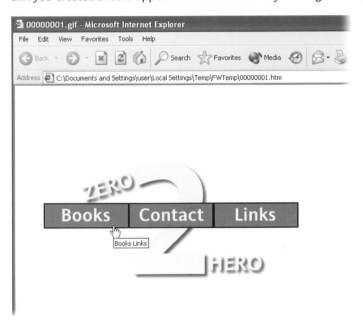

Fireworks sets up the necessary files in a temporary location that will vary depending on your computer and operating system. You can see this location in the browser's address bar. In this example, which uses Windows XP Professional, it was set up like so:

C:\Documents and Settings\user\Local Settings\Temp\FWTemp\00000001.htm

If you maneuver to this folder, you should see the following files. When were the additional slices made?

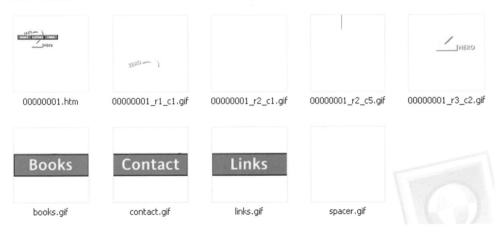

Notice the separate GIF files for each of your three slices.

You may also want to view the source files with the browser by using the View ➤ Source menu option. Don't worry if you don't understand all of the code. Suffice it to say that Fireworks did set up the HTML tables properly and made sure the proper graphic files ended up in the right place.

Creating a simple rollover

Let's create a simple rollover effect that, while relatively simple, will show you the concepts behind almost all behaviors.

1. Open zero.png (from the download files).

   As stated at the outset, frames play a strong role in behaviors. In most rollover cases, you're going to take the image in one frame and swap it for the image in another frame. Actually, you let Fireworks write the JavaScript code to do it for you.

2. Make a note of the x and y coordinates of the graphic (200 and 225 pixels respectively).

3. Open the Frames panel (Window ➤ Frames or *SHIFT+F2*). The current image, by default, is located in Frame 1.

4. Click the New/Duplicate Frame button at the bottom right of the Frames panel to create a new frame, and then select it in the panel. You shouldn't be able to see the contents from Frame 1 now.

5. Select File ➤ Import, import Hero.png from the download files, and click the blank canvas.

6. Use the Property inspector and position the Hero button at (x:200,y225). This locates it in the exact position as the Zero button.

   The Zero button graphic is in Frame 1 and the Hero button graphic in Frame 2. You want the Zero button to change to the Hero button when the mouse rolls over it. The only problem is that there's nothing to instruct the browser to do this. You need to use a programming language called JavaScript, but don't get scared; Fireworks handles it all for you. You don't need to get your hands dirty programming code.

7. Make sure you're back on Frame 1 (select it in the Frames panel and you should see the Zero button graphic again).

8. Open the Behaviors panel (Window ➤ Behaviors/*SHIFT+F3*).

9. Click the + button at the top left of the Behaviors panel. You'll see a strange message:

A slice partitions a graphic, or part of a graphic, but it's also used to include an entire graphic. It defines the area you want to slice or to apply a behavior to in order to apply a behavior or special export. In this case, the JavaScript code necessary to create the rollover effect will be connected to the slice. Furthermore, slices reside in the Web Layer (discussed in Chapter 3).

10. Click the Slice button and two things happen:

★ The graphic is now surrounded by the Slice guides.

★ The Behaviors panel options menu is available.

11. For this exercise, select the Simple Rollover behavior from the options menu. This behavior swaps the image in Frame 1 for the image in Frame 2. (The Swap Image behavior allows you to select which frame you want to swap with.)

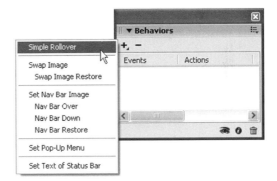

The onMouseOver behavior should now be added to your Behaviors panel.

12. You're all set! Click the Preview tab to preview the rollover in the document. Roll your mouse over the button and it'll change from Zero to Hero. Fireworks handles all the messy programming details in the background.

Disjointed rollover

The techniques here will be nearly identical to the typical Swap Image behavior, but with a few variations. When you created the Simple Rollover behavior, you told the program to use the information contained in Frame 2. However, this may not always be the case. For instance, when you create a rollover, you may want to swap with Frame 3 instead of Frame 2. Also, you may want to attach an external file of some sort to the frame that appears in another part of the browser. Let's try an example.

1. Continuing with your navigation bar (or starting afresh with `swapping_start.png` in the download files), duplicate Frame 1.

   Notice that it now duplicates the frame as a new Frame 2. This throws off the previous rollover behavior and will be fixed in a moment. As you start working with multiple frames, things can get a little confusing, so it's a good idea to name your frames using the same naming conventions that you use to name objects.

2. Double click Frame 1 in the Frames panel and rename it "original". Likewise, rename the new Frame 2 as "rollover2" and Frame 3 as "rollover1".

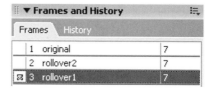

3. Frames can also be rearranged. Set things in order by dragging rollover1 above rollover2.

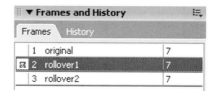

4. Draw a new slice in the rollover2 frame—your target slice. Draw it above the Links button and place some text or a graphic in it. Call the slice "rollover_slice_2".

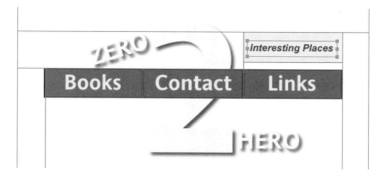

5. Click back on the Links slice and place the mouse cursor on the slice's behavior handle. Hold down the left mouse button, drag the handle over to the new slice you just created, and drop it there.

6. The Swap Image dialog box appears. Make sure that rollover2 (3) is selected in the drop-down menu and then click OK. You should see a thin blue line connecting the two images. This is called the **behavior line**.

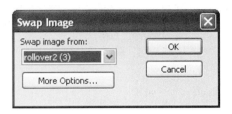 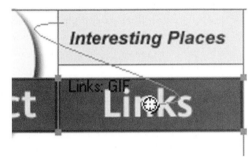

7. You're now ready to test all your hard work. Press *F12* to preview the file and move your mouse cursor over the Links slice.

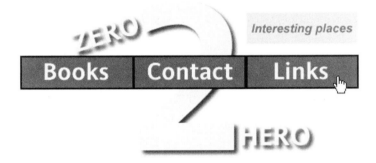

Again, if you feel so inclined, take a look at your source code in the web browser to see how it all works.

8. To remove a drag-and-drop rollover, simply select the slice from which you want to remove the rollover, and click the blue behavior line you want to remove. A dialog box then appears asking you if you want to delete the behavior. Click OK to remove the rollover.

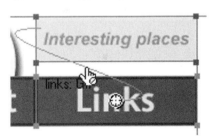 

Again, at the heart of the process are slices. In Chapter 5, you'll see how to use slice types and export settings.

Pop-up menus

Pop-up menus are a popular feature of website navigation. They allow you to maximize the amount of space on a web page by creating horizontal or vertical menus that pull out a hidden menu to reveal additional links. This also helps organize your links.

When you create a Pop-Up Menu behavior, Fireworks includes a file called `mm_menu.js` in your site folder. This JavaScript file is referenced in your HTML page and needs to be uploaded to your website at the same time. If you're wondering why this is created as an external file, it's so that if you use pop-up menus more than once (for example, in the same place on six different pages), you'll only need to reference this one file rather than repeat the extensive code six times.

How to create pop-up menus

1. Open `pop_up_menu_start.png` from the download files.

2. Select the books slice, click the behavior handle, and select Add Pop-up Menu....

   The Pop-up Menu Editor appears. Notice that the dialog box contains four tabs: Content, Appearance, Advanced, and Position.

   The Content tab contains the basic text, URL link, and target elements that comprise the menu structure.

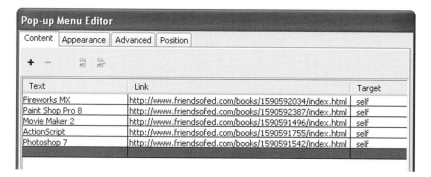

---

3. Double click under the Text column in the Pop-up Menu Editor and type in a name for the first element in your pop-menu.

4. Press the *TAB* key and type a URL link into the Link field (note that for the purposes of this exercise, you can leave it blank and everything will work fine).

5. Press the *TAB* one more time and select _self from the Target drop-down menu.

6. Now add some other items to your pop-up menu by pressing either the *TAB* key or by clicking the **+** button in the box.

To move an entry in the pop-up menu, simply drag the menu item to a new location in the list.

7. Now click the Appearance tab, which contains tools for customizing your pop-up menu's appearance.

Here you can set how your menu will appear. Notice that you have a choice of whether you want this appearance to be governed by HTML code or as an Image file. The Image file option does give you more options and greater flexibility; the only drawback is that it could add to the download time of the page.

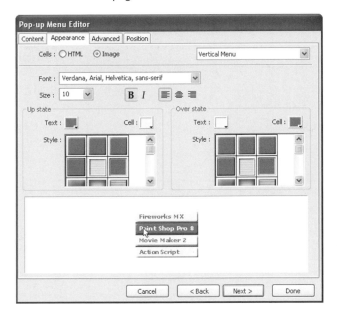

8. Create the cells with the Image option.

You can also choose whether your pop-up menu appears vertically or horizontally by selecting the appropriate option from the drop-down menu at the top right of the Appearance tab. Because the main three buttons in the navigation bar (Books, Contact, Forums) are arranged horizontally in a row, a vertical menu is the way to go here.

9. Finally, set the style of the pop-up menu cells. You can preview the styles on your menu in the preview pane, so go ahead and experiment with them until you find one you like.

10. Move on to the Advanced tab. Here you have a few more options to aid you in configuring your menu's appearance.

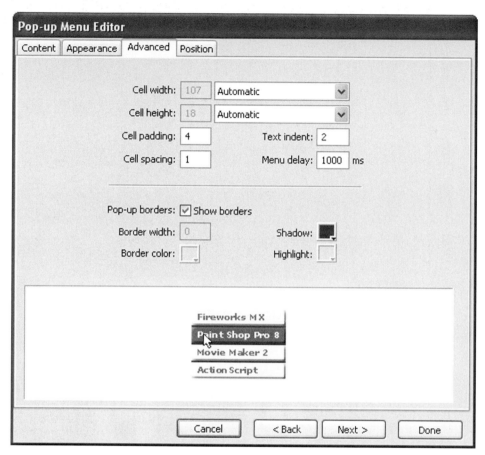

You can let Fireworks size the width and height of your cells automatically, or you can specify how many pixels you want them to be.

Cell padding refers to the amount of space surrounding your text within the cell, and Cell spacing refers to the amount of space between the cells themselves.

To the right of these options is Text indent, which describes how far to the right your text is indented within the cell, and Menu delay, where you can specify exactly how many milliseconds your pop-up menu will remain on screen after the mouse pointer has moved away from it.

You can also change the width, color, shadow, and highlight of the border, or uncheck the Show borders to remove them completely.

11. Click the Position tab, which determines how the menus and submenus are placed.

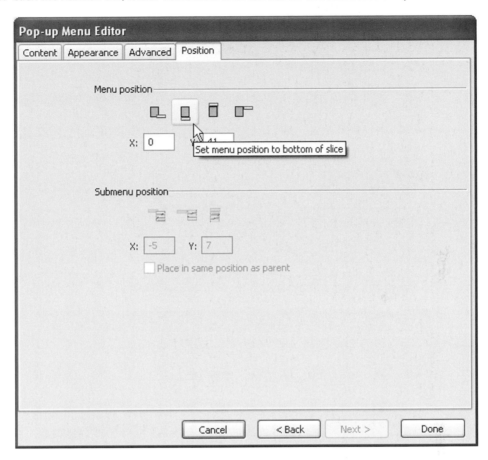

The pop-up menu can be placed in a variety of positions relative to the slice by selecting one of the four preset Menu position buttons, or you can specify the position yourself using the X and Y text boxes.

12. When you're finished working in the Pop-up Menu Editor, simply click the Done button to return to the canvas where you can now see the outline of your new pop-up menu.

13. Go ahead and give it a test run in the browser (*F12*):

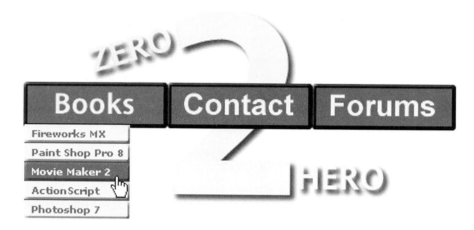

14. You can go back, if you want, and fine-tune the menu by clicking the Behaviors handle and selecting Edit Pop-up Menu. Back in the Pop-up Menu Editor, click one of the menu items, and press the + key twice to make room for two more items.

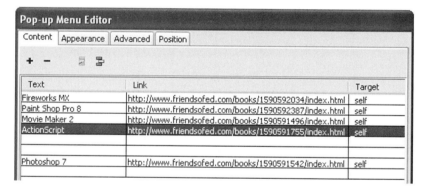

15. Add two more menu items and, after you've entered them, click each one and press the Indent Menu button. Modify any links, if you wish to reflect these new menu additions.

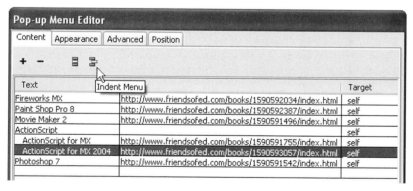

16. Now go to the Position tab. The Submenu position options should now be available. Select the option to put the new submenu to the right of the main menu.

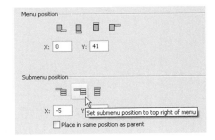

17. Hit Done in the Pop-up Menu Editor and test the file again in your browser.

You can create as many levels as you need. Go ahead and try to set up pop-up menus for the other buttons. You should see how easy it is. Don't be afraid to experiment with some of the options.

Summary

Well, there it is. You just became a behavioral superhero (and you didn't even need to get bitten by anything radioactive). This chapter should have given you a comprehensive and practical understanding of object behaviors. As you move along through the book, you'll learn how to apply this knowledge even more, and as you can see, you have a lot of behavior characteristics to work with in order to make your website as interactive and user-friendly as possible.

Five

Optimization and Exporting

In this chapter

Optimization and exporting are two related topics. Before **exporting** a graphic, it needs to be **optimized** to ensure that it's the best quality graphic with the smallest possible file size. Maintaining a low file size is essential to reduce the time it takes to download your images. Quality and file size are influenced by file type, the number of colors used, and compression, and all these factors need to be taken into account when optimizing images.

Throughout this chapter, you'll learn how to optimize your work and then export it out of the Fireworks environment. Here are the topics that will be discussed:

★ Optimizing Fireworks projects
  ★ Creating custom settings and using presets in the Optimize panel
  ★ Previewing your settings
★ Exporting Fireworks projects
  ★ Exporting slices
  ★ Exporting frames and layers
  ★ Exporting selected areas
  ★ Using the Export Preview
  ★ Working with the optimizing and exporting wizards
  ★ Exporting HTML
  ★ Using the Quick Export button
  ★ Exporting XHTML
  ★ Becoming familiar with CSS layers

Optimizing your projects

Open the Optimize panel (Windows ➤ Optimize/*F6*).

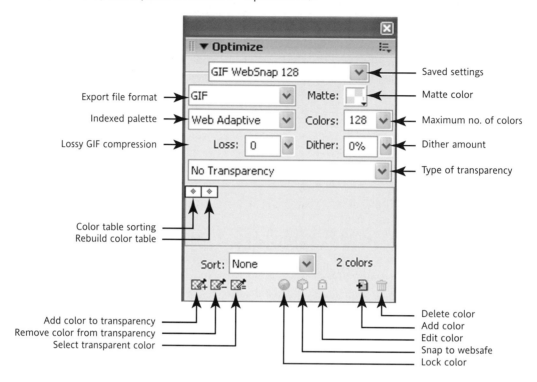

There's no such thing as a free ride: an image with a large number of colors will also have a large file size. However, when you reduce the number of colors you'll find a corresponding reduction in the quality of the graphic. Optimizing can be a delicate balancing act where you must make some careful decisions.

To help in this decision-making, Fireworks has preset optimization settings, which take a lot of the guesswork out of optimizing your graphic. You can find them by clicking the Saved settings drop-down menu at the top of the panel.

Let's take a closer look at these settings. The first set applies to GIF file formats.

★ **GIF Web 216** makes each color conform to the web-safe palette of 216 colors. It changes those colors that are not web-safe to their nearest web-safe equivalent.

★ **GIF WebSnap 256** uses the 216 colors of the web-safe palette along with 40 other custom colors. The word "Snap" means it will snap non-web-safe colors to their closest web-safe equivalent.

★ **GIF WebSnap 128** reduces the number of possible colors in your graphic to 128. Again, the word "Snap" means that the non web-safe colors are snapped into web-safe colors.

★ **GIF Adaptive 256** means that you're limited to 256 colors, but that non-web-safe colors will not be snapped to web-safe colors.

> *The web-safe palette is a palette of 216 colors common to both Windows and Macintosh computers. This palette is called "web-safe," or "browser-safe," because it produces fairly consistent results on different platforms and with different browsers. Although you should understand this feature, it's becoming less important with modern computers capable of displaying millions of colors.*

The next group of presets refers to the JPEG file format.

★ **JPEG - Better Quality** means the file will be exported into the JPEG format of the highest quality (and therefore the largest file size).

★ **JPEG - Smaller File** does just what it says: it produces a JPEG file format of a smaller size (and, as I'm sure you've guessed by now, that means a loss of quality).

★ **Animated WebSnap** refers to animated GIFs, which are detailed in the next chapter.

Creating custom settings

You can change the number of colors allowed in the graphic, as well as whether the settings you use are Adaptive or WebSnap, which can have a significant effect on the size and quality of your graphic.

Its fine to use the optimization presets, but what happens if you have a particular optimization, specific to your work, that you use over and over again? You could set it up manually each time (time consuming) or, better, create your own preset.

In the Optimize panel, manually set the settings you need (color, file format, dither, and so on). When you are through making your settings, select Save Settings... from the Optimize panel's options menu, and you'll be prompted to name your setting.

Once you've given your setting a name, from that point on, your custom settings will appear in the Saved Settings drop-down menu. What could be easier?

Previewing your settings

Now you've looked at the settings on the Optimize panel; let's see how these settings work differently when you go to export your graphic. Open sunset.png from the download files.

You can preview how the settings will affect the graphic by clicking the Preview tab at the top of the canvas. This screen has some new information for you to consider.

Most significant, is the information in the lower-left corner: the file size and potential download time using a 56kbps modem as a benchmark. Of course, you also can see this in the Original view. Here, however, you can start to compare it to the original.

Just to show how dramatic the settings in the Optimize panel can be, with the GIF WebSnap 256 preset, the file size is 10.09k, and it takes approximately one second to download.

Now change the Optimize setting to GIF Web 216. First of all, you'll probably see a considerable reduction in graphic quality but, also, the file size more than triples in size (to 33.33k in this example). You may find this a little counterintuitive. Lower quality and yet more file size—why?

To answer this, you need to remember that GIF Web 216 allows an unlimited number of colors and then converts them to web-safe colors. So, in actuality, it is working with more potential colors, which bloats your file size. In addition to this, because your file size increased, the download time increased to five seconds. It's a safe bet that you wouldn't use this setting!

As a last test, change the Color palette to Exact. The file size drops back to around 10.76k and the download time to approximately one second because, once again, you're only working with 256 colors.

You can experiment with the Optimize panel and the Preview view to find the best quality image with the smallest file size, but Fireworks takes these tools a couple of steps further.

Click the 2-Up tab at the top of your canvas.

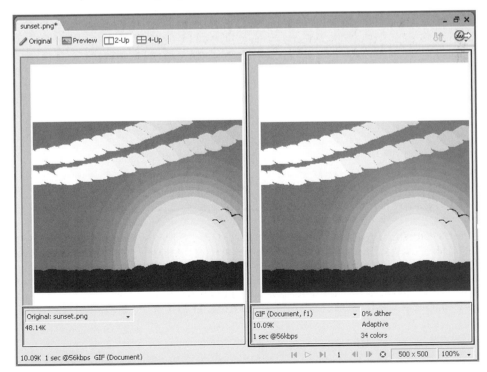

129

You can click either image to make it active, use the Optimize panel to make changes, and then compare the graphic before and after these changes. In the preceding screenshot, the left graphic is the original and the right window shows the graphic optimized with the GIF WebSnap 256 preset. You can see the difference in the statistics at the bottom of the window.

Note that you can change either graphic back to its original settings by using the drop-down menu at the bottom.

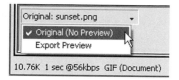

If you like, you can even view four previews simultaneously using the 4-Up tab.

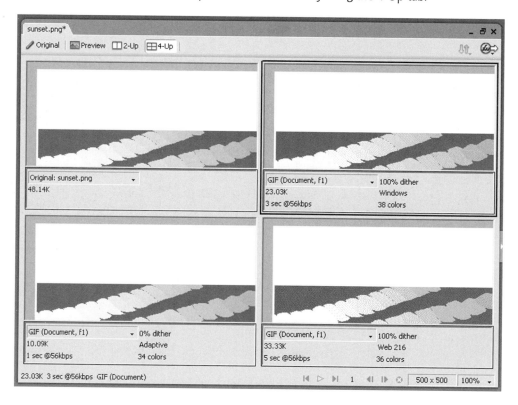

Again, click the preview you want to make active and change the settings in the Optimize panel.

Optimizing with JPEG formats

The process of optimizing a JPEG image is a little different than that of a GIF. The main concerns here are compression and smoothing. To follow the example in this section, open `australia.png`.

Choose JPEG – Better Quality in the Optimize panel. Change to the Preview view, and you can see that the file size is around 200k and the download time is 34 seconds. By web standards, this is way too large. Try switching to the JPEG - Smaller File and look at how the statistics have changed: your file size is reduced to around 90k and the download time to 14 seconds.

The difference is caused, primarily, by the Quality setting in the Optimize panel. JPEG is a lossy format and, in order to compress it, some of the data must be thrown out. Most of the time, reducing the quality from 80 percent to 60 percent will not result in an appreciable difference. Even if you adjust the quality to, say 30 percent, you'll see a small drop in quality, but a considerable drop in file size and download time. You need to make a decision balancing download time against image quality. Every picture presents its own challenges.

Quality is not the only tool available here. Hard edges do not compress well in a JPEG file and add to the file size. You have two controls to handle edges: one softens the edges and the other sharpens them.

In order to lessen the impact of hard edges, use the Smoothing control in the Optimize panel.

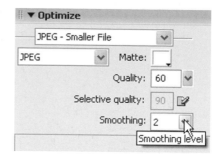

As an example, with a Quality of 60 percent and Smoothing of 0, your file is approximately 98k and takes about 15 seconds to download. By changing the Smoothing factor to 3, the file size is reduced to about 85k with a 13 second download. In many cases, you'll not see an appreciable difference in image quality.

You can also do just the opposite and ask Fireworks to sharpen the edges even more. To do this, choose Sharpen JPEG Edges from the Optimize panel's options menu.

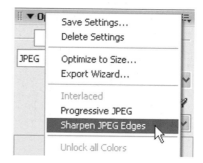

Another interesting tool is the Optimize to Size... menu option. Select this tool from the Optimize panel's options menu and you can set a target size for the file. It'll look for an optimal setting of the other features you've seen already (edges, quality, and so on).

In many cases, you may want to focus the viewer on just a portion of the image. In this australia.png example, the focus is the bridge, not the water beneath it. An interesting compromise to compressing the entire image and to emphasizing the important aspects with a higher quality is to compress only a portion of the image. This is only possible with the JPEG compression settings.

To do this, first ensure that you're on the Original view and then use the appropriate Marquee tool to select the area you want to compress. In this example, select the water:

Next, choose Modify ➤ Selective JPEG ➤ Save Selection as JPEG Mask, and you should see the selected area change color slightly.

Now enable the Selective Quality button in the Optimize panel. You'll then see the Selective JPEG Settings dialog box.

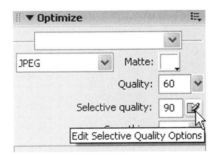

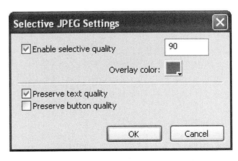

Here you can preserve any text or button properties that might be in the selected area, thus keeping them uncompressed and of the highest quality. After clicking OK, you can change the optimize settings for the selected area using the Selective quality field in the Optimize panel.

For illustrative purposes, try making the Selective quality field 40. You should not see a noticeable difference in the quality of the water, but your file size should go down to about 66k with a 14 second download time.

You can edit your selective quality area by choosing Modify ➤ Selective JPEG ➤ Restore JPEG Mask as Selection.

Exporting in Fireworks

Now that you've completed the first part of the process, optimizing, let's turn to the second job: exporting. In Fireworks you can either export to one of the standard exporting formats, or you can export just the images or a combination of image and HTML files.

If you want to export a single image once all your optimizing decisions have been made, it's a pretty straightforward process. First, select File ➤ Export to bring up the Export window, the primary interface for exporting your work.

Your optimization settings determine the file extension so all you have left to do is choose a location to save the file, and to choose an appropriate setting from the Save as type drop-down menu. In the screenshot here, we're indicating that just a single image is being saved by selecting Images Only. Once the name and settings have been made, click Save.

If you're exporting work for an in-progress website, then it should be exported to the root folder. This means that if you use the Edit button in Dreamweaver, then it'll know where to find the source file. When you export, Fireworks adds a note that tracks the source file to the exported location.

Note that selecting Images Only *here still allows you to export any slices that might be contained within your whole document.*

As you'll notice, there are several other options available in the Save as type drop-down menu. These apply to situations where you're exporting different types of files. Let's spend some time looking at the different types of files you can export, and how to do it.

Exporting slices, images, and HTML

You may recall from Chapter 4 that the process of slicing involves breaking the web document out as separate sliced files. You can export these sliced files separately using the HTML and Images option and have them reassembled in the web browser as an HTML table.

In order to export a document in which you use slices, you need to export both the images and the corresponding HTML. You can do this by first selecting File ➤ Export.

After navigating to the working folder and naming the file, select HTML and Images from the Save as type drop-down menu.

The Selected slices only checkbox is used if you only want to export certain slices, rather than the whole document. If this is the case, before checking it, you need to select the slices you want to export by *Shift*+ or *Ctrl*+clicking them, and then unchecking Include areas without slices.

Check Include areas without slices and uncheck Selected slices only. It's interesting to note that these are not mutually exclusive features. By doing it this way, Fireworks gives you the ability to set up a wide range of situations and to address a number of scenarios. For instance, you may encounter a situation where you want to export the non-sliced area of the document and only selected slices.

A quick and effective way to export either one slice or multiple selected slices, is to right/*Ctrl*+click a slice and choose Export selected slice. In the Export window, Selected slices only is checked by default using this method.

Many web designers feel that it's better file management to separate the program files from the image files. If you want to do this, check Put images in subfolder. You'll need to designate the folder with the Browse button (if you don't, then a new folder is automatically created for you).

However you configure the detail of your export, when you click Save, you'll end up with several groups of files:

★ A file containing the HTML code (created automatically by Fireworks).

★ A group of images of the main document (unless you're only exporting particular slices).

★ A group of the images of each of the slices, using the same name you used in the Property inspector when you were naming the slices.

So when do you need to export HTML? Well, it's often necessary to export HTML along with your images, as this allows Fireworks to create an entire web page for you. Also, you can export any behaviors attached to your images by incorporating the behaviors into the HTML.

For example, rollovers have JavaScript code attached to them. You can export just a navigation area using HTML and Images and the result is a working navigation system in its own table. This in return can be nested inside a table in Dreamweaver.

You can export in one of two ways. The first method involves selecting File ➤ Export and then choosing HTML and Images in the Save as type drop-down menu. This activates the HTML field where you can either export the HTML to a file or copy it to the clipboard.

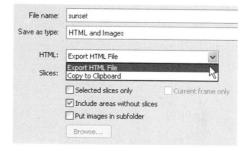

The second method involves the Quick Export button, which we'll look at later in the chapter.

Exporting frames and layers

You can easily export frames and layers as separate image files (using a chosen file format and optimization setup of your choice). Again, this helps designers adjust to any situation that may arise and aid optimization. The image file is assigned the same name as the frame or layer.

First, you need to select File ➤ Export, and then choose either Layers to Files or Frames to Files from the Save as type drop-down menu. Fireworks breaks these out as separate files using the names you assigned to the frames or layers. This discussion of exporting layers, frames, and slices highlights the importance of naming these components during the construction process.

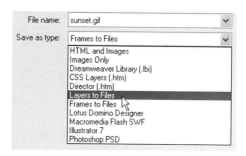

Exporting selected areas

Often, you may want to export just a small part of an image, rather than all of it, or just selected slices. For example, in the example australia.png, you may decide to export just the bridge part of the image and get rid of the water.

You start by selecting the Export Area tool. Next, simply click and drag around the area of your image you want to export.

Notice that the selected area now has eight transform handles located around it, which can be used to resize the selected area. Also, if you place your mouse pointer within the selected area, it changes to a four-headed arrow, which, when you click and drag it, allows you to reposition the selection area.

Once the area is selected, double click within it to open the **Export Preview** dialog box.

Here, you can actually edit your work while previewing it for export. Notice that it has nearly all of the optimizing tools contained in the Optimize panel.

In addition, just beneath the preview pane, there are the familiar Pointer, Zoom, and Crop tools. Also, you can use the buttons to the right of these to choose whether you have one, two, or four previews of your image for comparison purposes.

Once you've finished previewing your image and making your adjustments, click the Export... button. This opens the familiar Export panel where you can finish off your adjustments, and export your work.

The Export Preview can be accessed directly by selecting File ➤ Export Preview.

Optimize and Export Wizards

You can use two wizard tools to optimize your graphics as you export. These are opened with the two buttons at the bottom left of the Export Preview dialog box. At the left is the Export Wizard, and to the right is the Optimize to Size Wizard. Let's take a closer look at them.

Export Wizard

Based upon the information you provide it, coupled with an analysis of the image, the Export Wizard determines the best format and optimization settings for your file.

Once you have opened the Export Wizard (you can also open it with File ➤ Export Wizard), it asks if you want it to select the best export format, or analyze the current settings to see how they could be improved (if at all). If you need to constrain your file to a certain size, you can specify that size here, and Fireworks will do all the analysis necessary to achieve your target.

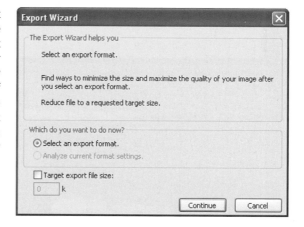

Select an export format, and press Continue to go to the next screen. Here, you select how the finished export will be used.

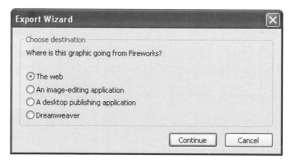

Once you've made your selection, press Continue again to see the **Analysis Results** screen.

Fireworks gives you its initial recommendations. If you chose Web or Dreamweaver as the destination, it recommends JPEG, GIF, or both. The other options normally have a recommendation of TIF. By clicking Exit, you'll return to the Export Preview window, set to the dual preview mode, to see the results of the recommendation.

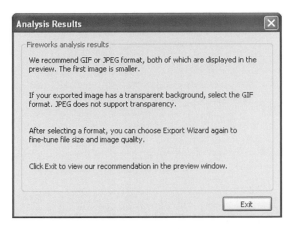

In this particular example, Fireworks recommends either a Better Quality JPEG or GIF Adaptive format for the best results. Of course, this is only a suggestion. You need to decide what is appropriate for your situation. If you want to accept one of these settings, click it and then click Export….

Exporting XHTML

One of the major issues in web coding today is the next generation of HTML called XHTML. This incorporates elements of HTML and XML and will be used in the next generation of portable devices for Internet access. Also, XHTML is case-sensitive.

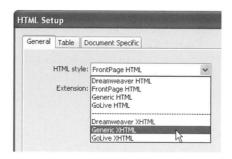

You can begin to export XHTML by first selecting File ➤ HTML Setup.... You can select either HTML or XHTML from the HTML style drop-down menu.

CSS Layers

Another major issue in contemporary web design is the use of Cascading Style Sheets (CSS), which are used to control the formatting and appearance of a web page. In Fireworks, you can export slices, layers, or frames as CSS Layers. You can then choose whether these layers are visible or invisible.

To do this, first select File ➤ Export....

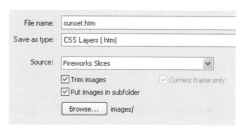

In the Source drop-down menu, you can select whether you want to export the layers, slices, or frames as CSS Layers.

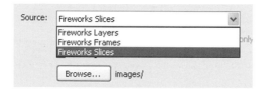

Quick Export button

You've come across this button several times already in the book. It's located at the upper-right corner of the working canvas.

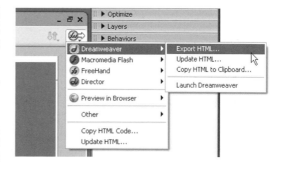

You can send your code to Dreamweaver with the first option.

You can export HTML to Dreamweaver, update an existing HTML file, copy the code to the clipboard, or launch Dreamweaver using the active file.

As you can see, you can also export to most of the standard web design programs and all of the Macromedia product line. Each of the features presents its own option screens, which will be pretty self-evident if you know the product to which you're exporting.

Notice that you can also update an existing HTML file.

Exporting to Flash

In Chapter 6, you'll learn how to build animated GIF files. As indicated at the beginning of this chapter, animated GIFs are a series of frames displayed sequentially at high speed; much like an animation is an ordered series of cells displayed quickly to create the illusion of motion. However, many web designers favor Macromedia Flash as the tool of choice for animation and motion graphics. Flash gives you more sophisticated graphics control coupled with smaller file sizes and quicker download times.

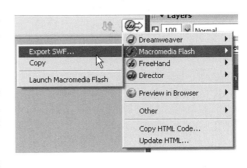

Fireworks has a handy tool to convert an animated GIF into a Flash SWF file (the output format of a completed Flash movie that's played back through the Flash Player inside a browser).

Assuming that you have an animated GIF file open (you'll try this out in depth in Chapter 6), click the Quick Export button and select Macromedia Flash.

If you select Export SWF…, it'll prompt for a name and location. The file extension .swf is automatically added.

Using Windows Explorer or Finder, you can see that a Flash file was created.

If you double click the Flash Movie file, it'll open it up in the Flash Player (provided it's already installed on your computer). As an interesting side note, the Flash file shown here is only 637 bytes in size. The original animated GIF used to create the file was 30.1KB. For web designers, this is a tremendous advantage.

If you don't have the free Flash Player installed on your computer you can download it from www.macromedia.com/downloads.

The other options allow you to copy a Fireworks graphic into Flash and to launch Macromedia Flash from within Fireworks.

Other quick exports

Macromedia Director is the heavyweight of graphic programs, used extensively for animating 3D graphics and game design. Fireworks allows you to convert your layers and slices to a format that can be used in Director.

Macromedia FreeHand is a dedicated vector-drawing program. For instance, if you want to design a storyboard for your website or use your graphics for print, Quick Export allows you to convert your Fireworks file to a .fh11 format used by FreeHand.

In addition to the ability to convert your Fireworks file to other Macromedia products, you can also convert them to other popular non-Macromedia graphic program formats. If you select the Other option in the Quick Export menu, you can see them:

You can convert your Fireworks file to three popular Adobe programs: Photoshop, GoLive, and Illustrator. As a designer, this gives you great flexibility in using the tools that you need to create a finished product.

In addition, you can export your file to Microsoft FrontPage.

Summary

In the world of web design, size is everything. The goal is always to reduce file size while maintaining quality in order to deliver the best, most visually appealing, websites within the shortest possible download time. With this in mind, you can see just how much of a crucial role both optimization and exporting play. A good tip is to test your work on as many different browsers and bandwidths as possible, as this allows you to check to see if you have managed to successfully balance quality and file size.

In the next chapter, things move up a gear with the world of animation, and you'll see how Fireworks can transform your static images into charismatic animated graphics.

Six

Animation

In this chapter

Two accepted standards exist for web animation today: GIF and Flash. Without question, web animation is increasingly dominated by Flash, Macromedia's dedicated animation application. However, most web designers still need to understand and work with traditional web animation technology: the **animated GIF** file. This is an Internet standard and is supported by virtually all web browsers. Therefore, you know that most visitors to your site can see the animation working properly without needing to download and install an additional plugin.

Because Fireworks can handle both vector and bitmap file formats, it can produce both Flash and animated GIF formats easily. You can export an animation as a Flash **SWF** file and then import it into Flash, for example. In some cases, you can even eliminate the first step and import the Fireworks PNG file directly into Flash. However, if you're not planning to use Flash for your animations, then you must create the animation in Fireworks and export it as an animated GIF file.

Here are the topics we will cover in this chapter:

★ Exploring the continuing importance of Fireworks, in an increasingly Flash world

  ★ Working with the GIF format

★ Introducing animation principles

  ★ Creating a simple animation

  ★ Achieving smoother motion in your animation

  ★ Exploring symbols and keyframe animation

  ★ Creating special effects

  ★ Exporting animations

Animation principles

In many ways, the basic concepts of animation haven't changed since the earliest days of Disney. Traditionally, an artist draws individual pictures called **frames** on clear plastic acetate material. Each frame is slightly different from the previous one and, when the sequence of frames is played at a high speed to the viewer, the brain connects the sequence of pictures together and is fooled into seeing motion. In addition, the acetates are layered so that each component of the scene is in its own layer and can be edited without affecting the other components.

This "flip-book" method of animation is still common in animation houses today. The only real change is that now a team of artists works on a project rather than just one. Within this team, usually one or two head animators draw the most important frames (known as **keyframes**) of the animation. These frames are those that introduce new images or define important points in the action.

Imagine that you want to animate a ball bouncing from left to right. The keyframes would be

★ The starting point of the ball at the left

★ The point at which the ball hits the floor in the middle

★ The point at which the ball completes its bounce at the right

All the frames in between the keyframes are called **tween** frames (derived from "in-between frames"). They simply portray the passage of the ball to its next destination, and are drawn by a team of apprentice animators.

In Fireworks, you can use both the frame-by-frame method (where you need to draw every single frame) and the more modern keyframe method. First, let's look at the more basic method.

Producing a basic frame-by-frame animation

In this section, you'll discover how to build each frame of an animation by hand. The main advantage of manual animation is that you have greater control. You can fine-tune details such as slight color alterations, shadows, and irregular movements, which could serve to create more startling effects. This approach is fine if you're creating something short and simple, but as your animations become more complex, it can make for very slow work!

When creating basic animations, start by ensuring that you have enough frames for your needs. There's no magic formula to determine how many frames you need. It just takes experience.

1. Open a new 500×500 canvas and go to the Frames panel (Window ➤ Frames or *SHIFT*+*F2*).

2. To add frames, click the options menu at the top right of the Frames panel and select Add Frames… to open the Add Frames dialog box.

3. Specify the number of frames you want in your animation using the Number field, and use the radio buttons to define where you want to insert the new frames. These radio buttons are very useful when you're adding new frames into an existing animation.

4. Once you click OK, the new frames are added to the Frames panel.

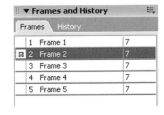

From this point on, you need to be careful to always know what frame you are currently working in. Keep an eye on the Frames panel while working with animations.

5. Highlight Frame 1 in the Frames panel and move back to the canvas to begin your animation.

6. Draw a small vector shape at the top left of your canvas (this completed example is basic_animation.png in the download files). Position it at x:25 and y:20.

7. Copy the object (Edit ➤ Copy or *Ctrl/Cmd+C*).

8. Click Frame 2 in the Frames panel. The object has disappeared, so paste the copied object here.

9. In Frame 2, change the object's position to x:95,y:130.

10. You now need to copy the object to all the other frames in the animation (you can just paste because it's in the clipboard already). Use the following coordinates:

    Frame 3: x:180,y:220

    Frame 4: x:275,y:310

    Frame 5: x:385,y:400

    The final position in Frame 5 should be the lower-right corner of the canvas.

Now that you've finished animating your object, it's time to test the animation. Notice the VCR-style playback controls at the lower-right corner of document window.

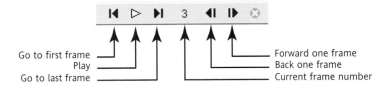

You can change the number of loops you want your animation to run through by clicking the **GIF Animation Looping** button at the lower-left side of the Frames panel and specifying the number of repetitions you want to cycle through.

If you play your animation now, it will loop forever. The number of repetitions only takes effect when you export your animation to its ultimate destination. You'll learn how to export animations at the end of this chapter.

How to delete frames

Deleting frames is very easy. Simply select the frame you want to remove in the Frames panel, and then click the trashcan button at the bottom of the Frames panel.

Tweaking your animations

If you found the previous techniques a bit tedious, don't worry, help is at hand. You can use several techniques to make the motion much smoother and more realistic. Let's take a look.

Onion skinning

This technique can be used when you're manually creating an animation; it helps you smooth out and monitor the movement of your objects across frames. To use it, click the onion skinning button on the Frames panel and select Show All Frames from the menu that pops up.

Now you can see the all the objects on each of your frames at the same time.

The object on the active frame is solid, whereas the others are opaque. You can edit the objects on all frames as normal.

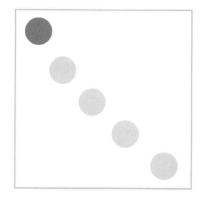

Duplicating and distributing frames

A great alternative to onion skinning is duplicating and distributing frames. Again, it's most useful when you're creating your animations manually. It might make your frame arrangement even easier.

1. Open a new 300×300-pixel canvas with a white background.

2. First determine how many frames you want in your animation. Let's say, for example, you want ten frames. Go the Frames panel and, using the New/Duplicate Frames button, put Frames 1–10 into your panel.

3. Click back on Frame 1 and draw a circle.

4. Duplicate your circle (Edit ➤ Duplicate or CTRL/CMD+ALT+D) and move it slightly along the path you want the animation to follow.

5. Repeat this process until you have all ten circles on your canvas arranged along the path that you want the animation to follow.

6. When you have all the objects arranged, select all of them and click the Distribute to Frames button in the Frames panel.

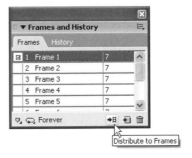

> Remember, this is a sequential process. You must draw your objects on the canvas in the order you want them to appear. If you rearrange this order, the path will still look correct, but the animation will be erratic.

7. Play your animation through now. Each of the circles has been given its own frame.

So, is it best to use onion skinning, frame distribution, or both? Well, there's no real advantage of one technique over the other, or both together; it's really a personal choice and depends on the style you develop.

Controlling time

It's important to get the speed of your animation right. If you have it too fast, too slow, or too constant, your audience won't believe the movement. You can control your speed with the **frame delay** setting.

> It's important to note that this isn't the case with animation symbols. The speed of these must be controlled by the number of frames used, as described in the "Using symbols" section.

1. Take a look at your Frames panel. You'll notice that each frame has a number to the right of it (the default is 7).

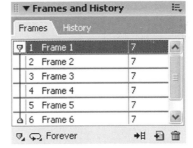

Fireworks measures frame speeds in 100ths of a second. The default of 7 means that each frame is visible to the viewer for 7/100ths of a second. You can change this setting for the entire animation or individual frames.

2. To change the frame delay, first select the frames you want to change and then double click the time at the right of each frame in the Frames panel. Change the numerical Frame delay value, and press *ENTER* to confirm the change.

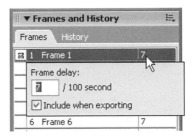

We use this technique to give a more realistic effect to our animations. For example, if we were animating a bouncing ball, we'd make it gain speed on the descent and lose speed on the ascent.

Using symbols to produce keyframe animation

Although the basic frame-by-frame animation technique is effective, it's certainly not the most efficient way to animate from a design or file size point of view. Copying and pasting objects means that you end up with several copies of the same object, each in its own location. If your animation required dozens or hundreds of frames, the number of objects it has to reproduce would mean that the file size would become way too large to use on the web.

To overcome this problem, you can use **symbols** in your animation. Using symbols means that you have only one copy of the object, located in a central library. Each frame that needs to display this object reads from the central library and places the object at the predetermined location. Efficient use of symbols results in dramatically smaller file sizes.

When using symbols, you specify the location you want the symbol to start from by positioning it on the canvas, and then you specify the other points you want it to travel through in the same way. These are the **keyframes**. Fireworks then creates all the in-between (tween) frames automatically.

By using this keyframe animation method, you remove much of the drudgework from animation. You're the lead animator creating the keyframes, the important points in the action, and Fireworks automatically draws the tween frames for you. Easy!

Let's take a look at an example to see this process in action. Let's redo our previous example, only this time, we'll do it a little differently.

Animating with symbols

1. Open a new 300×300 canvas with a white background and save the file as `animation_symbol.png` (the completed file is in the download files for reference).

2. Select Edit ➤ Insert ➤ New Symbol... (*CTRL/CMD+F8*). Name your symbol "Circle" and make it a Graphic symbol.

   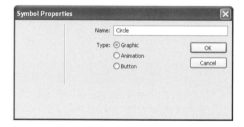

   Press OK and you'll be taken into the Symbol Editor. Notice the cross in the center; this will help centralize your symbol objects.

3. Draw a circle with your own choice of fill in the center of the Symbol Editor.

4. Click the Done button once you've drawn the circle.

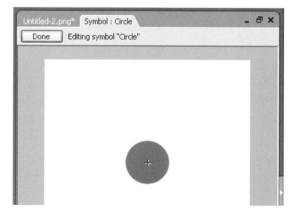

5. Your circle now appears on the main canvas. Select it and move it to the upper-left corner.

By positioning your symbol, you've specified where you want your animation to start from and you've created your first keyframe. However, to make an animation, you need at least two keyframes. Let's make another one.

6. Because you've created a symbol and placed it in a central library, you don't need to create it again. Just open the Library panel (*F11*) and click and drag your Circle symbol onto the main canvas. Place it at the lower-right corner.

This serves as your second keyframe. Now the animation needs its tween frames, the small steps between the keyframes, which will give it smoothness and continuity. As you learned earlier, Fireworks can create the tween frames for you.

7. Select both the object symbols on the canvas and then select Modify ➤ Symbol ➤ Tween Instances.... The **Tween Instances** panel opens, where you can decide how many Steps (tween frames) you want in your animation. For this example, type 10 into the Steps field and check Distribute to frames.

Fireworks creates 12 frames (2 keyframes, and 10 tween frames).

8. Play the animation through and enjoy your work.

> *If you don't check* Distribute to frames, *Fireworks will add all the tween instances into the frame you currently have open. Although your objects are all in one frame, there will be no animation; you'll simply have several copies of the same object in one frame.*

Another advantage to using the symbol Library is the ease with which you can add more keyframes to your animation. Symbols are reusable and you can drag as many as you like onto the canvas, thus building tweens to create animation. Just remember that you can only tween symbols from the same library. If you try to tween symbols from different libraries, you'll get a warning message that stops you.

Animated GIF banner

One of the most common uses for animated GIF files is in creating banners. Most animated banners are 468×60 pixels and usually have a constant background of a photograph or logo with some form of animation over them.

1. Create a new 468×60-pixel canvas and, if you want, give it a light color background (the example has white background to make it easier to see). Save the file as animated_banner.png.

2. Select the Text tool and click the banner (precise placement isn't important right now). Set the font size to 50 and choose a text color. Type in the word "Welcome".

3. Reselect the text box with the Pointer tool and select *Modify* ➤ Animation ➤ Animate Selection.

4. This opens the **Animate** dialog box. Frames determines how many frames it'll take your animation to complete its action. The more frames you add, the slower the animation will move. For our purposes, let's set it to ten frames.

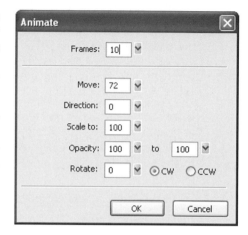

5. *Move* determines the distance your animation will move in pixels. As you'll see shortly, the number you set here initially isn't critical. Leave it at the default setting and click OK.

6. You should see this dialog box asking if it's OK to add the new frames. Select OK.

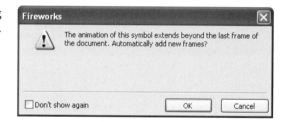

Your banner should look something like this (don't worry, you'll be making adjustments):

Notice that the text now has a beaded line with ten beads in it. This is called the **motion guide** and it is used to control the distance and direction of the animation, with each bead representing a frame. At the left side is a green bead, which indicates the beginning of the animation. To the right is a red bead representing the end of the animation.

7. Slide the text to the left of the banner area so that it is off the work area.

8. Using your mouse, drag the red bead to the center of the banner area (you can use the *SHIFT* key to keep it perfectly horizontal).

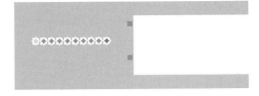

Remember, pixels determine the distance traveled. By stretching the guide, you're adding pixels. You can determine whether you have placed the guide in the right place by clicking the last frame button (in the VCR buttons at the bottom of the document window), or by clicking Frame 10 in the Frames panel.

9. Using the Frames panel, add a new frame (frame 11) and select it. Your canvas should be blank.

10. Repeat the process from step 2 again, but this time for the word "To". Once again, set the animation for ten frames.

11. As mentioned earlier, the motion guide controls distance *and* direction. Drag the To text below the banner area and drag the red bead so that it is once again in the middle of the banner area.

Again, you can use the last frame button to test the position. It's starting to shape up already.

12. Add a new frame (frame 21) to the Frames panel. In the banner area, type "The New".

13. Select Modify ➤ Animation ➤ Animate Selection.

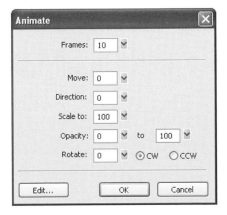

14. This time you're going to do something a little different. Use ten frames once again, but don't move the text—set Move to 0.

15. Let's start off with the text completely invisible and make it fade in. Set the left (start) Opacity field to 0 and the right (end) value to 100.

16. Click OK and test your animation now. It should be starting to look really professional.

17. Add a frame 31 to your Frames panel and select it.

18. Type the text "Fireworks MX 2004" onto the canvas. Once again, open the Animate dialog box and, this time, set Scale to to 0. Again, use ten frames and set Move to 0.

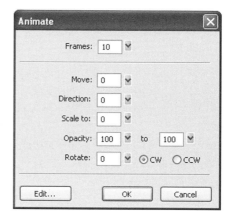

19. Try your animation now. It's looking really nice now.

Let's do one quick task to finish things up a bit.

20. Add a frame 41, select it, and type "Fireworks MX 2004" again (you could drag this text out of the symbol Library). Don't add any animation because this text will remain visible after the animation has completed.

Before previewing the animation in the browser and then exporting it, you need to ensure that it's set to be an animated GIF. If you're going to animate, you have two choices: animated GIF or Flash.

21. Go into the Optimize panel and choose the Animated GIF Websnap 128 preset. All the other settings fall right into place.

In this example, the animation is set to play through just once and then stay on the last piece of static text. However, when you click the play button to test it, the animation loops continuously. This is because the canvas doesn't have the ability to read the controlling code.

22. Return to the Frames panel and click the GIF Animation Looping button. To make the animation play through once and then stop, choose No Looping.

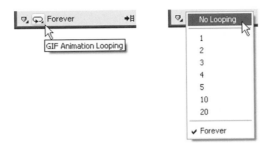

23. You're now ready to test the simple animated banner. Go ahead and use the Quick Export button and then choose ➤ Preview in Browser ➤ Preview in Primary Browser.

You should have a pretty nifty-looking animated GIF now. If you feel it runs a little fast, you can use the Frames field in the Property inspector to add frames at key points. This can sometimes be a little tricky for several reasons. First of all, as you add frames, you have to keep track of where the action is changing. What was frame 31 before could be frame 36 now. Also, you have to click the object you are animating, even if it is outside of the work area.

Exporting your animations

Unless you're planning on admiring your work of art in private, you'll want to export, or publish, your masterpiece on the Internet for the rest of the world to see. To make this happen, you need to do two things:

★ Produce an animated GIF file, which compiles the animation (frames and all) into a package that makes it much easier for another computer to play it back.

★ Produce an HTML file, which allows a browser to find and use the animated GIF file.

Thankfully, Fireworks can produce both files at the same time with little effort on your part.

Normally, when the animation is part of a larger web project, you would export the files to an HTML editor such as Dreamweaver, but for this exercise, you're going to bypass that and send it to its destination directly (see Hero One for a whole project on integrating Fireworks with Dreamweaver). Let's export the `animated_banner.png` file created earlier.

1. Select File ➤ Export Preview....

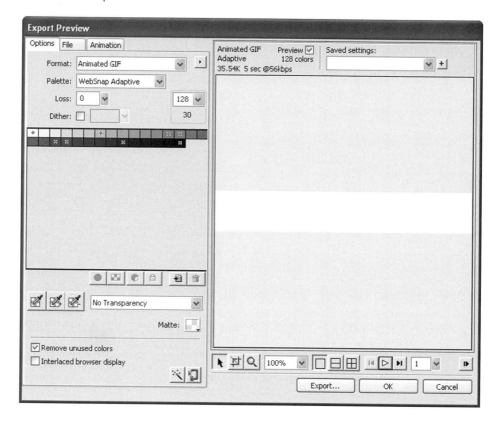

You've seen many of the options already in previous chapters. However, there is something important to note here: the export Format must be set to Animated GIF; otherwise you'll end up with an unanimated graphic.

2. Click the Format drop-down menu, select Animated GIF, and then select the Animation tab. This contains a wealth of information about your graphic. You can preview the animation using the playback buttons or by checking the content in each frame.

In addition to being able to do a frame-by-frame review, this tab tells you that the animation will take about three seconds to run, in this example. There are also two buttons to adjust the repetitions:

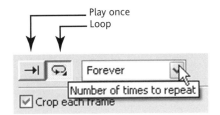

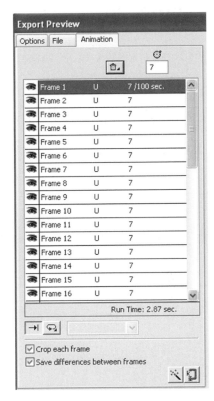

Clicking the left button sets the animation to run only once. With the Loop option, you can specify the number of repetitions.

3. Click the Export... button, which brings up this dialog box.

Here you have Save as type: set to HTML and Images. Remember, your animated GIF file must run in a browser and the browser needs the proper HTML coding to find the file. If you don't want to export all your HTML with the animation, you can also send it to an HTML editor of your choice (including Dreamweaver).

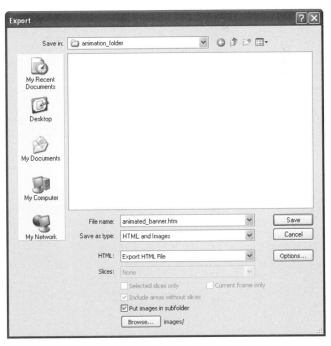

4. Navigate to your working directory, where all your files are kept, if you're not there already. Give your file a name and choose HTML and Images in the Save as type: dialog.

   This way, Fireworks creates two files for the price of one: `animated_banner.gif` and `animated_banner.htm`.

5. Click the Save button and your animation is now ready for the web.

6. Finally, open your browser and use the File ➤ Open menu option to navigate to the `animated_banner.htm` file and try it out.

Summary

In the first part of this chapter, you learned how to create frames manually, use keyframes, and animate a symbol to produce a basic animation. You also discovered how to use the onion skinning technique, duplicate and distribute frames, and utilize the frame delay option to tweak your animations. You also now know how to export the HTML code to publish your work on an actual website.

Seven

Working with Vectors

In this chapter

You're going to take a closer look at the Vector tools introduced in Chapter One. You can use these tools to make a variety of shapes to enhance your designs, particularly when you use them in conjunction with the Combine Paths operation. In this case, you'll learn how to draw a basic heart shape before making a more complicated decorative ornamental shape. You can make some shapes using the new Auto Shapes, but when you know how to use the Vector tools to make your own shapes, you'll unleash the true power of Fireworks. Also, knowing how to make custom designs may help you discover how to edit the Auto Shapes to make your own custom shape.

In this chapter, you'll explore the following:

★ Using the Rectangle and Pen tools to make tabs

★ Working with Auto Shapes

★ Enhancing your designs and making custom designs with vector tools

★ Editing vector paths using the Reshape, Freeform, Path Scrubber, and Knife tools

Making tabs

Tabs are a popular design feature used on many websites and are quite simple to make using the Rectangle tool. Though an Auto Shape called the Rounded Rectangle tool exists, you'll see how easy it is to obtain the degree of roundness you prefer using the Rectangle tool. You'll add these tabs to a folder later in the chapter. To begin with, let's make some simple tabs.

1. Open a new 600×100 document and select the Rectangle tool (*U*).

2. Draw a rectangle that's 110 pixels wide and 30 pixels high.

3. In the Rectangle roundness field in the Property inspector, choose a Rectangle roundness of 100.

4. Select Solid from the Fill category drop-down menu. Click the fill color box and change the fill color to #666600.

5. Aligning the tabs is easiest using guides. If your rulers aren't already visible, go to View ➤ Rulers and then drag out guides to the left, top, and bottom edges of the rectangle. Choose View ➤ Guides ➤ Snap to Guides.

> *A small bevel looks nice on these tabs as well. Try* Bevel and Emboss ➤ Inner Bevel *from the Effects menu. Choose* Smooth *for the Bevel edge shape and use a size of 5.*

6. Duplicate the rectangle four times so that five objects are present on the canvas. Change the color of each tab and arrange them, as shown here:

7. Once your tabs are all arranged correctly, drag out a vertical guide to the right edge of the rectangle furthest to the right.

8. Draw a rectangle between the two vertical guides and position it about halfway up the tabs.

This is just one way of making a tab, which is relatively quick and easy. You'll make what we think is a better looking tab using the Pen tool later in this chapter.

Using the Union operation

A design often calls for a shape with rounded and square corners, like the tabs at the top of a folder. You could make such a shape using the Pen tool, but it's more complex (using the Pen tool is detailed in the next section). Instead, you're going to make the shape using the Union operation along with the Rectangle tools, and then you'll also see how to use the Auto Shapes Rounded Rectangle to make the same shape. As you might expect, the Rectangle tool gives you the square corners and the Rounded Rectangle tool creates rounded corners (or the optional shape changes using the control points). Let's get started.

1. On a new canvas, draw a 180×60 rectangle with a Rectangle roundness of 50, no stroke, and any color fill.

2. Draw another regular rectangle with square corners that's 180×20. Position this rectangle over the rounded rectangle.

3. Select both shapes and then choose Modify ➤ Combine Paths ➤ Union.

Auto Shapes Rounded Rectangle

Auto Shapes are new to Fireworks MX 2004. The Rounded Rectangle tool can be used to easily make a shape with rounded and squared corners by following these steps:

1. Start a new canvas.

2. Select the Rounded Rectangle tool from the Auto Shapes area of the Shape menu and click the canvas.

    By default, the corners are rounded. You can change the corner shape by clicking one of the corner control points if you like.

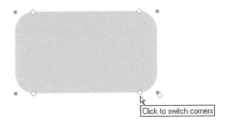

> *The Beveled Rectangle, Campfer Rectangle, and the Rounded Rectangle shape tools all have the same three shapes available. The difference between them is the default shape that is drawn.*

3. Fill the shape with your preferred color. In the Property inspector, change the stroke to Basic ➤ Hard Rounded and make the stroke width 1. Set the stroke color as you like.

4. Press the *ALT/OPTION* key and drag the bottom right control point (that says Click to switch corners) to the right until you have a square bottom corner.

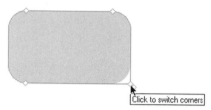

5. Repeat step 4 for the bottom-left corner of the rectangle.

Making a tabbed folder

As mentioned earlier, you're now going to make a nicer looking tab. Here, you'll draw a custom shaped tab and add it to a folder.

1. Open a new document, select the Pen tool, and draw one half of a tab. This image has been magnified so that you can see the placement of the points.

2. To make the curve on the left, press *ALT/OPTION* and click and drag the bottom-left point, as shown here.

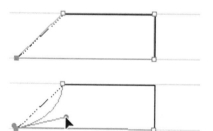

3. Choose Edit ➤ Clone and then Modify ➤ Transform ➤ Flip Horizontal. Align the two halves together by pressing the right arrow key.

4. Select both halves and choose Modify ➤ Combine Paths ➤ Union. Remove the stroke and add a fill.

5. Adjust the size of your tab if necessary. This example is 150×30.

6. Duplicate (Edit ➤ Duplicate) your tab twice, change the color of each tab, and arrange them side by side. Add some button text as shown here:

7. Double click the Home text in the Layers panel and rename the text object "home". Repeat for the other words.

8. Draw a rectangle to be used with the tabs and make it long enough to span the length of all three tabs.

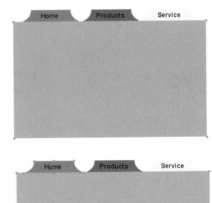

9. Open the Frames panel (*SHIFT+F2*). Select Duplicate Frame from the Frames options menu. Type in 2 for the number of frames (or more if you have more tabs) and check After current frame.

10. In Frame 1, *SHIFT*+select the first tab and the large rectangle.

11. Choose Modify ➤ Combine Paths ➤ Union. The tab and rectangle are now one shape but your Home text disappeared! It's now behind the new tab shape.

12. In the Layers panel, drag the home text above the new shape. Because I drew my rectangle over all three tabs, the other two are behind the new shape. If yours aren't, rearrange your Layers, as shown here.

13. Repeat steps 11 and 12 for both Frames 2 and 3.

14. To make these tabs work, you need to add a swap image behavior. In Frame 1, select the Rectangle Hotspot tool and draw a rectangle over the Home tab. In the Property inspector, name the hotspot "home".

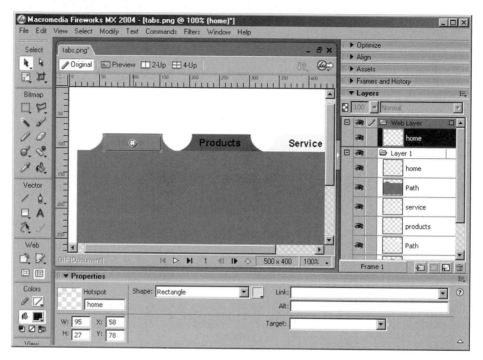

15. Press *ALT/OPTION*, select, and drag a copy of the hotspot over the Products tab and repeat for the Service tab. Name each hotspot appropriately in the Property inspector.

16. Right/*CTRL*-click the combined tab shape and select Insert slice. The slice will cover the entire tabbed interface. Name the slice "tabs" in the Property inspector.

17. Open the Optimize panel, use GIF as the file export format, and choose 8 colors, with no transparency. This sets the optimization for the entire slice.

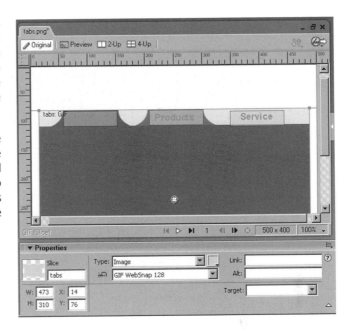

18. Choose the Select Behind tool (in the Pointer tool fly-out). Select the home button and you'll see a little white circle. Click it and select Add Swap Image Behavior.

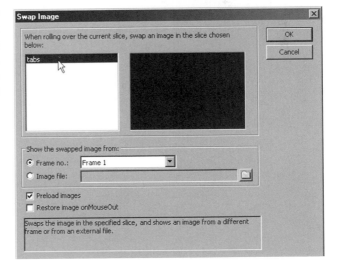

19. The Swap Image Behavior dialog box opens. Select the slice you want to swap (there's only one to select), change the Frame no. to 1, and uncheck Restore image onMouseOut.

20. In the Behaviors panel (*SHIFT+F3*), click the little down arrow and select onClick instead of the onMouseOver behavior.

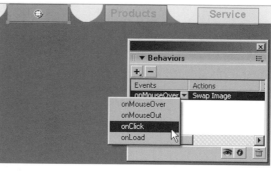

21. Repeat steps 18, 19, and 20 for the other two buttons, substituting Frame 2 for Products and Frame 3 for Service.

22. To prepare for exporting, choose Modify ➤ Canvas ➤ Fit Canvas. This removes all the extra canvas you don't want in the interface, leaving just the sliced area.

23. The interface is now ready for exporting. Choose File ➤ Export. Save as HTML and Images, uncheck Current frame only, and put your images in a subfolder.

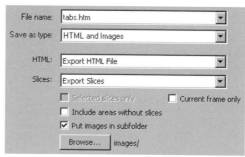

24. Test out your tabbed folder file in a browser. (A working version called tabs.htm is in the tabbedFolder folder in the download files.)

Make an L shape with a curve

A very popular shape for web page design is an inverted L shape with a curved interior corner; you can make this in a number of ways using Fireworks. The **Punch** command is a wonderful method for achieving all kinds of custom shapes.

1. Open a new 800×400 document with a white canvas.

2. Draw a 775×130 rectangle and another that's 130×300. Align the tall rectangle to the top left of the canvas and the wide rectangle to the top of the canvas, overlapping the other rectangle slightly, as shown:

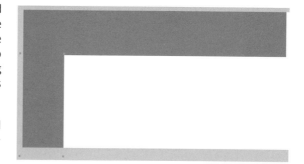

3. *SHIFT*+select both rectangles and use Modify ➤ Combine Paths ➤ Union to form one shape.

Now for the curved inside corner.

4. Draw a rectangle with a Roundness of 30 and make it 745×345 so that it's large enough for the curved corner to fit into the inside corner formed by the two existing rectangles and for the other rounded corners to reach beyond the straight portions of the L. Change the color of this rectangle to make it easier to see.

5. With your rulers turned on, drag a vertical guide to 100 and a horizontal guide to 100. Drag the rounded rectangle to the intersection.

6. *SHIFT*+select both shapes and choose Modify ➤ Combine Paths ➤ Punch.

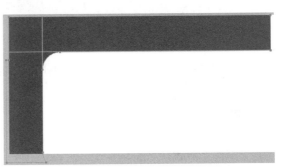

That's it. You now have a rounded-off L shape. How easy was that? Just imagine the innovative shapes you can achieve using the Punch command. You could add a bevel and/or a drop shadow if you'd like.

> You can also use the Auto Shape L-Shape tool, but it doesn't offer the same options, such as the curved inside corner.

Drawing a heart shape

Before moving on to create a more complex shape, let's quickly make a heart shape using just the Pen tool and a Transform command.

1. Open a new document and select the Pen tool.

2. Pull a guide to the center of the document. Click a point on the guide for the heart's center and click and drag a second point for the heart's tip. For the heart in this example, you can see the handles are pulled out quite a way, creating a steep curve.

3. With the first half of your heart selected, go to Edit ➤ Clone (*CTRL/CMD+SHIFT+D*).

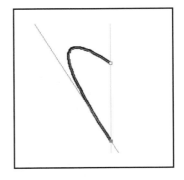

4. Now choose Modify ➤ Transform ➤ Flip Horizontal and move the second half into position.

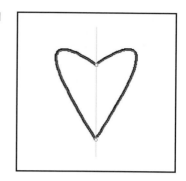

5. Next, choose Select ➤ Select All (*CTRL+A*) and then Modify ➤ Combine Paths ➤ Join. Fill the heart with red and remove the stroke. We've added a drop shadow as well.

6. If you want to draw a fuller heart, add an extra point. This way, you can adjust the curve in two directions.

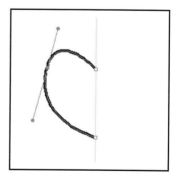

7. Once you've added the extra control handle, repeat steps 3 through 5. This is how the completed heart looks:

Making a decorative ornament

This project demonstrates the use of the Vector tools to produce intricate designs, such as this ornament:

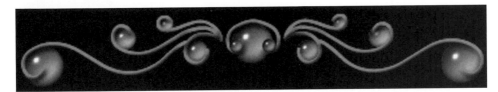

The following project is an adaptation of a Photoshop PSD file, and it demonstrates how you can convert many of the Photoshop tutorials available on the web into usable Fireworks techniques. This particular ornament didn't have a tutorial, but the PSD file gave enough detail to reproduce the ornament. It's printed here with Shafgat Ali's (the original designer) permission.

Creating the small spheres with highlights

First, you're going to make a sphere and then alter it for use in the ornament.

1. Open a new 130×130-pixel canvas with a black background.

2. Select the Ellipse tool. Press the *SHIFT* key to constrain the ellipse to a circle and drag the shape out on your canvas. Don't worry too much about the size at this stage (the size used in this example is 64×64).

3. Go into the Property inspector and choose Gradient ➤ Radial from the Fill category drop-down menu.

4. Choose Black, White from the gradient Preset drop-down menu. The only reason you're doing this is to ensure that you have only two color fill boxes in your gradient; otherwise, you'd need to delete the extras.

5. Click the first color box at the bottom left of the gradient color ramp and select the white swatch in the pop-up color palette.

6. Next, click the second color box (at the right beneath the gradient color ramp) and choose any color you like. The color in this example is #D89495. Press *ENTER/RETURN* when you're happy with your gradient.

7. Select the sphere and you'll see the gradient handles. Click and drag the circle to move the white area to the upper portion of the sphere.

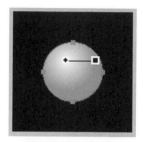

8. Select the Ellipse tool again and draw another smaller ellipse inside the circle, as shown here. Make this new ellipse 37 pixels wide and 31 high.

9. Move this second ellipse so it is at an angle. Select the Scale tool and, if you hover your cursor on the outside of the ellipse, you'll see the Rotate icon appear; click and drag it to rotate the ellipse.

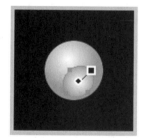

10. This second ellipse is going to be another highlight area, but there isn't enough white. Click the gradient fill in the Property inspector and drag the first square handle out just a little leaving a bit of pink.

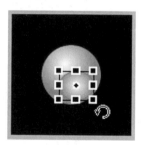 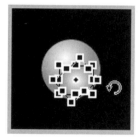 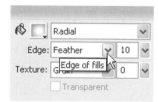

Once the shape is rotated, the size will change to about 46×26. The exact size isn't important. Just place it so that it looks good. A copy of this sphere with the highlight included is in the ornament *folder in the download files named* sphere.png *if you want to check it out.*

11. Select Feather from the Edge drop-down menu and choose 10 for the amount. You can experiment with the amount of feathering to see if you prefer more or less.

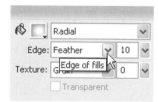

Notice that the edges are not as smooth as they could be. Even though the background is black, a small black stroke can help define this sphere.

12. Make sure only the large sphere is selected and, in the stroke area of the Property inspector, choose a Basic ➤ Soft Rounded stroke with a tip size of 2 and black color.

Now the sphere is complete. (You can find the completed sphere sphere.png in the download files.)

Sphere variation

For a sphere with more depth and a glassy look, try these steps:

1. After you draw your ellipse (steps 1 and 2 in the previous example), fill it with a solid fill instead of the gradient. Try the fill color #874A4A.

2. In the same position where you moved your first white highlight (step 7 of the previous exercise), place a tiny white circle with a feather value of 1.

3. Repeat steps 8 through 11 of the previous exercise with one exception—edit the gradient color and change the pink to a dark burgundy, (hex #874A4A). The finished variation is also included in the download files called glassysphere.png.

A variation of this sphere will be used to make the web page ornament, so remember to save it!

Preparing all the spheres

Look at the picture of the ornament at the start of this chapter, and you can see that quite a few spheres are used in the design. In this section, you'll create, change the color of, and resize all the spheres you need.

1. If you closed glassysphere.png, open it again or open the copy in the download files.

2. Select all the ellipses and group them (*CTRL/CMD+G*).

3. Open a new 200×200 black canvas. Copy the glassy sphere you grouped in the last step and paste it onto your new canvas.

7

4. Select the sphere and, in the Property inspector, make it 31 pixels wide and high.

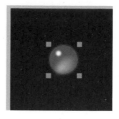

> *The original PSD file has shadows with all the spheres, but because you're working on a black background here, they're not necessary. For your information, the shadows are not drop shadows, they're ellipses with a feather applied. If you'd like to use this ornament on a different colored background, then add these shadows. Use ellipses that are 10 pixels larger in diameter than the sphere itself, fill with black, and select a feather of 5.*

5. The glassy sphere is already the right color, but you'll need some more of them so select the sphere, then press *ALT/OPT*, and drag out three more copies. Place three spheres at the top of your document out of the way and move the fourth to the center of the canvas.

6. Select a copy of the burgundy sphere and change both the width and height to 17. In the Effects menu, choose Adjust Color ➤ Hue/Saturation. Set Saturation to −100, and Lightness and Hue to 0 (if they're not already set that way). Click OK to produce a gray sphere.

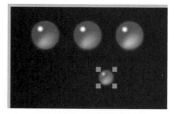

7. *ALT/OPT*+drag out three copies of the gray sphere. Move two of the gray spheres out of the way and select the other two.

8. From the Effects menu, choose Adjust Color ➤ Hue/Saturation. Set the Hue to 41, Saturation to 17, and the Lightness to 11. Click OK and move your finished gold spheres out of the way for now.

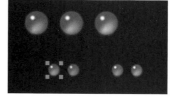

9. *ALT/OPT*+drag a copy of the gold sphere. You now need a green sphere, so select the copied sphere and choose Adjust Color ➤ Hue/Saturation again from the Effects menu. Give this sphere a Hue of 86, Saturation of 11, Lightness of −8 to make it green.

10. The green spheres need to be a bit smaller. Select the sphere and change the width and height to 11.

11. *ALT/OPT*+drag one additional copy of the green sphere onto the canvas.

12. The last two spheres you need to make are the two little ones in the center of the ornament. *Alt/Opt*+drag a copy of one of the large original burgundy spheres onto your work area. Change the width and height to 11 and *Alt/Opt*+drag out one additional copy.

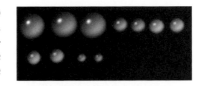

13. You're now finished creating all the spheres. Save this document so that you can use it to complete the ornament (the file complete to this point is in the download files as `spheres.png`).

> *If you're using the shadows, then place each sphere over its shadow and group it with its sphere.*

Making the basic shape

Here's the basic shape you're going to be drawing:

To draw this shape, you could use a variety of tools (Pencil, Brush, or Pen), depending on how you prefer to draw. You could even draw the shapes freehand using the Pencil or Brush tools. The easiest way to do this is to draw your design on paper first and then trace it using a drawing tablet. Another option is to use the Pen tool and trace around the shape. This is the technique you'll use here.

1. Open `ornamentbasicshape.png` from the download files.

2. Choose Lock All from the options menu in the Layers panel and add a new layer to work on without affecting the original image.

Because the technique involved for drawing all the curly lines is the same, the following steps are given for the large, bottom, left line only. You'll need to repeat these steps for the other lines in the image.

3. Select the Pen tool. Set the stroke to Basic ➤ Soft-Line, tip size to 2, and also set a highly visible color like red. Click with the Pen tool at the starting point, as shown here:

4. This image shows where to place the second point. To place this point, make it a curve segment by clicking and dragging to fit the curve as best you can. Don't worry too much about being perfect.

5. Now, to place the third point, click and drag this point as well.

6. Next, simply click to place the following three points.

7. Add the last two points by clicking and dragging to conform to the curves. Because the stroke is a different color, you can see how close your design lines up with the original. Remember that you can pull the handles in either direction with the Subselection tool to make alterations.

8. Once you're happy with your shape, choose Modify ➤ Alter Path ➤ Simplify…. For this path, enter an Amount of 2 and click OK. A setting of 2 maintains the shape's integrity and reduces the number of points to just 4. The less complicated the path, the smaller the file size will be, which is important if you end up using this as a vector in a program such as Flash.

9. Repeat this process for all the shapes on the left side of the design, and then work on the center shape. When you're finished and are satisfied with all the shapes, select all of them except for the center shape and choose Modify ➤ Join.

10. To make the second side, simply select the joined portion you just made, choose Edit ➤ Clone, and then Modify ➤ Flip Vertical. Move this half into position over the original background.

11. Press *CTRL/CMD+A* to select everything and choose Modify ➤ Join. Change the stroke color to gray (hex #999999) to get your basic shape:

12. Delete the original layer you used as a tracing guide and save the file with a different name.

Adding depth

Now let's move on to add some depth and dimension to the basic shape.

1. Continuing with your shape drawing from the previous exercise (or ornamentbasicshape.png from the download files), select your basic shape and add a duplicate layer. Change the name to "color".

2. Change the stroke color to hex #B0987C. Zoom in close and, with the Color layer selected, press the down arrow and the right arrow once each. Now deselect the image so that you can see the result. Just a small amount of the gray is showing.

3. To add dimension to the bottom side of the shape, select the color shape and choose Duplicate Layer from the options menu in the Layers panel. Choose After current layer. Rename the layer "shadow". (If you use the Add/Duplicate layer icon to add a layer, it will be placed above the selected layer, so just move it below the color shape.)

4. Select this new layer and change the stroke color to white. In the Effects menu choose Shadow and Glow ➤ Drop Shadow, and set the Distance to 7, Softness to 6, Angle to 323, and Opacity to 100%. Also check the Knock out option, which leaves only the effect, not the original shape. Place the shadow as seen in the following illustration. You'll notice a bit of white highlight showing too.

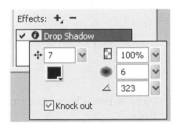

5. Change your canvas color to black (Modify ➤ Canvas Color) and save your file (this is finishedbasicshape.png in the download files).

Assembling the ornament

You'll need to open two files to complete the ornament: the finishedbasicshape.png and spheres.png file.

1. Make the finishedbasicshape.png file active and select Layer 1. Copy the large burgundy circle and paste it onto the spheres.png canvas.

2. In the Layers panel, drag the sphere below the basic shape. Position the sphere on the bottom left curl so that the white top highlight remains white. If you get it too close to the shape, the shadow (if you're using one) will dull the highlight.

3. Now repeat the previous steps for the right side of the shape. You may want to rename object names in the Layers panel to make them distinctive.

4. Repeat steps 1 through 3 for the gray, gold, and green spheres.

5. Copy the large burgundy sphere from the spheres.png canvas and paste it to the center of the ornament.

6. The two tiny spheres for the center shape go on top of the curly ends (not under) so select the Color layer and copy the small burgundy spheres from the spheres.png canvas, paste them, and move them into place (on either side of the large center sphere). Here is the finished ornament.

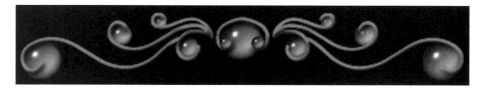

Using vector editing tools to make boring shapes interesting

In this exercise, you'll see how you can quickly transform the L shape you made earlier in the chapter into a totally different shape simply by editing it with the vector tools.

1. Open lshape.png from the l_shape folder in the download files.

2. The first thing you'll do is add a curved shape to the bottom of the left vertical side. Select the Reshape Area tool. In the Property inspector, set both the Size and Strength to 80.

174

3. Click inside the left side and drag down.

The side is much too short, but you want to keep the bottom's new shape, plus you want to add a bit of imagination to the shape.

4. To do this, pull a horizontal guide to just above the bottom shape and then select the Knife tool.

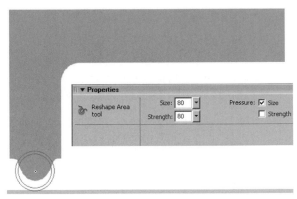

5. *SHIFT* and drag the knife across the shape.

6. Deselect all and now select the bottom shape. Use the arrow keys to move down a couple of inches. If that moves it off the canvas (and it will if you're using the sample file), choose Modify ➤ Canvas ➤ Fit Canvas.

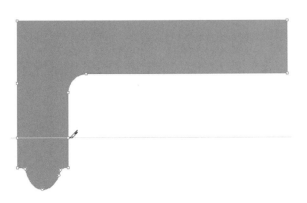

We use this command so frequently that we made a custom keyboard shortcut for it. We use CTRL+F to automatically fit the canvas.

7. Select the Arrow shape tool (in the Auto Shapes) and draw an arrow to fit in the space you just created. Make the arrowhead extend beyond the rectangle shape. You could also try a star or any other shape you like. We've also changed the color of the arrow here.

8. With the arrow selected, choose Modify ➤ Ungroup.

9. Select the Freeform tool. Set the Size to 72 and leave Pressure checked in the Property inspector.

10. Place your cursor inside the arrow, click and drag up, then drag down to make the shape shown here.

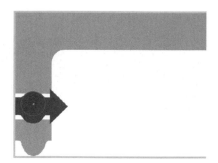

11. Use the Arrow shape tool to draw another arrow. Place it over the right top end of the main shape. Click the connector point to adjust the arrowhead size to fit the end of the main shape.

12. Drag the new arrow to the bottom of the stack in the Layers panel so that it's below the main shape.

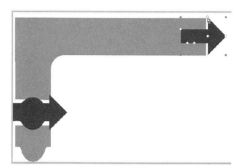

13. Select the top large portion of the shape and add a texture (I added 50 percent hatch). Add a texture to the bottom too. You now have a funky new interface design that you can continue to distort to your heart's content.

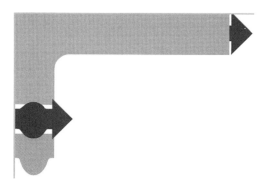

Summary

In this chapter, you started out creating some basic shapes using mainly the Rectangle tool. You then went on to create more complex shapes through the addition of the Pen tool along with your shape tools. You also looked at how to use the Combine Paths functions when you're working with vector shapes.

Once you finished creating the different vector shapes, you moved on to learn how to use the Vector editing tools; you looked at how different you can make even the most basic rectangle or line by using the Freeform and Knife tools. By using these, you can turn a dull image into something warped and creative. Now it's up to you to play and explore where you can go with these tools.

Spectacular Text Effects

In this chapter

You'll transform normal everyday text into something nice enough to be the main graphic element of a web page. Using text effects and specially treated text is a popular way to enhance a web page. Whether the text is a title, a subhead, or even a logo, it can be a very important part of your message.

In this chapter, you'll look at the following:

★ Using the Text tool and the Property inspector

★ Converting text to a path

★ Creating text effects such as 3D text with rust, metal textures, special bevels, and glows

★ Filling text with an image

★ Making small fonts readable and clear on a monitor

We've experimented with different text effects and have found that the most realistic by far have been those made using Photoshop. But Photoshop is primarily a bitmap image-editing program, so how can those techniques be translated into a Fireworks text effect? As you work through this chapter, you'll begin to see the true power and flexibility of Fireworks.

The vector capabilities of Fireworks are one of its huge benefits. Not only can you make many of your images using vectors that are fully scalable, they also remain completely editable. A huge number of effects normally possible only with bitmap images can be used on vector images too. You'll learn some tips and tricks for manipulating your text to look like bitmaps while retaining all the advantages of remaining as a vector. You can easily edit and make changes to an image when you keep the PNG source file in a safe place. With the original file, you can access the settings used for all the effects, strokes, and fills applied. But if you convert the image to a bitmap at any point, the ability to edit those elements will be lost.

Text tool and the Property inspector

As you saw in Chapter One, text is handled right in your open document. If you select the Text tool, all the normal text-editing options are displayed in the Property inspector: font, size, color, leading, kerning, and alignment. You'll also find options for horizontal and vertical orientations of the text and several options for paragraph text, such as Space Preceding Paragraph, Space After Paragraph, and Paragraph Indent.

Smoothing text edges

To smooth out the text edge, you need to **anti-alias** it. Anti-aliasing controls the appearance of edges by mixing pixels along the border of an image, thus creating a crisp line.

With your text field selected, go into the Property inspector and choose one of the following options from the Anti-aliasing level drop-down menu: Crisp, Strong, Smooth, No Anti-Alias, System, or Custom. Practice with all the options until you find the level that gives you the text results you want.

You can also access the majority of text options through the Text menu, including the option to open the Text Editor. In practice, though, because it's so handy to have all the text controls right in the Property inspector, you usually don't need to use the Text menu. However, a few special text-handling techniques, such as attaching text to a path or reversing the direction of the text on the path, are found in the Text menu, rather than the Property inspector, along with a useful spell checker.

Converting text to a path

Why would you want to convert text to a path, and what is the purpose of a path? First, text is a vector object and you can alter the entire word, sentence, or each individual letter's properties, but you can't make any physical shape changes to the individual letters themselves. If you have a great script font but would like to alter the ascender a bit, you need to convert the text to a path (Text ➤ Convert to Paths) before you can edit it. Once the text is converted to a path, you'll see the individual nodes that make up the path of each letter. Fireworks keeps the group of nodes for each letter as a group after the conversion to a path. To see the individual nodes, you have to select the text and choose Modify ➤ Ungroup.

Cutting text out of an image

You can convert text to a path, ungroup it, and then use Modify ➤ Combine Paths ➤ Union to make it into one vector shape. This is very useful when you want to cut text from another image or object. After text is converted into a path, it can be used just like a cookie cutter. By placing the converted text on top of another path object, you can punch it out, leaving a see-through hole.

1. Open a new a new 300×300-pixel canvas with a background color of your choice.

2. Draw a rectangle to fill the whole canvas. Place your cursor outside the canvas area and click and drag to cover the entire area.

3. In the Property inspector, select Pattern ➤ Other from the Fill category drop-down menu (you need to scroll all the way to the bottom of the patterns catalog). Browse to the folder where you saved the download files for this chapter and choose shellback.png. The canvas should now be filled with the shell background.

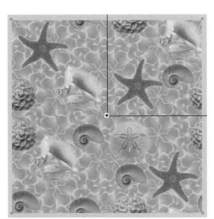

> If you have a pattern that tiles, select the circle handle and drag up to the top-right corner to fill the canvas with just one image instead of four.

4. Add a duplicate layer in the Layers panel.

5. Select Layer 2 and select Pattern ➤ Other (all the way on the bottom) from the Fill category again, and browse to the sand.png image in the download files.

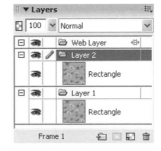

6. Now type in some text that you want to use as a cookie cutter. The settings used in this example are

> *The Tarzan font is available from* www.buyfonts.com *and costs $2, though feel free to use an alternative.*

★ Font: Tarzan
★ Point size: 62
★ Color: Black
★ Align: center
★ Anti-aliasing level: Smooth Anti-Alias

7. We wanted the text to cover more of the surface so we distorted it. You can do this by going to Modify ➤ Transform ➤ Free Transform and dragging the bottom center control handles.

8. To make the text into a punch, choose these commands:

  a. Select Text ➤ Convert To Paths.

  b. *SHIFT*+select each letter with the Subselection tool.

  c. Once you've selected each letter, go to Modify ➤ Ungroup.

  d. Be careful not to select the rectangle and go to Modify ➤ Combine Paths ➤ Join.

9. *SHIFT*+select the text and the rectangle and choose Modify ➤ Combine Paths ➤ Punch.

10. The hole is punched through the sand object and the shell object becomes visible through the cutout. Click the shell object and position it below the cutout text until you like the colors below the text.

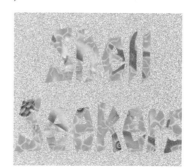

11. Select the sand object. In the stroke area of the Property inspector, make the following settings:

★ Air Brush: Basic
★ Tip size: 4
★ Color: #996666 (dark brown)

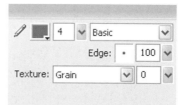

> *In this example, it's difficult to see the changes in real time on the canvas because the path has so many points. To see clearly, deselect by clicking outside the image area and then reselect before applying or making changes to the effects or strokes.*

12. Choose Shadow and Glow ➤ Drop Shadow from the Effects menu with these settings:

   ★ Distance: 4

   ★ Opacity: 65%

   ★ Softness: 3

   ★ Angle: 315

   ★ Color: black

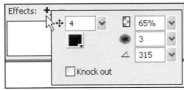

Placing text on a circular path

Here you'll place text on the top and bottom of a circle independently. To do this, the path has to be cut in half, forming two arcs, and then the direction of the bottom type reversed.

1. Open `birdlogo.png` from the download files. This is the object that you'll place text around.

2. Draw an ellipse around the outside of the image, completely surrounding it. Don't use a fill and choose a 1-pixel black stroke.

3. Type the word "Exotic" just above the ellipse. I used the following settings:

   ★ Font: Tarzan (downloaded from www.fontfreak.com)

   ★ Point size: 55

   ★ Color: Black

   ★ Edge: Smooth Anti-Alias

   ★ Alignment: Center

> The text alignment makes a difference to the position of the text when you place it on the circular path.

4. Type the word "Birds" beneath the ellipse using the same text settings. The exact position doesn't really matter here.

5. Place a horizontal guide where you'd like to slice (I put it in the center). Select the ellipse and choose the Knife tool (Y). To cut a straight line, press the Shift key as you slice horizontally. You can slice anywhere you want—it doesn't have to be in the center. In the image here, I moved the bottom arc down a bit so you can see the cut, but it'll be moved back into position.

> If you want to move the path you just sliced, click in your document to deselect the path. Next, select the path you'd like to move, and click and drag it wherever you'd like. Notice that you now have two open paths instead of one closed path.

6. *SHIFT*+select the Exotic text and the top arc and choose Text ➤ Attach to Path.

> If your text automatically jumps to the left or right edge of the arc, then you need to check your text alignment; the text should be center aligned.

7. Even though the text is attached to the path, you can still change the font attributes without removing it from the path. Select the text and change the kerning to 20 percent to add a bit of space between each letter.

> Select the word in order to apply a kerning range, which affects every letter. If you only wanted to add space between two letters, you'd insert your cursor between the two letters and then apply the kerning value.

8. Select Birds and add 20 percent kerning to it. Now *SHIFT*+select the Birds text and lower arc and choose Text ➤ Attach to Path. The Birds text is now upside down, but you can remedy this with Text ➤ Reverse Direction.

9. Highlight the Birds text with the Text tool and, in the Property inspector, change the baseline shift to −30.

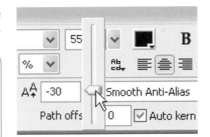

If you select the text on the path with the Pointer tool, the Property inspector shows a stroke icon, but if you select the text with the Text tool, the Property inspector changes and the baseline shift (two As) becomes visible.

10. Save the file as mybirdlogo.png and leave it open for the next exercise.

Pasting an image inside text on a path

Yes, you've read the title correctly. You can paste an image inside text even after it has been attached to a path, but you can't paste an image inside the text *prior* to putting it on a path. You put the text on the path first, then drag it on top of the image you want within it, and proceed as normal.

1. With your mybirdlogo.png file open from the last exercise, go to File ➤ Import and select birdbackground.png from the download files (or use your own image).

2. Click to place it over the Exotic text. Where you place the image depends on what portion of the image you want to see in the text. We wanted the brighter colors on the bottom, so we lined the bottom up with the bottom edge of the text.

> To help place the image, lower the image's opacity in the Property inspector so that you can see through to the text below. Once the image is in position, be sure to return the opacity to 100 percent.

3. With the birdbackground.png selected, go to Edit ➤ Cut (CTRL/CMD+X), select the text, and then choose Edit ➤ Paste Inside (CTRL/CMD+SHIFT+V).

4. Choose Shadow and Glow ➤ Drop Shadow from the Effects menu and use the default settings.

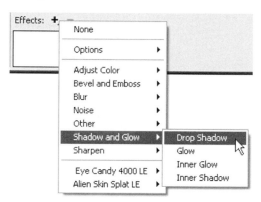

5. Repeat the steps 1 through 4 for the Birds text.

.

6. To complete your image, you could change the canvas color to a complimentary color (Modify ➤ Canvas Color) and then sample a color from the text.

3D text

In this exercise, you'll use a pattern file and several effects to produce text that appears as if it's rusted. You can change the look by changing the pattern, the offset of the lower layer, and even the shadow.

1. Open a new canvas that's 400 pixels wide and 150 pixels high with a tan (#FFCF9C) canvas color.

2. Add the text "Rusty" to your canvas. The font used in this example is 96-point Whimsy TT in black. This first text object is going to be used as the edge of the final text layer.

3. Click the fill color box in the Property inspector, click the Fill Options… button, and choose Pattern from the Fill drop-down menu. Scroll down and choose Other…. A dialog box opens allowing you to locate the pattern to fill with. Select rusty.png from the download files.

> The completed file for this exercise (rustytext.png) is included in the download files. If you open this file or any other file containing a font you don't have installed on your computer, a dialog box opens giving you the option to change the font or maintain its appearance. If you choose to maintain the appearance, the text is converted to a bitmap image.

4. Staying in the Fill Options dialog box, choose Line-Horiz 1 from the Texture drop-down menu and set it to 100%.

5. To bring back a bit of the color that was lost by applying the texture, open the Effects menu in the Property inspector and choose Adjust Color ➤ Hue/ Saturation with the following values:

   ★ Hue: −13

   ★ Saturation: −35

   ★ Lightness: −37

6. Choose Edit ➤ Clone. To remove the existing effects from the cloned text, click to select the Hue/Saturation effect in the Property inspector and then click the minus symbol (−).

7. Go back into the Fill Options dialog box and change the Texture amount to 0%.

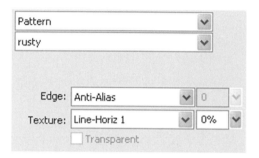

8. Using the keyboard arrow keys, move the cloned copy up and to the left by 3 pixels. (The amount you nudge the top text object will depend on the size of the text.)

9. In the Property inspector click the stroke swatch, then click the Stroke Options button. Choose Charcoal from the stroke category drop-down menu, Soft for the stroke name, and a tip size of 2. The image on the right shows the top text object moved with a stroke added.

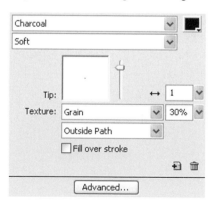

10. Choose Adjust Color ➤ Brightness/Contrast from the Effects menu in the Property inspector and set the Contrast to 20.

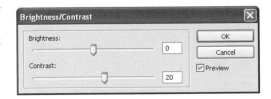

11. Select both the text objects and choose Modify ➤ Group (*CTRL/CMD+G*).

12. The final touch is to add a shadow. Choose Shadow And Glow ➤ Drop Shadow from the Effects menu with the following settings:

   ★ Distance: 10
   ★ Softness: 6
   ★ Opacity: 50%

> *You can select the top text object and change the layer blend mode to* Luminosity *to achieve another nice effect.*

Metal text

Here's another popular effect that creates realistic-looking metallic text.

1. Open brushedaluminum_45.jpg from the download files to use for your background.

2. It's a little light so let's darken it. Select the background image and choose Adjust Color ➤ Curves from the Effects menu. Click and drag the center of the line down until the image darkens a bit.

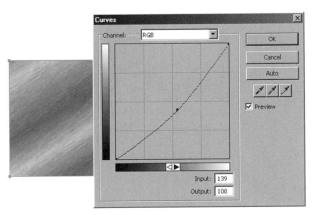

> *We are using the Curves control here because it darkens or lightens specific pixels instead of all of pixels in the image (as do the Brightness and Contrast controls).*

8

3. Type in some text using a large thick font. If the letters are too close together, increase the kerning.

4. In the Property inspector, click the Fill swatch and click the Fill Options button. Choose a Satin gradient from the fill category drop-down menus and click the Edit button. Place your gradient color swatches as shown here. The colors used are medium gray and white.

5. Once the gradient is added, you can move the gradient handles to reposition the white highlights if you'd like.

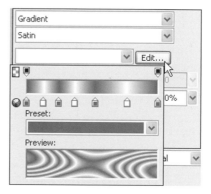

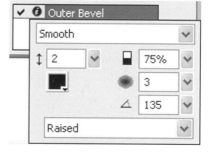

6. From the Effects menu, choose Bevel and Emboss ➤ Outer Bevel with these values:

   ★ Edge: Smooth
   ★ Width: 2
   ★ Color dark gray
   ★ Contrast: 75%
   ★ Softness: 3
   ★ Angle: 315
   ★ Raised

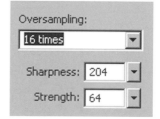

7. With the text selected, change the Edge in the Property inspector to Custom and select Oversampling of 16 times, Sharpness of 204, and Strength of 64. This makes the edges a bit sharper looking.

8. Now choose Shadow and Glow ➤ Drop Shadow from the Effects menu and just use the default values. It's looking pretty good.

If you want a bit more refraction, a quick fix is to use a third party plug-in, such as the Alien Skin (www.alienskin.com) Eye Candy 4000 Glass one. But we'll show you next how to do it yourself and for free.

9. Zoom in to the first letter. Select the Pen tool and, in the stroke area of the Property inspector, set the stroke to Air Brush ➤ Basic with a tip size of 2, an edge of 100, and the color white.

10. Draw a line down the outside of the first letter.

> You have to use the Air Brush because it's a tool that works with pressure sensitivity, which is required for the Path Scrubber tools. You also need a minimum of 2 pixels; otherwise, when you scrub, the entire line will disappear.

11. Select the Path Scrubber tool (subtractive) and click once near the bottom edge of the line and to the right.

12. Deselect the line so that you can see the result. Basically, the line has simply lightened and faded at the bottom end.

13. To add a bit of brightness to the top of the line, select the Line tool (color: white, size: 2, edge: 2, stroke category: Air Brush ➤ Basic) and draw a tiny line at the top of the previous one.

14. For the highlight inside the M use the Line tool, but this time, use a stroke size of 1. This one doesn't need to be faded.

15. Use the same procedures (2 pixel line, Path Scrubber tool [subtractive], add a small highlight) across the top of the letters E, T, and the side of A. Where you add the highlight depends on the font you've used. Also, if your font is curvy, then use a Bezier curve to follow the contours of the letter.

If you think you'd like to use this effect again, then make a style of it. The style will save everything except the lines you added for highlights.

16. Open the Styles (*SHIFT+F11*) panel and choose New Style from the options menu. Name your style. We've unchecked all the text options, otherwise the style would only work on the same text at the same size.

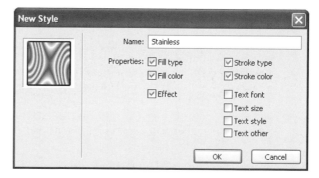

17. Click OK to close the New Style dialog box. Your new style will be added to the bottom of your Styles panel.

Filling text with an image

This effect is deceptively simple and very useful. Although you won't be able to change the letters of your text, you will be able to edit the effects and place images inside.

> *The techniques in this section apply not only to text, but to any vector shape.*

1. Open `seattle.jpg` from the download files.

2. Type the word "SEATTLE" on top of the image using a solid or thick font. We used the following settings:

   - ★ Font: Futura ExtraBold
   - ★ Font size: 110 points
   - ★ Color: Black
   - ★ Kerning range: 10%
   - ★ Smooth Anti-Alias

3. Place the text over an area of the skyline that you'd like to remain visible through the text.

4. Select the image layer and choose Edit ➤ Cut (*CTRL/CMD+X*).

5. Next, select the text object and paste inside (Edit ➤ Paste Inside or *CTRL/CMD+SHIFT+V*). We added a drop shadow to make it look even better. Notice where the arrow is pointing in the following image; this cloverleaf symbol alerts you that an image is pasted inside this vector object.

Now that was easy enough. Let's look at some variations of the same technique.

Filling only half of an image

Filling half of an image is very similar to what you just did in the previous exercise. Actually, you only need to add in one step to get a result that looks completely different.

1. Start by opening the seattle.jpg file again.

2. This time, instead of going on to add the text right away, use the Marquee tool to make a selection over the top half of the image. Fill it with white and deselect it.

3. Now continue with steps 2 through 5 of the previous exercise and you should end up with a result like this:

Filling a portion of an image with an uneven edge

When you see this technique, you'll begin to appreciate the real possibilities of what you can achieve with this effect. The Reshape Area tool is one that might seem intimidating, but it is very versatile and makes altering a path extremely simple.

1. Open a fresh version of seattle.jpg.

2. Draw a rectangle across the top portion of the image and fill with a light blue color.

3. Type the word "SEATTLE" using a solid or thick font and apply the same text settings as you used in the previous examples.

4. Place the text over an area of the skyline that you want to remain visible. The text object should be above the rectangle object in the Layers panel.

5. Select the Reshape Area tool with a size of 40 and strength of 80.

> *A warning should open saying that this tool works only on paths. This is a path, but rectangles are grouped in Fireworks, and it isn't being recognized as a path. Just choose* Modify ➤ Ungroup *(CTRL/CMD+SHIFT+G).*

6. Select the rectangle and use the Reshape Area tool to alter the top path of the rectangle. To use the tool, place your cursor outside the path and push up and around. Place the cursor behind some of the text and push to make a different shape.

7. Turn the text's visibility off and you'll see the result of pushing on the path with the Reshape Area tool.

8. When you're finished, group the rectangle and the bitmap together.

9. Select the image layer and choose Edit ➤ Cut (CTRL/CMD+X).

10. Select the text object and paste inside (Edit ➤ Paste Inside or CTRL/CMD+SHIFT+V).

> *You can move the image inside the text even after it's pasted in. Simply click and drag on the Cloverleaf icon and move the cursor around until it is positioned where you want it to be.*

Gold text with custom bevel

The bevel effect in Fireworks adds shadows and highlights but they are localized, which means that the shadowed or highlighted part is the top or the bottom of the text. However, by using gradients, you can produce highlights that look like light is reflecting off many parts of the bevel instead of just one area.

1. Open a new 400×300-pixel canvas with a white background color.

2. Type the word "Luxury" on to the canvas using a thick or heavy font. We used the following settings:

   ★ Font: Splash

   ★ Font size: 78

   ★ Kerning range: 5%

   ★ Color: black

> *If you like this font, you can find it at* www.buyfonts.com *for $2.*

3. Place the text near the top of the canvas and choose Edit ➤ Clone (*CTRL/CMD+SHIFT+D*).

4. Select the bottom text object and turn the visibility off for the top text object.

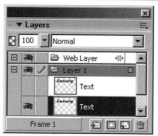

5. Now, increase the size of the bottom text object to allow for the bevel. To expand the text path, you need to convert the text to a path with the following commands:

   ★ Text ➤ Convert to Paths (*CTRL/CMD+SHIFT+P*)

   ★ Modify ➤ Ungroup (*CTRL/CMD+SHIFT+G*)

   ★ Modify ➤ Combine Paths ➤ Union

> *In this step, you converted the text to paths but each letter was grouped together. Because you can't alter a grouped path, you ungrouped it and then combined all the letters into one shape. Although this object is still a vector, you can no longer edit the text as text.*

6. Choose Modify ➤ Alter Path ➤ Inset Path. In the Inset Path dialog box, select Outside and enter a value of 4 in the Width field.

> **Photoshop tip:** *If you're more familiar with Photoshop, then you may see similarities between using Inset Path or Outset Path in Fireworks and expanding or contracting a Photoshop selection, but keep in mind that this is a bitmap method. You can do it this way in Fireworks, but by using the Inset and Outset method, you make the most of Fireworks' vector capabilities. So why not just scale the text? You can test this easily yourself. Scale the text (Modify ➤ Transform ➤ Scale) and notice what happens. Scaling doesn't follow the contours of the shape, whereas Inset Path and Outset Path do, making them a perfect way to increase or decrease the size of an object.*

7. Choose a linear gradient fill and click the fill color box. Add new color points and colors as shown here:

★ Set the first color swatch on the left to #937500.

★ Set another color pointer and make it #FFD015.

★ Alternate the colors along the gradient—dark, light, dark, light—working across from left to right.

> *Once you have the first two colors set, you can press the ALT/OPT key and drag a copy of a color box over to where you want it.*

8. Adjust the gradient angle so that the light rays are slanted.

9. Add a new layer and repeat steps 2–8, substituting the word "Edition" for Luxury and reducing the font size to 68 points. When you get to step 8, change the direction of the gradient on the word Edition.

10. Turn the visibility back on for both of the black text objects. It doesn't look too bad as it is. Notice the highlights on the bevel. We think they need to be lightened some.

You could alter the gradient color, but there's an easier way that offers more options: **Levels**.

11. With the bevel still selected, open the Effects menu in the Property inspector and choose Adjust Color ➤ Levels. We pulled the two end sliders in, which changed the Input values for the shadows (left side) to 27 and the highlights (right side) to 218.

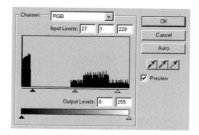

Although the text looks great with just the bevel added, you can go all out and make the entire text gold by simply filling the black text with a gold gradient.

12. Select the black text and choose a linear gradient fill. Click the Edit... button, set the first color swatch to #937500 (the same dark color of the bevel), and set the last color swatch to #FFD015 (the highlight color).

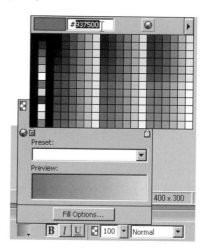

13. Adjust the gradient for the word Luxury so that the dark portion is on top and the highlight is on the bottom. Reverse the gradient for the word Edition—light on top and dark on the bottom.

14. To complete the effect, you could even try a black canvas color.

> *You can change any charac-teristic of this text except for the font. You can change the font on the black or top text, but not the one with the gra-dient, because, if you recall, that text was combined into one vector shape. But all the gradients, levels, and fills are editable. Because this is a vector object, you can also increase or decrease its size without degrading the image.*

Text with bevel and glow

In this exercise, you'll add a bevel using a different method and you'll produce a glow. You're going to vary the results by using layer blend modes.

1. Open a new 400×150-pixel file with a black canvas.

2. Type the word "Adventure". I've used the following settings:

   ⭐ Font: Ruzicka Freehand RomanSC

   ⭐ Kerning range: 10%

   ⭐ Point size: 58

> *Ruzicka Freehand RomanSC is an Adobe font (www.adobe.com).*

3. Fill the text with a black and white linear gradi-ent. Adjust the gradient so that the white is at the top of the text and the black is at the bottom. Name this object "text 1".

4. Clone the text (Edit ➤ Clone) and move it below text 1. Name the clone "text 2".

5. Now make the text 2 objects slightly larger by choosing these commands:

   ⭐ Text ➤ Convert to Paths (*CTRL/CMD+SHIFT+P*)

   ⭐ Modify ➤ Ungroup (*CTRL/CMD+SHIFT+G*)

   ⭐ Modify ➤ Combine Paths ➤ Union

   ⭐ Modify ➤ Alter Path ➤ Inset Path… (**Select Outside… and give it a Width of 1.**)

6. To now apply a bevel and emboss to text 2, **choose** Bevel And Emboss ➤ Raised Emboss from the Effects menu in the Property inspector. Set a Width of 2 and Softness of 2. Use the default contrast and angle.

7. Select text 1 and clone it (*Ctrl/Cmd+Shift+D*). Move the clone below text 1 and name it *COLORED*.

8. Expand this text as follows:

   ★ Text ➤ Convert to Paths (*Ctrl/Cmd+Shift+P*)

   ★ Modify ➤ Ungroup (*Ctrl/Cmd+Shift+G*)

   ★ Modify ➤ Combine Paths ➤ Union

   ★ Modify ➤ Alter Path ➤ Inset Path… (**Select Outside** and set a **Width** of 3.)

9. Fill the text with a linear gradient using these colors (from left to right), which are also shown in the screenshot:

   ★ #000000 (black)

   ★ #9966FF (purple)

   ★ #9933CC (lighter purple)

   ★ #FF0000 (red)

   ★ #FFFF00 (yellow)

   ★ #FF0000 (red)

   ★ #000000 (black)

   Your colored text should now look like this:

10. Choose Blur ➤ Gaussian Blur from the Effects menu in the Property inspector and enter 4 for the Blur radius.

11. Use the keyboard down arrow to nudge the colored text down by 5 pixels.

12. Set the blend mode of the colored object to Screen (or try out several different blend modes to see how they perform and which one you prefer).

Creating a reflection

In this exercise, you'll experiment with making a custom perspective shadow for a piece of text. The result will be text that appears to stand up on a reflective surface. The shadow portion of this text, however, will become a bitmap because of the selections that are made.

1. Open a new 400×300-pixel file with a white canvas color.

2. Add the text "Standing Alone" to your canvas. (I used Arial with a point size of 38, black color, bold, and block capitals).

3. Choose Edit ➤ Duplicate.

> The Duplicate command places the new object slightly below and to the right of the original object. The Clone command places the object exactly on top of the original object.

4. Select your duplicated text and choose Modify ➤ Transform ➤ Flip Vertical. Line up the two text objects as shown here:

5. Select the lower text object, and choose Modify ➤ Transform ➤ Distort. Click and drag each of the lower corner control handles to add some perspective.

6. Now drag in each of the top control handles to line up the top and bottom text objects' edges. Notice that as you pull in, the letters shift under the top text. Be careful not to lower the text as you drag or the text won't touch. If it moves away, simply click and drag the control handle until you get the text to look something like what is shown here. Double-click to complete the transformation. Your text doesn't need to be exact, just something close to this.

> The bottom text is being converted to a bitmap because that's the only way you can select just a portion of the text to apply blur and feathering to. If you were to apply just the blur or just the feathering to the entire object, it could remain as a vector.

7. Select the lower text object and choose Modify ➤ Flatten Selection.

8. First apply a small blur to the entire reflected text. Choose Filters ➤ Blur ➤ Gaussian Blur and use a Blur radius of 1.5.

9. Using the Marquee tool, draw a rectangle selection around the bottom third of the text—the part closest to you. Choose Select ➤ Feather and enter a Radius of 10.

10. Choose Filters ➤ Blur ➤ Gaussian Blur and a value of *4*.

11. Use the up arrow and move the marquee selection two-thirds of the way up and choose Filters ➤ Blur ➤ Gaussian Blur and a value of *2*.

12. Draw a Marquee selection three-quarters of the way up and choose Filters ➤ Blur ➤ Gaussian Blur and a value of *2*.

The shadow now appears more blurred as it moves away from the base of the text. This type of shadow is more realistic than just the standard drop shadow.

13. Draw a rectangle to cover the canvas and drag it to the bottom. Add any kind of gradient you'd like. We used blue and rotated the gradient to 90 degrees.

14. To make the effect stand out even more, we added a medium gray stroke with a Custom Anti-alias edge. We used Oversampling of 16 times (which determines the amount of detail used for creating the transition between the text edges and the background), Sharpness of 199 (which determines the smoothness of the transition

between the text edges and the background), and Strength of 164 (which determines how much the text edges blend into the background).

Producing clear small type

When you use small type, you'll find that it can sometimes be difficult to read. If you're using this type for navigation purposes—on buttons or navigation bars, for example—it's even more important that the words are clear and sharp. When you're faced with the problem of fitting 6- to 10-point text on a button and ensuring that it's readable, try these tricks:

★ Turn off the anti-aliasing option. Anti-aliasing adds a small amount of blur, which can make small text more difficult to read.

★ Use a font designed for small text such as the Silkscreen font included in the file download. Other good choices include Verdana or Trebuchet.

The following image shows a button with text in 10-point Trebuchet. The top button has Smooth Anti-Alias turned on, whereas the lower button text is set to No Anti-Alias. It doesn't look very good in print or enlarged, but it looks considerably better on screen. Try it out.

If you find yourself in a position where you have to use a font for small type that isn't suitable for easy viewing, try this:

1. Type your text larger than necessary, perhaps 36 points.

2. Choose Modify ➤ Flatten Selection.

3. Choose Modify ➤ Transform ➤ Numeric Transform and scale it to about 30 percent or so.

4. If the text looks a little weak, make a clone and place it on top of the original. Reduce the opacity of the top clone as needed, say about 50 percent.

Some custom made small fonts have been designed for use on the web. We've included a font called Silkscreen, which is in the download files. Jason Kottke of www.kottke.org provided both the PC and the Mac versions.

Adding copyright and trademark symbols

To add special symbols in Fireworks, you need to know the key combinations. To access the Character Map in Windows, go to Start ➤ All Programs ➤ Accessories ➤ System Tools ➤ Character Map or run the CHARMAP.EXE file and you'll see the key codes for all the Windows characters. Select the character you want—in the lower-right status bar you'll see the key combination.

On Mac OS X, choose Applications ➤ Utilities ➤ Key Caps. Hold down the *OPT* key to see the extended characters and use *SHIFT+OPT* to see even more. Here are some useful key combinations:

★ In Windows, pressing *ALT+0169* produces the copyright symbol and pressing *ALT+0153* produces the trademark symbol.

★ On a Mac, the copyright symbol is *OPT+G* and the trademark symbol is *OPT+2*.

To add the symbol in Fireworks, select the Text tool, press the *ALT/OPT* key, and type in the key combination.

Summary

In this chapter, you've seen how to use text creatively in Fireworks and you've explored the possibilities offered by converting text to paths. We then rounded the chapter off by looking at some of the impressive text effects that you can create using Fireworks. Text is such an important element of any website—exciting text carries a great deal of impact. However, remember not to go over the top and distract from your message. Now it's up to you to use these techniques to explore your ideas and make your text come alive.

Nine

Creating Interfaces

In this chapter

You're going to look at how to make a basic interface for a website. Initially, you'll create a metal-themed interface with buttons and a navigation bar. Once you've created the buttons and navigation bar, you'll then incorporate them into pop-up menus to aid in the navigation around the interface.

After completing the basic interface, you're going to take it further, making it more creative and adding animation to it. You'll look at the following in this chapter:

★ Creating metallic buttons using gradients and textured fills

★ Adding a button to the Symbols folder

★ Creating and exporting a navigation bar with metallic buttons on it

★ Adding pop-up menus to the navigation bar file

★ Making a much more creative interface using images, hotspots, and disjointed rollovers

★ Animating a banner ad and sliding buttons

Make a metal button

The first thing to do is make the brushed aluminum texture you'll need for the metal buttons. This is the button you'll be making.

1. Open a new 400×400 canvas with a white background.

2. Draw a 200×200 rectangle. In the Property inspector, choose Gradient ➤ Linear from the Fill category.

3. Open the gradient editor by clicking the fill color box and set the gradient as shown here. The color box on the left is a medium gray, the center is white, and the box on the right is black.

4. Select the Gradient tool (toggle to it with G). It's very difficult to get a straight horizontal gradient instead of the vertical one by moving the gradient handles. It's easier to use the Gradient tool, press and hold *SHIFT*, place your cursor above the top center of the button, and drag down to reverse the direction of the gradient.

5. Open the Styles panel (*SHIFT+F11*) options menu and select New Style. Name it "alum", accept the default settings as seen here, and click OK. Notice that the new style is added to the Styles panel. You'll use it again later.

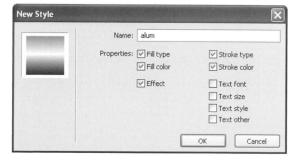

6. Select Noise ➤ Add Noise from the Effects menu in the Property inspector. Check Color and use an Amount of 98 (color noise will give a nicer brushed look than monochrome).

7. Select Blur ➤ Motion Blur… from the Effects menu. Set the Angle to 180 and the Distance to 14.

8. Select Adjust Color ➤ Hue/Saturation from the Effects menu. Set Hue to –100, Saturation to –100, and Lightness to –12.

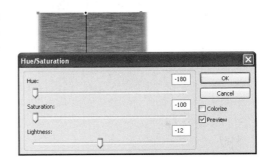

9. In the Property inspector, set the opacity to 60 percent.

> *Normally after performing all these steps for a style, we'd suggest saving it as a style to reuse. But in this case it won't work as a style because of the blurred edges. Even if you crop the edges prior to saving the style, the blur is still saved with it.*

10. Use the Crop tool to crop off the blurred edges of the button.

11. Export the image as a JPEG (an exported copy called `brushed_alum.jpg` is in the images folder of download files, so is the original PNG file if you want to check the different settings used for the effects). You can close this file now.

12. Open a new document (300×300 will do) and draw a 150×50 rectangle. Open the Styles panel and click the alum style you made. Ensure the opacity is at 100 percent in the Property inspector.

13. To use the saved aluminum as a texture for the button, select Other from the Texture pop-up menu in the Property inspector (you need to scroll all the way to the bottom). Navigate to your saved `brushed_alum.jpg` (or use the copy in the images folder of the download files). If you don't see the image, be sure you have All Files selected for Image Type.

Although this texture is now available in the Texture drop-down menu, it's only available for this document. If you want it to be in the menu permanently, copy it to the Textures folder in the Fireworks application folder.

14. Set the texture opacity to 90 percent.

15. Draw a 130×30 rectangle and set the Rectangle roundness in the Property inspector to 100. Apply the alum style from the Styles panel. To change the gradient, use the Gradient tool and drag up from the bottom to the top of the rectangle to reverse the gradient. Drag the square handle up a little to have less black in the button. Center this rounded rectangle over the first rectangle.

16. With just the small rounded inside part of the button selected, go to the Effects menu in the Property inspector. Select Adjust Color ➤ Levels. Drag the white output slider (on the right) to the left to darken the oval (Output levels of 0 and 211).

17. In the Layers panel, name this rounded rectangle "buttonInSet". Copy the oval and paste (or make a clone with *CTRL/CMD+SHIFT+D*).

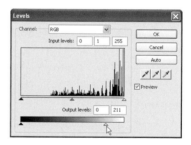

18. With the top copy selected, choose Modify ➤ Alter Path ➤ Inset Path. Set the Direction to Inside, make the Width 5, and click OK.

19. Apply the alum style. In the Layers panel, name this shape "button". This illustration shows where you are at this point. Notice the different objects in the Layers panel.

20. Select the Rectangle tool. Change the Texture opacity to 0, the fill color to a solid white, and the Edge to a Feather of 2.

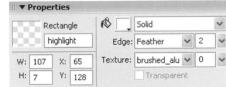

21. Draw a small rectangle (107×7) and place it at the top of the button to use as a highlight. Name it "highlight". Deselect and check the highlight's appearance. If you think it needs to be smaller or larger, adjust the width. It should fit on the button without overlapping.

22. Select the button object and add a black drop shadow with a distance of 5, a softness of 4, and an opacity of 80%.

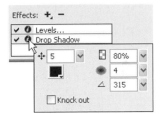

23. Type the text "Home" on the top of the button and center it. This example uses the Verdana font at size 18 and Crisp anti-alias.

24. Change the canvas color (Modify ➤ Canvas ➤ Canvas Color) to black.

> *Note that the button's look will vary depending on the color placement and intensity of the gradients used. The source files in the download file are* `metalbutton_done.png` *and* `metalbutton2.png`*. They are simply different variations of the gradient for the button.*

25. Save the file as `metalbutton.png` (a copy is in the download files).

Making the metal button a symbol

1. Open a new 300×300 canvas with a white background.

2. Choose Edit ➤ Insert ➤ New Symbol (*CTRL/CMD+F8*). In the New Symbol dialog box, name it "Metal button", and choose Button type.

3. Choose File ➤ Import (*CTRL/CMD+R*) and navigate to your `metalbutton.png` (or the copy in the download files). Click in the Symbol Editor to place the button.

4. Click the Over tab. Click the Copy Up Graphic button to place a copy of the Up state in this window.

5. Select the button object and then choose Adjust Color ➤ Hue/Saturation... from the Effects menu. Check Colorize in the Hue/Saturation dialog box and choose a color you like.

6. Next, click the Down tab and then click the Copy Over Graphic button. Select the button object again and, in the Effects menu, click the little check mark next to Hue/Saturation to turn it off.

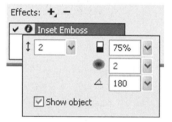

7. Select the text and choose Bevel and Emboss ➤ Inset Emboss from the Effects menu. Use the default settings, but change the angle to 180.

8. Click the Done button in the Symbol Editor. Your metal button is now a symbol complete with a rollover effect. To preview the button, click the Preview tab in the document window and try rolling over the button.

9. Open the Optimize panel (*F6*) and set the export file format to JPEG with a Quality setting of 80.

10. Save the file as metalbutton_done.png.

Navigation bar

Now you're going to use the button symbol to make a complete navigation bar (or nav bar for short). This nav bar will have special JavaScript code to display the Down state of each button, indicating which page is currently being viewed.

1. Create a new 800×200 canvas with a black background.

2. Open the Library panel (*F11*) and select Import Symbols... from the Library panel's options menu.

3. Navigate to where you saved `metalbutton_done.png` (or select it from download files) and click Import.

4. Drag five instances of the symbol onto your canvas from the Library panel.

5. Click the Hide slices and hotspots button in the Tools panel.

6. Select the first button on the left. In the Property inspector, delete the name that's currently in the Button field and name it "index". For nav bars, the button name has to be the same as the link name in order for the Down state to show on the page being viewed.

7. In the Link field enter index.htm and add some Alt text. Leave the Home text on the button as it is.

> *You can only use the* `.htm` *extension for nav bars, not HTML.*

8. Check Show down state on load.

9. Select the second button from the left and, in the Property inspector, change the button name to "products", type "Products" in the Text field, change the Link to products.htm, add some Alt text, and check Show down state on load.

Notice how the text of the button on the canvas is updated when you change the Text field in the Property inspector? This doesn't break the link to the symbol.

10. Repeat step 9 for the remaining buttons using the following properties:

★ **Button 3:** Text: Services, Button name: services, Link: services.htm

★ **Button 4**: Text: About Us, Button name: aboutus, Link: aboutus.htm

★ **Button 5:** Text: Contact Us, Button: contactus, Link: contactus.htm

11. Choose Modify ➤ Canvas ➤ Fit Canvas to leave just the nav bar.

12. Save your file as navbar.png and leave the file open for the next tutorial.

Exporting the navigation bar

Now it's time to export this special nav bar with all its code intact.

1. The optimization settings for the button should already be set, but if you haven't set them, use JPEG with a quality of 80. This particular nav bar is being optimized as a JPEG because of the gradients used.

Prior to exporting, you have to make a setting in the HTML setup in order for the nav bar to export properly.

2. Choose File ➤ HTML Setup and click the Document Specific tab. The only thing you're concerned about is the Export multiple nav bar HTML files (for use without frame sets) option. Select it.

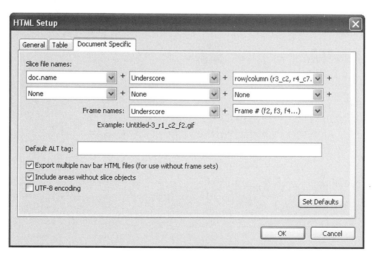

As you don't want to export the entire Fireworks page (just the nav bar), you don't want Fireworks to generate a table with additional cells and rows in it. You can tell Fireworks how to export your tables.

3. Select the Table tab. Choose Single Table, No Spacers from the Space With drop-down menu. Choose None from the Contents drop-down menu and then click OK.

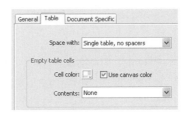

Now when you export, you'll export your buttons and code, and the pages that they link to will be generated for you by Fireworks.

4. Choose File ➤ Export. Set the Save as type to HTML and Images and Slices to Export Slices. Uncheck Include area without slices; you want to export just the nav bar.

5. Check Put images in subfolder. A lot of images will be generated, so it's easier to manage them if they're kept in their own folder. Click the Browse button and add a folder named "navbar" wherever you saved your buttons. We have it exported into the navbar folder in the download files. When you're done, click the Save button to export.

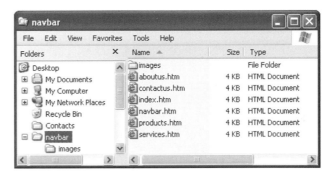

6. Open the folder where you exported the files. Notice the folder named navbar that contains the images and the source PNG files that have been saved throughout this session. Do you see the additional HTM files added? Fireworks made these automatically.

7. Double-click the index.htm file. If your browser is the default HTM viewer, you should see your nav bar in the index.htm file. Notice that there's no rollover state for the Home button. Look closer and you'll see the inset Home button indicating you're on the home page. Click one of the other buttons and notice that it opens its page and the button is in the Down state. Pretty cool and simple as well!

Pop-up menus

Fireworks includes a very easy way to add pop-up menus to your buttons. These are the menus that drop down when the user passes their mouse over a link.

This menu will also function as a true nav bar showing the Rollover and the Down state of the page currently being viewed. In order to do this, the button names and links are named index and index.htm, and so on, for each button as discussed in the *Making a navigation bar* section.

> *We have saved the brushed aluminum styles for the buttons and for the metal text tutorial. Copy the styles from the downloaded files and place them in the* Styles *folder of the Fireworks program folder.*

Considerations

You should consider a few things prior to deciding to use a Fireworks pop-up menu:

★ The JavaScript file that is exported with the menu is between 25 and 30KB.

★ If you place your menu in an area that contains HTML forms, Flash movies, or Java Applets, when the menu opens, it will go behind these items. If you want to use this menu, you'll have to design your page so that these elements aren't in the same place as the pop-up menus.

★ Pop-up menus don't cross over frames.

★ The submenus themselves can't be searched by search engine spiders. You need to have alternative text links somewhere, such as in the footer area, for this to work.

★ The pop-up menus aren't accessible.

Building the pop-up menu

1. Open the pop-up_start.png file from the download files.

2. Select the Products button and open the Behaviors panel. Click the plus (+) sign and select Set Pop-Up Menu, which will open the Pop-Up Menu editor.

3. Double click in the field below the Text heading. Type in "Metal Products" and click the + button to add the menu item.

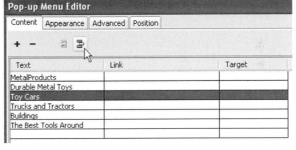

4. Repeat for the following items:

   ★ Durable Metal Toys

   ★ Toy Cars

   ★ Trucks and Tractors

   ★ Buildings

   ★ The Best Tools Around

5. Click Toy Cars and then click the Indent menu icon to make the entry a submenu.

6. Repeat Step 5 for Trucks and Tractors and Buildings.

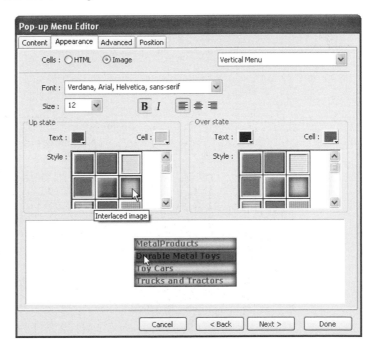

7. Now, click the Appearance tab. The first option is whether to use an HTML menu or one with an image. We normally use HTML because the file size is less. The pop-up menu's JavaScript has a size of about 25KB on its own, so size is a serious consideration. If you have a design that isn't really that large in file size, go ahead and use the image.

8. Click the Image option and choose Vertical Menu from the pop-up alignment drop-down menu. Choose the Arial font with a size of 12 that is bold and left aligned.

9. For the Up state, set the text color to #55656C and the Cell color to #ADDB9B3.

10. For the Over state set the Text color to #000066 and the Cell color to #55656C.

11. Click the style shown in this figure (we've noticed for other menus that the styles aren't always in the same position).

12. Now, click the Advanced tab (or use the Next button). Leave the Cell Width at Automatic but change the Cell Height to 22 and select Pixels from the drop-down menu.

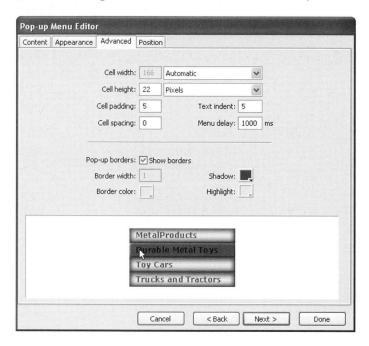

13. You can see the effect of your settings in the preview area. The menu items are a bit close together, so enter 5 for the Cell padding and 5 for the Text indent (to keep the text off the left edge).

14. Finally, check Pop-up borders, but only use the Shadow with a dark gray color.

We normally don't use this option at all because, with an HTML menu, we like the flat menus with no bevels or borders. We're using Shadow only because this option puts a line between the menu items.

15. Click the Position tab. You can select one of the icons for the Menu position or you can enter your own x,y coordinates. For this menu we used x:4,y:50.

For the Submenu position we used 0 for both x and y coordinates so that the submenu lines up evenly with the menu. The default is for the submenu to overlap the menu. Click Done.

16. Back in your document, if you now select the Products button, you'll see an outline of the pop-up menu's position. You can also reposition your menu here. Simply click and drag to place the outline where you'd like your menu to be, and then preview it in a browser. To edit your menus, double click the outline and the Pop-Up Menu Editor will open.

17. Repeat steps 2–16 for the Services button with these exceptions:

For the Content tab (step 3) use these link names:

★ Custom Orders

★ Repairs

★ Metal Cutting

★ Stainless (submenu)

★ Aluminum (submenu)

★ Other (submenu)

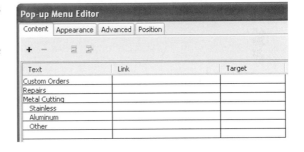

On the Advanced tab, change the Cell width to 150 pixels instead of Automatic. When you preview this menu, notice that the submenu is also 150 pixels. If it were set to Automatic, the menu would fit the button. You're using 150 so that the menu fits under the Services button and looks better visually.

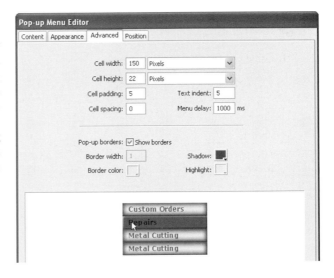

18. Click the Done button and preview the menu.

Exporting the pop-up menu nav bar

Because you're using a nav bar, you have to perform an extra step to choose to export the Multiple nav bar HTML pages.

1. Choose File ➤ Export and click the Options button.

2. Click the Table tab and be sure that the Space is set to 1-Pixel Transparency with the Contents set to Spacer Image. You're exporting everything including the non-sliced areas and need the spacers to hold the table together.

3. Click the Document Specific tab, check the Multiple nav bar HTML pages option, and click OK.

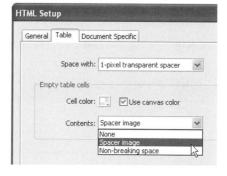

4. You're now returned to the Export dialog box. Refer to the following image for the settings to use. Most of them are entered properly by default. Check Include areas without slices and check Put images in subfolder.

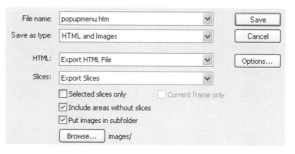

> *You can click the* Browse *button to locate a folder for the images, or Fireworks will make the folder inside the folder you export to. If this were for a real site, you'd need to export to the root folder of your site. The* mm_menu.js *file needs to be in the same location as the HTML pages that use it.*

5. Click Save and your menus are ready to view. Go to where you exported your files and preview the `index.htm` page in a browser. Notice that the Down state is shown on the button you click and the pop-up menus work. The best of both worlds!

Creative interfaces and navigation

In this case, you're going to create a post with a birdhouse and rustic wooden signs. Also, you'll add the buttons and turn the whole piece into a symbol. After you've finished with the birdhouse, you're going to look at how to use different navigation methods with hotspots and disjointed rollovers.

Birdhouse button graphic

The first thing you are going to do is make a wood button to use on a birdhouse graphic.

1. Create a new 300×300 canvas with a transparent background.

   In this example, the buttons will be rough wooden boards. You could draw a rectangle, fill it with a wood texture, and skew the shape, but we had a photo of barn wood that we liked and the angle was about right for what we wanted to do. Besides, it's more organic looking then a canned wood texture.

2. Open `woodslats.png` from the Chapter 9 birdhouse folder.

3. Select the Polygon Lasso tool and draw a selection around one the boards, as shown here:

4. Copy the selection and paste it into your 300×300 document (you can close `woodslats.png` now).

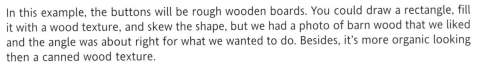

5. The board's edges are little bit jagged. With the Magic Wand tool, select the transparent area and choose Select ➤ Select Inverse (*CTRL/CMD+SHIFT+I*) and then Select ➤ Contract Marquee by 2 pixels.

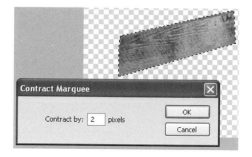

6. In the Property inspector, set the Edge to Feather with an amount of 4. Choose Select ➤ Select Inverse again, press *DELETE*, and deselect all (*CTRL/CMD+D*).

When you click *DELETE*, notice that the edges clean up a bit. It's a very subtle fix. A feather of 4 is slight, but it does give you a cleaner looking edge.

7. To smooth some of the jaggies off the edges even further, select the Smudge tool (from the Blur tool's flyout menu) and, in the Property inspector, set the Size to 8, the Edge to 50, the Shape as round, and be sure Smudge color is unchecked.

8. Zoom in and smudge along the edges to make the board much smoother. This removes the jagged edges from the slanted portions of the board. Be careful smudging though; you don't want to alter the shape.

9. Flip the board with Modify ➤ Transform ➤ Flip Horizontal.

10. In the Property inspector, resize the board to 110 pixels wide by 53 pixels high.

11. To darken the light areas a little, select the Burn tool with a Size of 20, a Range of Midtones, an Edge of 100, and an Exposure of 50. Brush over the light areas to add a touch of black to the wood.

12. Select the board again and choose Bevel and Emboss ➤ Inner Bevel from the Effects menu in the Property inspector. Use a Flat bevel edge, a width of 4, a Raised preset, an Opacity of 75%, and an Angle of 135.

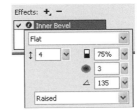

13. To add a nail, make a small rectangle with the following properties (you'll need to zoom in):

   ★ Size: 4×10

   ★ Stroke: Dark brown or gray

   ★ Fill: Linear dark brown to rust or dark gray to light gray

   Then draw a small ellipse with the following properties:

   ★ Size: 8×8

   ★ Stroke: Dark gray

   ★ Fill: Radial, medium gray to dark gray

14. Place the ellipse on the rectangle and group them together (*CTRL/CMD+G*). Place the nail at the top center of the board, as shown in the preceding illustration.

15. Select everything on the canvas (*CTRL/CMD+A*) and choose Modify ➤ Symbol ➤ Convert to Symbol (*F8*). In the Symbol Properties dialog box, check Button, name it "woodslat", and click OK. The button will now appear on your canvas with a green overlay if your View slices option is selected in the Tools panel, or just as an object with a little arrow in the bottom-left corner if the View is off.

16. To edit the symbol and add text to the woodslat, double-click the button on the canvas to open the Button editor. Align the button to the center using the Align panel.

17. Select the Text tool and, in the Up state, add your text. We used the following text settings:

   ★ Font: Verdana

   ★ Size: 18

   ★ Kerning: 5

   ★ Align: center

   > *Even though much nicer fonts are available and are more appropriate for this design, we choose Verdana so that the sample file that we included wouldn't ask you to replace fonts if you use it.*

18. Select Modify ➤ Transform ➤ Free Transform (*CTRL/CMD+T*) and rotate the text so that it looks like the screenshot shown here. Double click to accept the transformation. You can always repeat the rotate if need be.

19. Use the align panel to center the button.

20. With just the text selected, choose Bevel and Emboss ➤ Inset Emboss from the Effects menu in the Property inspector with a width and softness of 2, an angle of 135, and an opacity of 75%.

21. Select the Over tab and then click the Copy Up Graphic button. Change the font color to gold and leave the Inner Bevel settings the same.

22. Move on to the Down tab and then click the Copy Over Graphic button. Change the font color to orange and change the Inner Emboss width to 3. Click Done.

A copy of this button symbol is saved as woodslatsymbol.png in the birdfolder folder of the download files.

Navigation symbol

In this exercise you'll use the birdhouse background, add the buttons, and make the entire navigation element one reusable symbol.

1. Open a new 300×500 canvas with a transparent background.

2. On the new canvas, choose Edit ➤ Insert ➤ New Symbol. Name it "birdhousenav" and make it a Graphic symbol.

3. Choose File ➤ Import and import the birdhouse.png file. Center it in the Symbol Editor.

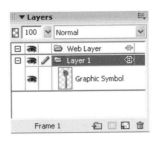

4. Choose Share This Layer from the options menu in the Layers panel. You need to share the layer because the button symbols you'll be using have three different frames involved. If you didn't share the layer, the rollovers wouldn't have the birdhouse graphic present. Also notice that to the right of the layer name, you can now see an icon that looks like a ladder, indicating that this layer is being shared.

5. Import the woodslatsymbol.png file and place it on the post. Use *Alt*+drag to create three more copies of the symbol.

6. Use the Scale tool to rotate the buttons until they look randomly placed on the post.

> *Leave the slice view on so that when you rotate you don't overlap any of the slices. It's okay to overlap a bit but not much. You'll need to preview in a browser to be sure that the slices don't affect the final result (cut some image out). The rotated buttons have larger slices.*

All that's left to do now is to change the button text.

7. Select the second button down and, in the Property inspector, change South to North in the Text field, enter a null link of javascript:;, and some Alt text. Repeat for West and East. The text is automatically changed for all states.

8. Import birds.png from the birdhouse folder in the download files and place them on the birdhouse. Click the Done button.

> *The null link (a placeholder for a real link) of javascript:; is preferred over the null link of the hash mark (#) because an hourglass appears in Netscape 4.x if a null link with a hash mark is clicked.*

221

9. You can now preview the interface in a browser. Your birdhouse and buttons are now one symbol. Try adding a canvas color if you like.

10. Save the file as birdhousenav_done.png and close it.

> You can export this symbol as Multiple HTML files. This way, when the button is clicked, the Down state will automatically be depressed on the next page.

Adding hotspots

Hotspots can be applied to any portion of an image. They're useful for adding links to a portion of an image without a specific slice, and you can also attach behaviors to a hotspot. You can use three hotspot shapes: Rectangle, Oval, and Polygon.

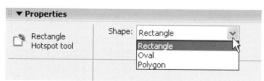

When you use the Polygon Hotspot tool, it will still export a rectangular shape around the polygon shape. Use polygon hotspots with caution. You'll find that you'll need a lot more slices to export a polygonal shape.

1. Open collage.png from the collage folder of the download files.

2. Select the Rectangle Hotspot tool.

3. Draw a rectangular hotspot over the word Buttons. Go into the Property inspector and name your hotspot "buttons" in the Hotspot field. Enter a null Link of javascript:; and Alt text of "Buttons".

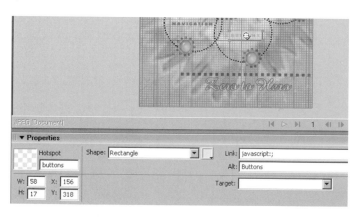

4. Repeat step 3 for the rest of the text links in the collage file.

The red lines are the slicing guides that Fireworks automatically adds based on the current slices of the buttons. This image has far too many slices and would need to be sliced manually to get the best results.

5. Save the file and leave it open to continue with the next section. (This file is also included as `hotspots.png` in the download files.)

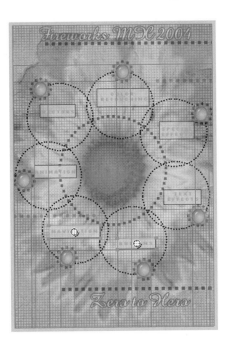

Making disjointed rollovers

When the mouse moves over or clicks a trigger area and an image (or piece of text) is displayed in a *different* part of the web page, a **disjointed rollover** has been used. You'll see disjointed rollovers used quite often on buttons. The button is the trigger area, but the target area displays a text description somewhere else on the page. In this exercise, you'll use the drag-and-drop behavior, which is a fantastic timesaver.

1. Continue working with your file from the previous example (or use `hotspots.png` from the collage folder in the download).

You'll now add some frames to the document. When you add a disjointed rollover, the image is stored in a frame. Each different image you use needs a separate frame, but no matter how many images you use, you still only need one slice for the area in which the image will display.

2. Open the Frames panel (*SHIFT+F2*).

3. Select Duplicate Frame from the Frames panel options menu. In the Duplicate Frame dialog box, enter 7 for the Number of frames. Check After current frame, if it isn't already checked.

4. In the Frames panel, select Frame 2 and you'll see the background and the Over state of the button symbols too. Click the other frames, and you'll see the background area and the circles for the buttons.

5. Add a new layer and name it "disjoint". The images you use for the disjointed rollover will go in this separate layer that isn't shared.

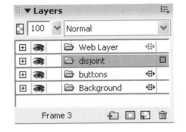

6. Select the Slice tool and draw a rectangle for the center of the flower. Set the width to 85 and height to 78. Place it in the center of the flower (x:108,y:175). In the Slice field, name it "disjoint".

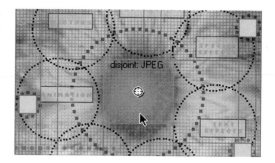

Let's add the images to each of the frames. Each button will have an image in a separate frame starting with Frame 2.

7. Select Frame 2 and then select the disjoint layer. Import buttons.png from the disjoint folder in the download files. Click in the slice area to place it, and position the image in the center slice area using the x and y coordinates. If you're using the supplied hotspots.png, then the coordinates are x:108,y:175.

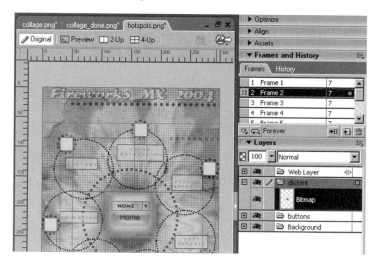

8. Select Frame 3 and the disjoint layer. Import nav.png from the disjoint folder in the download files and position it on the disjoint slice again. Repeat this for the remaining frames using these images:

★ Frame 4: animation.png

★ Frame 5: vectors.png

★ Frame 6: retouch.png

★ Frame 7: special.png

★ Frame 8: texteff.png

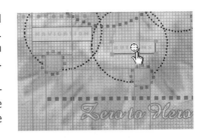

9. To add the behavior to make the buttons and hotspots work, first select the buttons hotspot. Notice the circle with the cross in the center. When you move the mouse cursor over it you'll see a hand.

10. When the hand is present, click and drag to the center slice, releasing the mouse when you pass over the slice. Notice the red line that now connects the hotspot to the slice. This indicates the behavior.

11. The Swap Image dialog box opens. Because the image you want for the button's hotspot is in Frame 2, click OK.

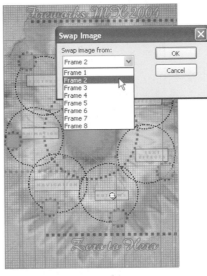

12. Toggle off the slice view and click the Preview tab in the document window. Pass your mouse over the buttons text. Now pass your mouse over the button. The image of a button sample should be in the center of the flower.

> *Only one slice is used. Do you see how you could have multiple rollover images? If you wanted to, you could add additional frames and have different images for the text and the button.*

13. Repeat steps 11 and 12 for the remaining buttons and button labels using these frames:

- ★ Navigation: Frame 3
- ★ Animation: Frame 4
- ★ Vectors: Frame 5
- ★ Color Retouching: Frame 6
- ★ Special Effects: Frame 7
- ★ Text Effects: Frame 8

14. Click the Preview tab to preview each button and to make sure each text label is working.

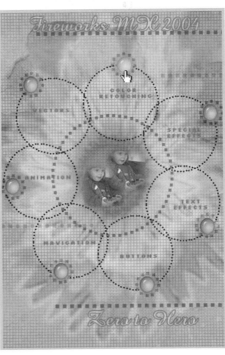

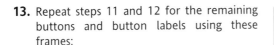

15. To see the behavior that was automatically added or to edit it, turn on the slice view and select the slice. Choose Window ➤ Behaviors to open the Behaviors panel. You'll see the Swap Image behavior has been added with an onMouseOver event.

> If you want the image to appear only if the user clicks, click the down arrow in the Behaviors panel and select OnClick. We didn't do this for our final file.

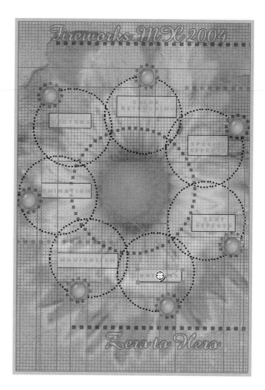

16. Save your file. A copy is also saved as collage_done.png in the collage folder of the download files.

Animation

Let's look at how animation can be used as part of an interface. You're going to use animation in two different ways in these last projects—an animated banner ad and animated buttons.

Animated banner ad

This ad will use several different animation techniques so that you can practice applying what you learned in Chapter 6. The following figure shows the animation so that you can get an idea of where you're heading. A working copy of the animation (called banner.gif) is also in the banner folder in the download files. If you open this file in your browser, you can see what you're going to make.

Prepare the background

1. Open bannerad.png from the banner folder. To make it a full size banner, choose Modify ➤ Canvas ➤ Image Size, uncheck Constrain Proportions, and change the width to 468 and the height to 60.

This photo would be best if optimized as a JPEG. But because the background is blurred and the flower has a lot of flat color, it's acceptable as a GIF. Another trick for making a photo look good as a GIF is to convert the photo to a vector in FreeHand or Flash. Or you could make a selection of the main image and apply a filter such as Watercolor (Photoshop 5's Watercolor works), or perhaps change the entire image to a sepia or two-tone.

2. In the Optimize panel (*F6*), change the export file format to Animated GIF and the number of Colors to 32. Now click the Preview tab of your document. Not bad at all because text will cover a good portion of this image.

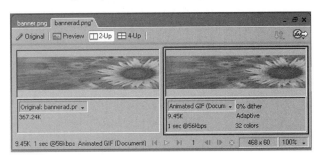 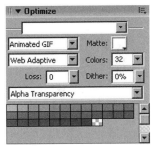

3. Double click Layer 1 (which contains only the background). Check Share Across Frames and press *ENTER/RETURN*. The background will now show up on every frame you add to the animation.

Add animated text

In this section, you'll animate a piece of text to make it appear as if it's zooming toward you, starting off small and growing in size.

1. Add a new layer in the Layers panel and name it "stop".

2. Click the banner and type the text "STOP" in block capitals. We used the following text settings:

- ★ Font: Bauhaus Md BT
- ★ Point Size: 42
- ★ Color: #D60C01
- ★ Stroke size: 2
- ★ Stroke color: White
- ★ Range Kerning: 10
- ★ Anti-aliasing level: No Anti-Alias

To change the stroke options, first select the text, then click the color box next to the pencil icon in the Properties inspector and click the Stroke Options button.

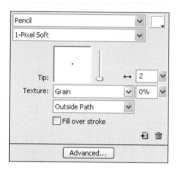

> *The other way to select text so that you can edit it is to use the Text tool and highlight it.*

3. With the text field selected, press *F8* to convert it to a symbol. Name the symbol "stop" and make it a Graphic symbol. Position the text as shown here:

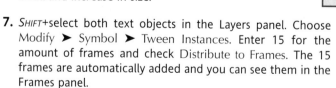

4. Select the text field, then choose Edit ➤ Clone to make a duplicate.

5. Make the copy 30 percent smaller with Modify ➤ Transform ➤ Numeric Transform (*CTRL/CMD+SHIFT+T*). Check Scale Attributes and Constrain Proportions.

6. Choose Modify ➤ Arrange ➤ Send to Back. The smaller copy is sent to the back so that the animation will begin small and increase in size.

7. *SHIFT*+select both text objects in the Layers panel. Choose Modify ➤ Symbol ➤ Tween Instances. Enter 15 for the amount of frames and check Distribute to Frames. The 15 frames are automatically added and you can see them in the Frames panel.

8. Let's make the animation play once and then stop. Click the GIF Animation Looping icon in the Frames panel and select No Looping.

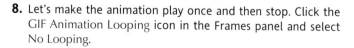

9. To make the animation play a little faster, the delay time needs to be changed. *SHIFT*+select all 17 frames in the Frames panel and select Properties... from the options menu. Change the Frame delay to 2.

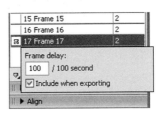

10. Double click the 2 in Frame 17 and change the delay to 100 and press *ENTER/RETURN*.

11. Add a new layer and rename it "smell". With Frame 17 still selected in the Frames panel, click the New/Duplicate Frame icon (+) to add a new frame (Frame 18). You'll now see just the background. With the Text tool add the words "And Smell The Flowers". These are the text settings we've used:

⭐ Font: Bauhaus Md BT
⭐ Point Size: 26
⭐ Color: FF9900
⭐ Stroke: Black (the default size)
⭐ Range Kerning: 5
⭐ Anti-aliasing level: No Anti-Alias

12. Place the text as shown in the following illustration and convert this to a symbol (*F8*). Name it "smell" and make it a Graphic symbol.

13. Choose Modify ➤ Animation ➤ Animate Selection. The following were the settings we changed:

⭐ Frames: 10
⭐ Move: 0
⭐ Opacity: 0 to 100

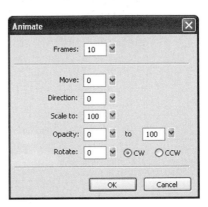

Click OK again when a window opens saying that frames will be added.

14. *SHIFT*+select frames 18–27 in the Frames panel, choose Properties... from the options menu, and change the frame delay to 20.

15. Click Preview to check your animation. Click the Play symbol on the bottom of the document area. You'll see "Stop" get larger, hold, then disappear. Next, "And Smell The Flowers" gradually fades in. You want this to hold for a bit as well, so change the last frame's delay to 100. The image here shows what your Frames panel should look like at this point.

16. Add a new layer and name it "tour". The last piece of text will enter from outside the canvas. To add it, select Frame 27 and click the New/Duplicate icon in the Frames panel. Add the text "Book A Tour". The settings we used are as follows:

- ★ Font: Bauhaus Md BT
- ★ Point Size: 26
- ★ Color: #FFCC00
- ★ Stroke color: Black
- ★ Stroke size: 1
- ★ Leading: 5
- ★ Anti-aliasing level: No Anti-Alias

17. Convert this text to a symbol (*F8*), name it "tour", and select Animation behavior.

18. The Animate settings become available. Enter 15 Frames, change Move to 288, and change the Opacity to 0 to 100.

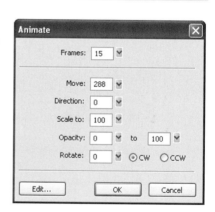

19. Move the text off your document to the left of the banner. To adjust the movement, click the red dot and drag it to the center of the flower.

20. *SHIFT*+select frames 28–42 and set the frame delay to 10. Preview the file in the browser.

21. In the Optimize panel, be sure the export file format is set to Animated GIF or it won't animate. Also, change the number of Colors to 64 and use Index Transparency.

22. Preview the animation and, when you're satisfied, choose File ➤ Export. Name and save your animation. (A copy called `bannerad.gif` is in the banner folder of the download files).

Making sliding buttons

For the last project, you'll make a sliding and transparent vector button.

1. Open `slidingbutton_start.gif` from the sliding_button folder in the download files.

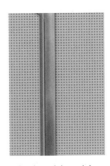

This file has a textured background and a metal bar to place buttons on. This starter file is so you can see the transparency. The only way the transparency will be visible is if it's exported over the underlying image. You can get true transparency (you can see through the button on to any background) by importing your PNG file into Flash.

2. Insert a new layer at the top of the Layers panel and call it "buttons".

3. Select the Rectangle tool. Use a Basic ➤ Soft Rounded stroke that's 4 pixels wide with a dark gray color (#666666). For the Fill, choose Gradient ➤ Linear. Set both gradient color boxes to the color #339999 and set both the opacity markers to 50 percent (the color boxes *above* the gradient preview).

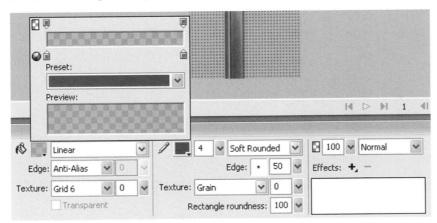

4. Draw a rectangle and make it 135 pixels wide and 25 pixels high. Change the Rectangle roundness to 100%.

5. Choose Bevel and Emboss ➤ Inner Bevel from the Effects menu. Use the following settings:

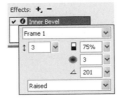

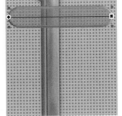

   ★ Bevel edge shape: Frame 1
   ★ Width: 3
   ★ Softness: 3
   ★ Angle: 201

6. Name the object "button".

7. Drag a vertical guide to just inside the curve of the button (see this image). Use the Pen tool to draw around the left side of the button. Use no stroke and the fill color #339999. Name the "objectShape1". Notice that the fill covers a bit of the black outline. We also used control handles to manipulate the curved area.

> The control handles for the curved area will be important later when you make an animation of the button with the dark color sliding closed. In the process, you may need to adjust the curve, and the control handles make it easier to do this.

8. Select the Pen tool. Change the stroke to white and make it 1-pixel hard. Click at the top of the button at the guide line. Press *SHIFT* and click at the bottom of the button. Name the object "whiteLine".

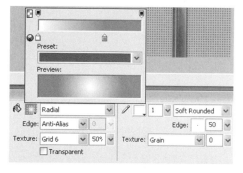

9. Use the Ellipse tool to draw a small 10×10 ellipse with a 1-pixel Basic ➤ Soft Rounded stroke in a medium gray color (#666666). Fill it with a radial gradient of white to light gray (#999999). Follow the placement of the color markers, as shown here.

10. Name this object "sphere".

You'll need to arrange the order of all the objects now so that the dark fill (button) is behind the frame of the main button. The color will actually change because in reality the dark portion will be behind the transparent button fill.

11. In the Layers panel, move objectShape1 below the button object. The whiteLine object should be above the button and the sphere should still be at the top of the layer stack. The white line should be 20 pixels high to fit within the frame of the button.

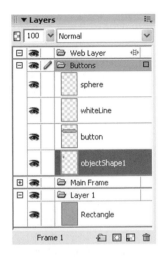

12. Open the Frames panel and select Duplicate Frame from the options menu. Enter 5 frames and check After current frame.

13. Select Frame 2. You need to gradually expand the objectShape1 to the right. Begin by selecting the shape and changing its width to 25.

14. Next, select both whiteLine and sphere objects and use the arrow key to nudge them to the right so that the whiteLine is on the edge of the objectShape1. Be careful not to alter the horizontal positions of the objects—it's easiest to select both of them in the Layers panel and use the keyboard arrow keys to nudge them into position.

The expanded objectShape1 can only be seen on Frame 2. You'll be expanding the objectShape1 on each of the remaining frames.

15. Select Frame 3. Change objectShape1's width to 50. The curve no longer fits snugly inside the left of the button. Use the Subselection tool to reshape the curve.

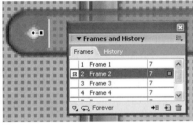

16. Select whiteLine and sphere objects in the Layers panel and nudge them into position.

17. Repeat steps 16 and 17 for the next two frames. In Frame 4, use a width of 85, and in Frame 5, use a width of 120.

18. Select Frame 6. Delete whiteLine and objectShape1.

19. Clone the button object (CTRL/CMD+SHIFT+D). Remove its stroke and change the fill color to solid #339999. Move this copy below the original button and move the sphere to the right side. You now have a fully closed button.

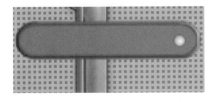

9

20. Let's preview the sliding button. Open the Optimize panel, set the export file format to Animated GIF, set the number of Colors to 32, and use No Transparency. Preview it in a browser, and you'll see that it moves really fast.

21. Select all frames in the Frames panel and double click the number 7. Change the frame delay to 22 to slow down the animation and check Include when Exporting. Also, click the GIF Animation Looping icon at the bottom of the Frames panel and choose No Looping.

> *When you preview the button in Fireworks using Preview, the animation will loop. If you preview in a browser, the button will close and stop.*

Right now the button closes at the end of the animation, but let's make it open back up again. To do this, you just need to reverse the direction of the animation.

22. Select Frame 5 and select Duplicate Frame from the Frames panel options menu. In the Duplicate Frames dialog box, leave the number of frames at 1 and check At the end.

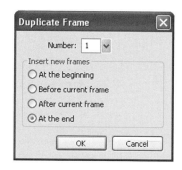

23. Repeat the previous step for Frames 4, 3, 2, and 1.

24. Now preview the button in a browser. It should slide open and closed. (This source file is `animatedbutton.png`.)

Adding actions

Now it's time to make the animation play in response to an onMouseOver action. To do this, you first need to add a slice.

1. Draw a 140×34-pixel slice. Place it at (x:1,y: 9).

2. Right/CTRL+click, choose Export Selected Slice, and save it in your folder for this project. If you're using the same folder as the download files, be sure to name it `myanimatedbutton.gif` so that you don't overwrite the original file.

3. To make the animation, let's use a static button. To make the button static, delete Frames 2–11 and save the file as `mystaticbutton_open.png`. You're using the name `open` because the static button is in the Open state.

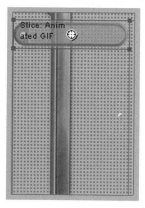

4. Select the slice and open the Behaviors panel (*SHIFT+F3*). Click the plus (**+**) sign and choose Swap Image. Frame 2 should be selected in the Swap Image dialog box. Click the yellow folder, navigate to the animated button you exported, and click OK.

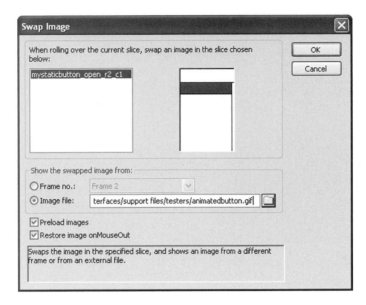

If you preview in a browser, your button should now open and close in reaction to the onMouseOver.

5. Save the file as mysliderbutton_swap.png and export this button as mysliderbutton_swap.gif.

Summary

In this chapter, you've covered a lot of detail involved in creating a variety of interfaces with Fireworks. You started by making basic buttons and built up from there to an interface with a navigation bar and pop-up menus.

After that, you went even further to look at how to make interfaces more creative and appealing by using images as buttons and navigation tools. You also added some hotspots and disjointed rollovers to liven up the navigation. Finally, you looked at adding animation to enhance an interface.

Ten

Extensibility and Automation

In this chapter

One of the best things about Macromedia's Studio MX 2004 products is the extensibility they provide through the Extension Manager and its useful accompanying resource: the **Macromedia Exchange**. The Exchange is an online community where developers and designers can share Macromedia product extensions—prewritten code, automated functions, extra filters, and much more—all managed through the Extension Manager software that ships with compatible Macromedia products.

Extensibility means that Fireworks never stands still. There's always something new being developed to automate a task, create new effects, or enhance workflow. Also, with the ability to save your own commands and ultimately create your own extensions, you don't even have to wait for someone else to do it. In this chapter, you'll see how to extend Fireworks by using these extensions and commands along with the Macromedia resources.

The following topics will be covered:

★ Extensibility in Fireworks MX 2004
★ The Commands menu
★ User-defined Commands
★ More automation tools
    ★ Using Plugins
    ★ Working with Find and Replace
    ★ Batch processing graphics files
    ★ Creating your own extensions

Extensibility

Extensions are a great under-used resource. Developed for a wide variety of purposes, they can range from simple time-savers to neat special effects. In short, they extend the functionality of Fireworks; they allow it to do something new.

As an example, the Align panel started life as an extension developed by Kleanthis Economou (www.projectfireworks.com). It became so popular that Macromedia bundled it with the MX version.

Once installed, an extension is simply applied in a suitable situation. Fireworks comes packaged with a whole bunch of built-in extensions, most of them visible through the Commands menu. You'll run through some of these later in the chapter.

Extensions are packaged as MXP (**M**acromedia e**X**tension **P**ackages) files, downloaded, and stored on your hard drive, where one double click opens the Macromedia Extension Manager.

Macromedia Extension Manager

The Extension Manager is all you need to install, uninstall, and organize your extensions. You can find out developer information and even read instructions within the tidy Extension Manager interface.

To open the Extension Manager, select Commands ➤ Manage Extensions....

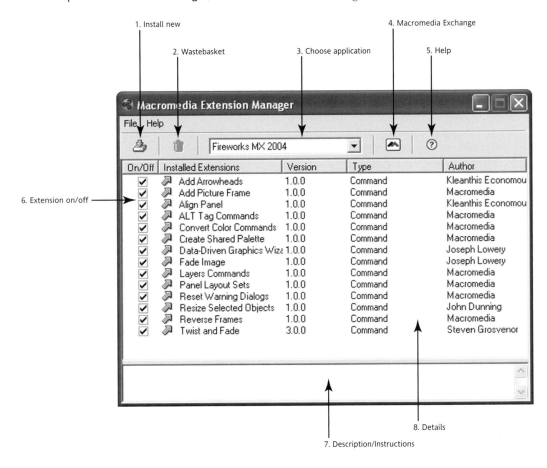

1. Install new

2. Wastebasket

3. Choose application

4. Macromedia Exchange

5. Help

6. Extension on/off

7. Description/Instructions

8. Details

Let's look at this in a little more detail, and then you'll download and install an extension to put it all into practice.

1. **Install New:** Use this to open a Browse dialog box so that you can search for an MXP file on your hard drive. The Extension Manager will then install it for you and add it to the list of installed extensions. Another way to install a new extension is to locate it first on your hard drive and then just double click it. The Extension Manager will open automatically and install the extension immediately.

2. **Wastebasket:** Use this to remove extensions selected in the Installed Extensions column.

3. **Choose Application:** The Extension Manager works for the Macromedia Studio MX 2004 products and also with previous Macromedia products. Choose yours from the drop-down menu and the Extension Manager will show you the extensions relevant to that application.

4. **Macromedia Exchange:** Click this to go straight to the Exchange.

5. **Help:** How long have you been using a computer? Next!

6. **Extension On/Off:** Some extensions use up a lot of system resources or just clutter your menus, so you might want to use this to temporarily disable them.

7. **Description/Instructions:** Here you'll find everything you need to know about your extension—what it does, how to apply it, and also any developer information, such as bug fixes or version improvements.

> *When you disable extensions, you're just temporarily turning them off. They remain in your Extension Manager and don't go anywhere near a wastebasket. They will, however, disappear from the Fireworks interface until you turn them back on.*

8. **Details:** This is the main section that lists your extensions in alphabetical order and also contains information on who developed them and what version they each are.

It's an easy-to-use interface for what is intentionally an extremely simple but very practical application. Time to pay a visit to Macromedia Exchange...

Macromedia Exchange

In the Extension Manager, click the Go to Macromedia Exchange button. This is the gateway to Macromedia's extension swap shop for Fireworks (or whatever program you're requesting extensions for).

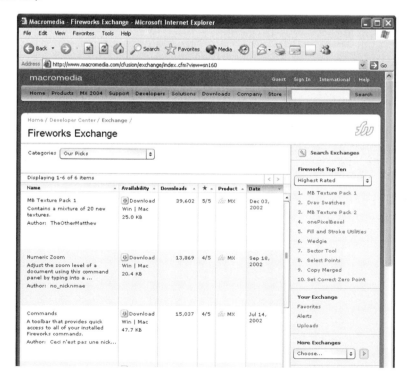

Note that this Exchange page is a work in progress and your screen may look considerably different than the figure shown. In this illustration, you're looking at Macromedia's picks, but there are other categories.

Take a break from reading and browse around. As I write this, over 40 extensions are available for Fireworks, covering areas such as texture packages, document handling, special effects, and 3D to animation.

The Exchange website also provides support forums, advanced searches, and sorting to help you find the right extension for you. When you're done browsing, you're ready to move on to the extension exercise in the next section.

Before you can download any extensions, note that you have to register with www.macromedia.com. *This is fast and easy and unrelated to any product or software registration. You just provide Macromedia with some basic details about yourself and then you're ready to go. Macromedia's privacy policy is TRUSTe approved, so you don't have to worry about them selling your details to SpamCorp of Illinois.*

Downloading and installing an extension

Let's download a sample extension—the MB Texture Pack 1 extension, in this case (or you can follow these instructions and download any one that catches your eye).

1. Click the name of your chosen Extension (in this example, MB Texture Pack 1) to bring up its detail page. (A link is sometimes provided to the author's site. It's a good idea to check it to see if you're getting the latest version. Macromedia is much slower at updating their extension list than the authors are.)

   Not only can you download from the details page, you can also find out information about the author, how many other people have downloaded it, what their opinion of it is, what the extension does, and what it costs, if anything.

10

2. When you click download, you'll probably be asked to sign in or create an account. (There's no charge for this service.)

3. Once you sign in, the standard download dialog box pops up giving you the choice to either open or save the file. I suggest you use Open for proper installation. Of course, you'll need to accept the licensing agreement.

4. Once the extension is installed, you'll be prompted to shut down Fireworks and reopen it for the extension to be available.

5. If you go to the Extension Manager once again, you should see your downloaded extension.

   Alternatively, you could have downloaded the extension to a folder of your choice and then used the Install New Extension button in the Extension Manager itself (or pressed CTRL+1) to browse to your folder and install it.

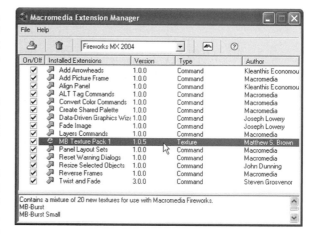

6. If you select your new downloaded extension and scroll down the lower window, you'll see what it does as well as instructions on how to use it.

   This tells you that your extension is now installed with the other textures you saw earlier in the book.

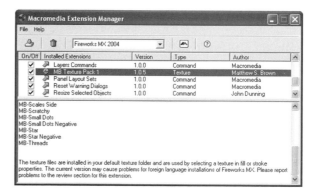

7. If you open Textures in the Property inspector, you'll see the new ones prefaced with MB (in this case, MB stands for the author, Matthew Brown).

That's all there is too it. Take a few moments and try downloading and using other extensions.

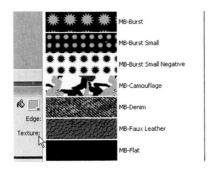

Creative commands

Fireworks ships with many built-in extensions, most of which appear on the Commands menu. Let's start by looking at the effects-related extensions (accessed with Commands ➤ Creative...).

Arrowheads

1. Start a new canvas. Type some text and add a vector line.

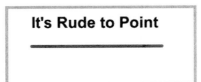

2. Select the vector line, and then choose Commands ➤ Creative ➤ Arrowheads to open a versatile little dialog box where you can add points and baubles at the drop of a hat.

★ You can specify whether to add the arrow to the start, end, or both ends of the line, and you can choose from 17 different arrow styles.

★ Solid fill and Apply stroke determine the attributes applied to the arrowhead. Apply stroke, for example, applies any softness in your stroke to the arrowhead when rendered.

★ Scale determines the size of your arrowhead.

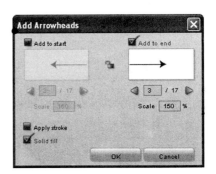

3. In this example, we only added the arrowhead to the end of the line; we chose the third style, and the scale has been increased to 150 percent.

> *As before, experimentation is the key to getting the most of these extensions. Now that you have an easy arrowhead, try applying some fill effects, a glow, or a drop shadow. Now that it's drawn, the arrow is a vector object for you to play with and incorporate into your graphics.*

Add Picture Frame

This is another prepackaged extension that's quite powerful. However, there are a couple of undocumented tricks for using it.

1. Open an image of your choice.

2. Select Modify ➤ Canvas ➤ Trim Canvas.

3. Select Commands ➤ Creative ➤ Add Picture Frame.

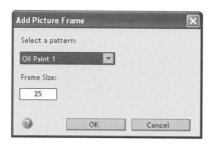

The settings are basic—you just select a pattern from the drop-down menu and frame size, and Fireworks generates the frame on a new layer.

4. Click OK to add the frame to your image.

5. To fix this the problem with the picture frame, select Modify ➤ Canvas ➤ Fit Canvas and then use the Pointer tool to properly position the picture in the frame.

It's worth spending a few seconds taking a look at the Layers panel.

Notice that the picture frame is in its own layer called Frame and the object is called Composite Path. The layer is also locked. So, if you want to edit the frame (which is rare), you need to unlock it first.

Fade Image

This extension is useful and you can manipulate it to create some great effects. Open up an image, select it, and then choose Commands ➤ Creative ➤ Fade Image.

At first, the effect makes your image practically indecipherable, but by dragging the handles around, you can adjust and stretch the **Vector Mask** and **Waves** pattern responsible for the effect.

You can achieve some pretty spectacular effects.

Twist and Fade

You really need to experiment with this neat effect to achieve the best results. As the name suggests, Twist and Fade turns the selected item(s) into a swirling vortex. This effect also has a multitude of customizable options. To try it out, type some text onto your canvas and choose Commands ➤ Creative ➤ Twist and Fade.

With Twist and Fade, you can use these four sliders to alter a number of the properties to shape your effect exactly the way you want it:

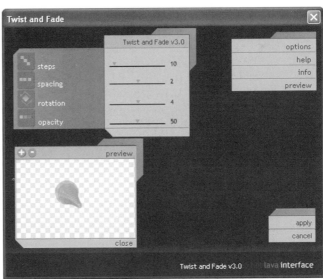

* **Steps:** The number of iterations of your object; essentially the number of stages the twist/fade goes through.

* **Spacing:** The space between those steps.

* **Rotation:** The amount each iteration of your object rotates during the course of the steps.

* **Opacity:** The starting transparency of your object.

The Preview tab helps you visualize what your graphic will look like and is especially useful at gauging the rotation.

The options tab has three additional features:

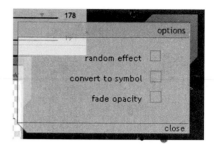

- ★ **Random Effect:** Picks a random set of values for you to use.

- ★ **Convert to Symbol:** Whereas normally your finished effect appears on your canvas as a horde of different objects (the number you specified in steps), this feature converts the entire effect into one solid symbol.

- ★ **Fade Opacity:** Here you can fade the object down to 0 opacity. Pick this for a true Twist and Fade effect.

Apply your choice of settings and check your output. We've been quite minimalist here with our choices, because we're using text.

If you are a little crazier with your settings, you can achieve more outrageous effects. Experiment to see what you can create using geometric shapes, text, or graphics. Remember that if you leave Convert to Symbol unchecked in the Twist and Fade options menu, each of these items will stay as a separate object, and you'll be able to adjust the effect later.

This logo on Joyce's site was created using this effect (www.joycejevans.com/tutorials/Fireworks/fwtutorials.htm).

> *If you look at the Frames panel, you'll see that each step was converted to a separate frame. You can add or delete frames to make some adjustments to the effect manually.*

Non-creative commands

As you've seen, Fireworks ships with a whole bunch of preinstalled extensions visible in the Commands menu. As you can see, there are many more than just the creative ones. Let's look at the remaining items on this menu briefly in turn.

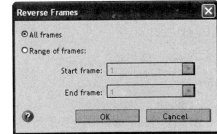

Document

The Document menu contains a number of automated tasks for your Fireworks projects.

★ **Distribute to Layers:** Takes each individual element in your PNG document and gives it its own individual layer. Using this is a great way to reorganize your document without separating the layers manually.

★ **Hide Other Layers:** Works great with the previous command, hiding all but the currently selected layer(s). Hide Other Layers is especially useful when your canvas is busy and you're trying to select or work with a particular object independent of its surroundings. If your document is cluttered and you want to view a few items/layers, remember that you can unhide others individually after you've run the command.

★ **Lock Other Layers:** Locks all but the present layer. It's a great command if you want to keep a tight reign on which elements you're currently editing but also want to see the whole document in context at the same time.

★ **Reverse Frames:** Unsurprisingly, this reverses the frames in your document, but a neat dialog box offers extra precision:

You can choose whether to reverse all frames or a specified amount. When you using frames in animation, this can be a great little tool for reversing your sequence (or parts of it).

Panel Layout Sets

The three options here—1024×768, 1280×1024, and 800×600—are preset panel arrangements depending on your monitor size.

Data-Driven Graphics Wizard

This is an advanced dynamic graphics generator that uses variables in your Fireworks file to retrieve images. It's unlikely that you'll need this so early in your Fireworks career, but it is a useful extension if you ever want to incorporate XML into your web graphics projects.

Save Panel Layout

You can also save your preferred panel arrangement to Fireworks' memory.

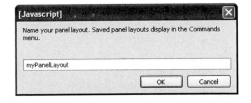

In the future, your saved layout will appear on the Panel Layout Sets menu alongside the preset options.

Reset Warning Dialogs

This is a neat housekeeping command that allows you to reinstate any warning dialogs where you may have previously checked Do not show this again. If you prefer to be told when you're about to do something important, irreversible, or risky, then use this simple command.

Resize Selected Objects

This command by John Dunning (johndunning.com/fireworks) is a precise and practical alternative to the Scale tool. There are three main advantages:

★ You can make pixel-by-pixel adjustments in any direction more easily and more precisely using John's cute interface.

★ Rectangles with rounded corners maintain their corner radii during the resizing process.

★ Selected objects are resized independently. In a similar way to the roundness, multiple objects maintain an **absolute** rather than **relative** relationship. So, if two objects are 20 pixels apart in height, and you resize both with this tool, they'll still be 20 pixels different. The Scale tool would produce different results.

The larger arrows on the interface, at the right of the screenshot, scale by ten pixels at a time, whereas the smaller arrows (highlighted by the bottom cursor) resize by one pixel at a time. This great command can save you time and frustration—keep it in mind!

Web

You'll find three web-related commands available here:

★ **Create Shared Palette**: With this command, you can create a new palette based on the average color settings of a specified folder of images. You need to navigate to the appropriate folder, and then Fireworks will look at the palettes of all of the images in the folder and average their settings into one new palette.

★ **Set Blank ALT Tags**: You can specify Alt (alternative) text for any currently empty Alt fields in any hotspots or slices in your document.

★ **Set ALT Tags**: Here, you can give all images in your Fireworks document the same Alt value.

User-defined commands

You can create, save, and reuse your own commands by using the History panel to "record" your actions and save the procedure as an automated command, which you can then apply from the Commands menu at any time. Saved commands have a number of practical applications:

★ Automate a series of steps applied to an object or text so that the same effects are easily reapplied.

★ Create a reusable self-contained object. Like a permanent clipboard entry, you can paste an object from the Commands menu as and when you need it.

Your saved commands aren't just limited to attribute changes and effects. You can save alignment and other properties, and your saved action history can include the application of other commands.

Using the History panel

Open the History panel with Window ➤ History or *SHIFT+F10*.

The History panel records every step you take in Fireworks. You can then select individual, or groups of, actions and either undo or redo them. To reexecute a group of steps, you select the appropriate steps and then click the Replay button. This is an excellent way to avoid performing the same actions over and over.

One thing to be aware of is that, by default, the History panel only remembers the last 20 steps you made. However, you can adjust this by selecting Edit ➤ Preferences... and changing the number in the Undo steps field.

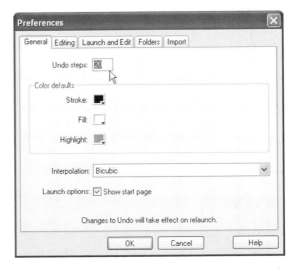

1. Open a new canvas and draw some simple vector shapes with strokes and fills.

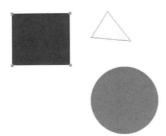

2. Now look at the History panel. Notice the slider control at the left side of the panel:

This is called the undo marker. As you drag it up, the steps become grayed out and undone on the canvas.

If you perform another step, the marked undone steps will be deleted and replaced with the new step. You can also drag the marker back down (provided you didn't perform any new steps) to undo the undo.

Now, let's move on to create a command that will help you quickly and effectively apply a specific group of effects and attributes to basic text.

Creating a command

1. Start a new Fireworks document (the size and properties aren't important).

2. Put some basic text in a large blocky font on the canvas and use the Align panel to align the text vertically and horizontally to the center of the canvas.

Notice how using the Align panel shows up as a Command Script in the History panel. This is because the Align panel is actually an extension itself (one that lives in the Window menu rather than the Commands menu).

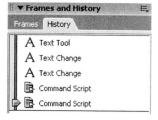

3. Go to the Effects menu in the Property inspector and add an effect you like. We've used a Shadow and Glow ➤ Glow, which has been customized.

4. Let's give the text more than one customized effect to demonstrate how much time a custom command can save. Add a Drop Shadow from the Effects menu.

5. Take a look at your History panel. Select all the actions you've performed from aligning the text to adding the effects. You can select the group by highlighting the first step and then *SHIFT*+clicking the last step in the range or by using *CTRL/CMD*+click to select/deselect actions you do(n't) want to include.

When making your own commands, if you see a history action separated by a solid black line, you'll be unable to include this. This is an action that involves you clicking or dragging an object and can't be saved.

For the purposes of this exercise, if your steps are in a different order, it's not critical.

6. With your selection made, click the little save icon at the bottom-right corner of the History panel.

7. Name your command (using the naming conventions discussed earlier in the book).

Time to test it all out.

8. Start a new canvas and type in some more text like you did earlier.

9. Select your new command from the Commands menu, which should be underneath the separator line.

10. With a single click, your text is colored, centered, and has a glow and a shadow—all because of the exact specifications you set up earlier. What could be easier?

This command isn't document specific, so it will be available in *all* the Fireworks projects you work on. Maintaining a good set of command files could save you hours of work.

11. Should you ever want to rename or remove any command, use Commands ➤ Manage Saved Commands....

Here you can rename or delete your command files.

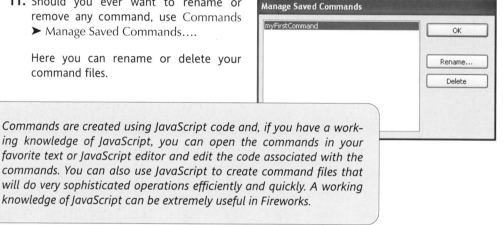

Commands are created using JavaScript code and, if you have a working knowledge of JavaScript, you can open the commands in your favorite text or JavaScript editor and edit the code associated with the commands. You can also use JavaScript to create command files that will do very sophisticated operations efficiently and quickly. A working knowledge of JavaScript can be extremely useful in Fireworks.

More automation tools

If you haven't realized already, you'll soon discover that designing requires a lot of repetitive work. For the busy designer, this isn't efficient. Fortunately, Fireworks has a number of tools to perform repetitive tasks automatically, leaving you with more time to concentrate on the fun bits. You've seen extensions and creating custom commands via the History panel—now let's look at some other methods of automation.

Plugins

Bundled with Fireworks MX 2004 is a sample package by Alien Skin Software. This company puts out a number of creative filters to enhance your graphics. As an example, open up cat.png from the download files.

Open the Effects menu in the Property inspector, and select Alien Skin Splat LE ➤ Edges....

In this example, Torn Paper is the Edge Mode selected whereas all other settings are at their defaults.

You can find a complete list of their filter packages at www.alienskin.com. The following images are examples of their various filter effects:

Installing third-party plugins

Adobe Photoshop is, without question, the industry standard. As a result, many third-party plug-in filters have been developed for Photoshop by a variety of vendors. Fortunately, most of these filters are fully compatible with Fireworks MX 2004.

You can handle the installation of these plugins in two ways. The easiest and most reliable technique is to install them in the following directory:

★ **Windows**: C:\Program Files\Macromedia\Fireworks MX 2004\Plug-Ins

★ **Mac OS X**: Macintosh HD\Applications\Macromedia Fireworks MX 2004\Plug-Ins

Once installed, you need to restart Fireworks for the new plugins to take effect.

The other technique is to use the Property inspector. Click the Effects + button and then choose Options ➤ Locate Plugins....

Maneuver to the folder where you installed the plugin. You should see the screen shown here:

Once there, the button at the lower left of the dialog box should reflect the name of the plugin. Once you select this, you'll be prompted to restart Fireworks in order for the new plugin to take effect.

Find and Replace

Another handy feature is the Find panel (Window ➤ Find or *CTRL/CMD*+F). You can search for text, colors, fonts, and URLs and specify replacements. You have a number of options here.

In the top drop-down menu you can choose the scope of the search:

★ Search Selection and Search Frame: Limit the scope of the find and replace to selected elements or the active frame.

★ Search Document: Makes the scope the whole document. Selecting Search Files... opens a dialog box where you can select the files to include in the scope of your search.

Once you've decided the scope of the find and replace, specify what you're searching for in the second drop-down menu.

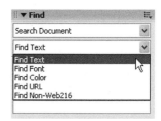

When searching text, you can specify case sensitivity, whether the string you entered is a whole word or a partial string, and also set the replacement value.

If you select Find Font, extra options appear in the lower half of the panel, enabling you to search for fonts, styles, and point style.

At the bottom of the panel, you can select the replacement value for your font once Fireworks has found it.

Find Colors allows you to use the various color tools you're familiar with to find and replace colors and to apply the replacement values to fills, strokes, or both.

With Find URL you can find and replace any URL references in your document. Its extra options are similar to those for the text search.

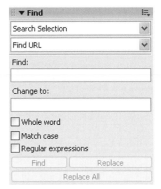

Finally, selecting Find Non-Web216 instructs Fireworks to look for non–web safe colors and replace them with the nearest web safe color. Again, like the Find Color option, you can apply it to fills, strokes, or both.

Batch processing graphic files

As a web designer, you may often find yourself performing tedious operations, such as changing file formats, resizing, or optimizing, for a large number of graphic files. It can be very time consuming to make these changes individually so, thankfully, you can instead use Fireworks' batch processing feature to process all of the files at once.

Begin the process by selecting File ➤ Batch Process... to open the batch processing window.

You can add the files you want to perform operations on by selecting them in the top pane and clicking the Add button. If you need to, you can use the Add All button to add all the graphic files in the folder.

Once you've selected your files, click the Next button. This brings up a new screen where you select the operations to perform on the files.

Similar to the Find and Replace panel, each operation you select reveals a set of extra options in the lower pane of the window. For example, in the screenshot here, we've chosen to export the files and have been given the extra option to use any of the standard formats.

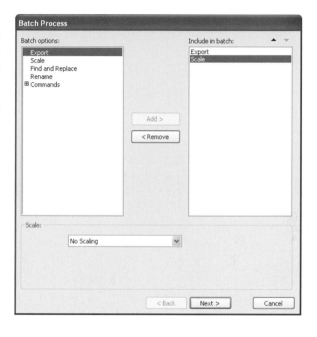

Let's quickly run through the other Batch options:

★ **Scale:** Allows you to adjust your graphics to a certain size, a certain percentage of their size, or to fit a certain area.

★ **Find and Replace:** Use this to batch find and replace throughout multiple files.

★ **Rename:** This does what it says—it batch renames all the selected files.

★ **Commands:** A list of JavaScript commands that perform additional operations. If you expand the list, you'll see the list of commands, the names of which are self-explanatory. This list will include your custom commands.

Once you've selected the operations you wish to batch perform, press the Next button.

Use this final screen to decide where the finished products will be placed. If you select the Backups option, you can instruct the program to name the files incrementally (myfile-1.png, myfile-2.png, and so on).

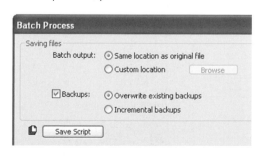

An interesting feature here is the Save Script button. It'll save this batch operation as a JavaScript command file.

> *It's interesting to note that JavaScript command files can be saved as a desktop icon. If you then drop that icon on the Fireworks icon, or an open document, the command script file will run!*

Summary

You've covered a lot in this chapter, and there was a lot to cover, because Studio MX 2004 is extensible like never before. You've seen how to find and download, apply and use, and manage extensions; and how to use and make your own commands. By fully exploiting the automation options, you can remove some of the repetitive tasks and improve your workflow immensely.

Eleven

Retouching and Enhancing Color

In this chapter

You'll learn how to enhance and retouch images in the Fireworks environment. This ranges from fixing broken lines in black and white images to creating complex color image compositions using photos and native Fireworks objects.

The following topics will be covered:

- Retouching images from a scanner or digital camera
- Using the Levels histogram to adjust color
- Anti-aliasing and reducing colors
- Adding color to a grayscale image
- Building a composite image using blending modes

When using photographs or other physical media in your Fireworks projects, the first task is to get them into the Fireworks environment itself. So, let's first look at how to use a scanner and digital camera with Fireworks MX 2004.

Using a scanner and digital camera

The prices of digital cameras and decent scanners have dropped dramatically in the last couple of years to something like $100 or less for a reasonable scanner, and to $200 (sometimes less) for low-end cameras suitable for web pages.

Once you've made this relatively small investment, the opportunities for new designs start opening up. Even just opening your refrigerator can reveal a whole new world of graphic ideas. Of course, if you use a traditional camera, you need to get the film developed before you can scan, but if you want that pinecone you spotted on your way home, you could simply place it on your scanner.

Whole books have been written on the subject of scanning and digital camera use, and it's impossible to cover it all in these pages. Instead, this section covers all you need to know to get started, and you can take it from there. If you're already at the level where you need more advanced information, I highly recommend that you pick up a copy of *Real World Scanning and Halftones* by Blatner, Fleishman, and Roth (Peachpit, 2004).

Before we look at how to scan or take a digital photo, let's consider what we need to do to prepare.

Resolution

When taking a scan or a digital photo that you intend to use in Fireworks, it's important to determine the level of resolution (see Chapter 1) your image will have. The higher the resolution, the more pixels/dots per inch (ppi/dpi), and the larger the image can be without degradation.

For example, if you have a photo that's 3×2 inches at a resolution of 266 dpi, and you stretched it to 11×9 inches, you would decrease the resolution to 70 dpi, thereby degrading the image. Also, if the original image only had 70 dpi to start with and you tried to make it larger, there wouldn't be enough data to work with.

When scanning line art, the resolution at which you scan also depends on the output device. For instance, if you plan for the scan to be viewed on a web page, you don't need more than 72 dpi (because a computer screen only has 72 pixels per inch), but if you plan to print it on a laser printer, scan at a minimum of 300 dpi.

Cleaning your scanner

The glass on your scanner needs to be clean and free of dust and dirt, otherwise it'll be visible on your newly scanned image. Be very careful when cleaning the glass—do not use traditional glass cleaners. Plain water and a lint-free cloth is enough to keep your scanner in good shape. You could also use eyeglass cleaner if the scanner glass is particularly dirty.

Making a scan

For this example, the scan we're making will be used for a web page, but because we want to touch up this line drawing in Fireworks, we decided to scan at a higher resolution of 300 dpi. It's more data than we need, but the image will be optimized after it's scanned and has been manipulated in Fireworks. The resolution has been decided and the scanner is clean. Let's get scanning.

1. The first thing you need to do is install your scanner software and hook your scanner up to your computer.

2. Place your artwork, photo, or object on the scanner. For artwork, try to place it as straight as possible so you don't have to do any further editing to straighten it in Fireworks.

3. If this is the first time you've used the scanner from within the Fireworks interface, go to File ➤ Scan ➤ Twain Select, and choose your scanner from the list. If you've installed digital camera drivers, they display here too. If your scanner isn't listed, check that your scanner drivers are successfully installed.

4. When you're ready to scan, choose File ➤ Scan ➤ Twain Acquire ➤ Import TWAIN Acquire. If you've already selected the scanner, then your scanner interface will open automatically.

   Scanner interfaces vary greatly, so at this point, refer to your scanner's manual to learn how to use it. You'll most likely see a preview of the item you're scanning. With some scanner software you can resize the image, use curves, or adjust brightness and contrast before scanning. If you're comfortable using these features, go ahead. However, we prefer to do our editing in a dedicated image editor.

5. Set the scanning resolution in your scanner software. You may also need to choose what type of media you're scanning (glossy, black and white, web, and so on). The choices really depend on your scanner software.

6. Finally, click the Scan button and your image will open in Fireworks. Now you can resize it for layout and edit it.

In a moment, we'll see how to capture an image from a digital camera. First though, let's take a look at the line drawing we scanned here, and see how to touch it up in Fireworks.

Removing artifacts from a black and white scan

A common problem when scanning a line drawing is lots of gray noise or trash in the image. Fortunately, it's simple to correct in Fireworks.

1. Open `astronaut_line.tif` from the download files.

2. Zoom in to the pack on the left side of the image near the number 2, or anywhere you can see a lot of gray particles.

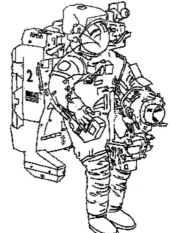

3. Select the image and choose Filters ➤ Adjust Color ➤ Levels.... In the Levels dialog box, you'll see a set of three eyedropper tools: shadow, midtone, and highlight color. To use them, select the one you want, and then click an area of the image.

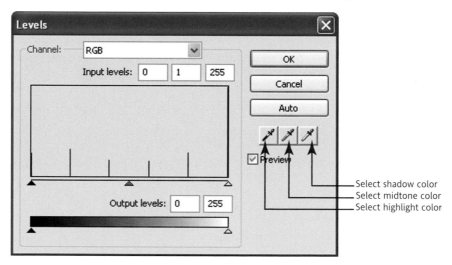

Select shadow color
Select midtone color
Select highlight color

★ With the shadow eyedropper, everything darker than the point you select will become black.

★ With the midtone eyedropper, the point you select will become the new midtone point in the image.

★ When you choose an area for highlights, anything brighter than the highlight area you select will become white.

4. Choose the Select highlight color eyedropper and click a gray spot. Just like magic, the spots are gone. Click OK.

5. You can darken some of the black lines in the same way. Zoom in to the middle of the left leg and you should notice that one of the lines seems broken as if some of it has been erased. This is caused by the fact that the drawing was made with a felt pen.

6. Select one of the lighter marks using the Select shadow color eyedropper tool and click OK to make the black lines a little more solid and continuous.

You may be wondering what the main diagram in the Levels dialog box is. It's actually the **histogram** and it shows you the balance of shadows, midtones, and highlights across your image. You can also use the histogram to edit this balance to get the best out of our pictures, which we'll see in a moment. First, let's walk through how to get your digital photos into Fireworks.

Shooting with a digital camera

Digital cameras work very much like a standard camera except that the images are stored digitally rather than on film. You take pictures with your camera, attach the camera to your computer (or use a card reader), and save the images directly to your hard drive.

Here are the steps that enable you to set up your camera so that it's recognized by Fireworks and then import your images (you can skip all of this if you have a card reader). You'll notice that this procedure is very similar to importing scanned images.

1. Be sure you have installed your camera drivers and connected the camera to your computer.

2. Choose File ➤ Scan ➤ Twain Select and choose your camera from the list.

3. When you're ready to get the images from the camera, choose File ➤ Scan ➤ Twain Acquire.

4. Your camera software will open. Choose the image you want and open it.

11

Adjusting color levels with the histogram

It's easier to read the histogram for a color image, so retire your astronaut and open `trees.png` from the download files. Open the Levels dialog box (Filters ➤ Adjust Color ➤ Levels…).

 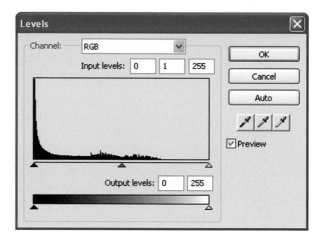

The spikes and peaks in the histogram show you where the detail in the image is. To the left are the shadows, in the middle are the midtones, and to the right are the highlights. Ideally, you want a balanced histogram because too many shadows hide the detail and too many highlights wash the image out. Equally, the image appears dull and lifeless if there are too many midtones.

When you see a histogram severely lacking in one or more of these areas, like the trees image here, it's a great candidate for tonal adjustment.

The sliders below the histogram add shadows (if you drag the left slider to the right), and highlights (if you move the right slider to the left). The center slider adjusts the midtones. A quick way to adjust tonal balance is to move the shadow and highlight sliders to the base of the "mountain range." At the moment, `trees.png` is looking pretty dull. Let's fix it.

1. Move the highlights slider (the clear one) to the edge of the mountain range where the highlight detail starts. There is already an abundance of shadows, so leave the left slider where it is.

 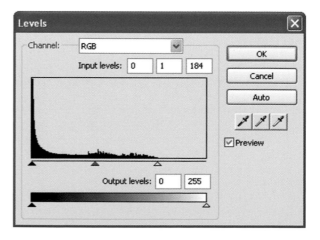

2. As you can see, the image is a little better, but it can still be improved. Because no "reset" button exists and you don't want these settings, click Cancel to close it and open the Levels dialog box again (Filters ➤ Adjust Color ➤ Levels…).

   This time, you're going to make tonal adjustments in individual color channels. Currently, you're looking at all channels at once (RGB), but you can specify the red, green, and blue channels individually in the Channel drop-down menu.

3. Select the red channel and move the right slider to the beginning of the highlight detail (the beginning of the mountain range). Repeat this for the green and the blue channels too.

4. Select the RGB channel again, and notice how the histogram has changed. There are far fewer spikes and peaks; it appears more rounded. Click OK to accept the changes.

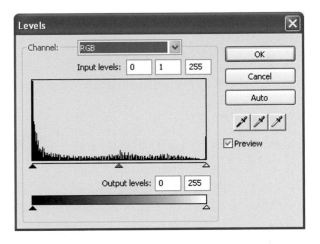

Setting highlights and shadows with the eyedropper

When cleaning the scanned image, you saw how to use the eyedropper tool to remove black flecks from a poor quality scan. You can also use the eyedropper tool to select different color values when changing the highlights and shadows in the histogram, but it works a bit differently when color is involved.

1. Open the Info panel (Window ➤ Info) and select RGB from the options menu.

2. Pass the Pointer tool over your image and try to locate the darkest point. As you move the Pointer over the image, monitor the RGB numbers in the Info panel. Locate the area where the RGB numbers are closest to 0; a range of 5 to 10 is fine. Remember the area.

3. Repeat the last step for the highlight area, this time watching for the higher RGB numbers, the closer to 255 the better. Take note of the location again.

4. To adjust the levels, open the Levels dialog box again, choose the Select shadow color eyedropper, and sample from the dark area you located in step 2.

5. Next, use the Select highlight color eyedropper and click the lightest area you located in step 3.

This should be enough to remove any color cast and fix the tonal adjustments. If the image is still a bit too dark or light, try adjusting the sliders at the bottom of the Levels dialog box.

6. When you're satisfied with the image, click OK.

Anti-aliasing and reducing colors

When you're dealing with vector images it's just as important to get a good line definition as it is to get good color quality in a photo. To keep your lines smooth, you can use **anti-aliasing**. This works by using transitional colors along the edge of the object, blending the background color with the stroke color. However, the addition of these extra colors can be costly in terms of file size, so you must reach an important balance here. Let's take a look at how to strike that balance.

Open the bitmap image `logosample.gif` from the download files. Notice that the edges are anti-aliased and smooth.

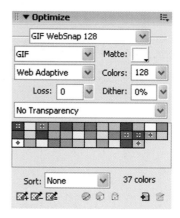

1. Open the Optimize panel and change the indexed palette to Web Adaptive. In the Color info area, click the Rebuild button at the bottom right of the panel. You'll then see that this image has 37 colors.

> *If you've used a version of Fireworks prior to MX, you'll notice that the Color Table has disappeared and the color information for GIF images now resides in the Optimize panel.*

2. In the Optimize panel, change the number of Colors to 16, and click the Preview tab in the document window. Nothing changes. While you're still on the Preview tab, change the number of Colors to 8 and then down to 4. Not much change results, but the edge is starting to get a bit more jagged. Because the image only appears to have two colors, drop the number of Colors down to 2.

Were the results unexpected? There are actually three colors in this image—the transparent background counts as the third color.

3. Change the Colors to 3 and change the transparency type to Index Transparency. In Preview mode, you'll now see two colors and the transparency. With the reduced colors, the anti-aliasing is removed and the edges are now jagged.

Reducing the number of colors also reduces the file size. If you want the anti-aliasing effect but also want to reduce the file size, try increasing the number of colors to 8. This isn't bad quality and is a lot better than using 37 colors. The exchange of image quality versus image size is a judgment you have to make.

Anti-aliasing will always add additional colors because the edge pixels are being "mixed" with the background pixels to make the edges blend in better. Zoom in close to your image and you'll see the varying shades of color on the edge of the image.

Using effects to change colors

In this exercise, you'll learn how to change colors of a bitmap image without making selections. Editing the color of a flattened image can be tricky when you don't have the original vector source file to work from.

1. The logo for this sample is an exported GIF image (a bitmap), not a Fireworks source file (vector), and it is called `logo.gif` in the download files.

If you had a logo like this on a website and decided you wanted to change the color of the word "to" or any of the other text, it could be quite difficult, especially if the logo was more ornate than this one, or you didn't have access to the original file or the font file. However, you can get around these problems by using effects to change the colors.

2. Select the bitmap and choose Adjust Color ➤ Color Fill from the Effects menu in the Property inspector.

3. Choose a bright blue from the color box with a Hue blending mode. Notice how only the word "to" has changed.

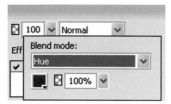 

4. Double click the Color Fill effect listed in your Effects menu to edit it and change the blending mode to Screen. Change the color if you'd like to experiment more.

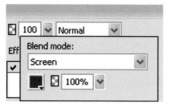 

Colorizing a grayscale image

Adding color to a grayscale image is relatively simple. In this example, you're going to use the Brush tool to paint the color back into the image, colorizing the large center flower to make it the focal point of the image.

1. Open the grayflowers.jpg file from the download files.

2. Zoom into the top of the flower, select the Brush tool, and set the following options in the Property inspector:

   - ★ Stroke color: gold (#FFCC00)
   - ★ Tip size: 30
   - ★ Stroke category: Air Brush ➤ Basic
   - ★ Edge: 100
   - ★ Texture: 0
   - ★ Opacity: 25%
   - ★ Blend mode: Tint
   - ★ Preserve transparency: checked

3. Paint over the larger petals of the foreground flower. Use a tip size of about 18 for the thinner petals and the tips. You can raise the opacity if you want more color.

4. Select a dark brown color (#633000) and a tip size of 100, and then paint the center of the flower. This is the finished result:

Adding color to black and white images can be good fun and can create some really interesting effects. Image modification in general is a fascinating area full of potential. Let's get a little more into it.

Image modification

Take this image, for instance. It could certainly do with some enhancing. First of all, the wall has to be cleaned up. Also, the area behind the girl's head blends too much with her hair. There's a hand at the left that has to be removed and, if you zoom in, you'll see that a lot of JPEG artifacts need to be removed too.

First of all, let's get the tone of the picture right. At the moment, it's a little dark.

Adjusting color tone

1. Open startingyoung_before.jpg from the download files (you can take a peek at how this image is going to end up—it's startingyoung_after.png).

2. Choose Filters ➤ Adjust Color ➤ Curves... to open the Curves dialog box, which you can use to adjust the brightness of pixels right across the tonal scale. The Input (horizontal axis) displays the original pixel tone you want to change, and the Output (vertical axis) displays the tone you want your pixel to change to. For example, pulling the diagonal line to the bottom-right corner of the grid changes your original highlights to shadows.

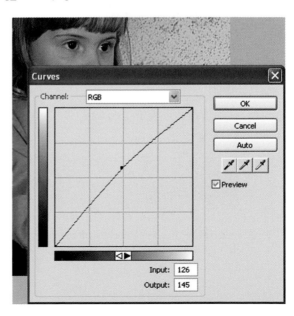

11

3. In this example, just click and drag the center of the curve slightly upward to lighten the midtones. The Input value is 126 and Output is 145.

4. Next, choose Filters ➤ Adjust Color ➤ Auto Levels. This automatically adjusts your color levels around the new midtone specification.

Removing unwanted objects from a photo

1. Select the Polygon Lasso tool (L) and make a selection around the contour of the hand and out into the green of the girl's sweatshirt. This selection will be used to conceal the adult's hand.

2. Once you've made your selection, copy and paste it. Use the Pointer tool and move the pasted piece toward the hand. Cover up as much of it as you can and try to match the crease at the elbow level. It's okay if a bit of the hand still shows.

> You could leave the piece separate, but every time you wanted to use the Rubber Stamp tool, you'd have to choose the Use entire document option and keep an eye on what object is selected. By merging, you don't have these concerns.

3. Select the copied piece in the Layers panel and choose Modify ➤ Merge Down (*CTRL/CMD+E*).

4. Select the Rubber Stamp tool (*S*) and set the Size to 28 with an Edge of 100 in the Property inspector. Use the Rubber Stamp to blend in the seams and fill the adult's hand. Remember, you take a sample with the Rubber Stamp tool by holding down the *ALT/OPT* key and then clicking with your mouse in the area you want to use.

You can see that the center part of the sleeve in the image here has a distinct pattern. To remove this, we sampled above the pasted area. If it's still too dark, you can select the Dodge tool (*R*) and click once or twice.

5. Once your sleeve is blended and the hand removed, check to see if your copied sleeve overlaps the black shadow below the girl's arm like ours did. If it does, select the area with the Polygon Lasso tool and fill it with black, or use the Rubber Stamp tool.

Cleaning up the wall

1. To clean up the dark spots on the wall, use the Rubber Stamp tool with a Size of 40, an Edge of 50, and Source aligned checked. Sample a clean area and stamp over any darker spot. The tone will still be uneven but this'll be fixed in the next step.

2. Select the Dodge tool (*R*) and set its Size to 49, Edge to 100, Range to Shadows, and Exposure to 50. Click and drag back and forth over the wall to lighten and even the tone.

3. To recolor the wall area behind the hair, use the wall pattern. Select the Rubber Stamp tool with a Size of 30 and an Edge of 50. You want the edge a bit sharper so that the hair edges don't look blurry.

Removing JPEG artifacts

JPEG artifacts are the blocky pieces of color you see when an image is overly compressed. If you look closely at your photograph, you'll notice several areas where the color could be smoother and more lifelike. Removing the artifacts helps you achieve this.

To remove the JPEG artifacts you can use a filter from Alien Skin called **Image Doctor**. You can download a demo version (it's 6MB) from www.alienskin.com. Once you've downloaded the demo, run `ImageDoctorDemo.exe` to install it. A dialog box asks you which program you want to use Image Doctor with (you can use it with multiple applications, but you have to install it individually for each program). If Fireworks MX 2004 isn't listed in the available programs, click Next and select the correct plugins folder to use. On Windows this is C:\Program Files\Macromedia\ Fireworks MX 2004\Plug-Ins. On a Mac this is Macintosh HD\Applications\Macromedia Fireworks MX 2004\Plug-Ins.

1. Select the image and choose Filters ➤ Alien Skin Image Doctor Demo ➤ JPEG Repair… and make the following settings in the dialog box:

   ★ Remove Artifacts: 10
   ★ Blur Edges: 3
   ★ Add Grain: 4

If you've downloaded and installed the Image Doctor demo with Fireworks open, you'll have to save your work, close, and reopen Fireworks for it to be listed in the Filters *and* Effects *menus.*

Play with the settings to see what they do. Notice that the image looks more like a water-color painting if you go too high. Reset to the values in step 1 and click OK.

2. Select the Blur tool (R) and give it a Size of 50 and an Edge of 100. Zoom in and click over areas that still need JPEG repair. Make sure you click and don't drag. If you drag, you'll get distinct blurring. All you want to do is smooth out the few blocky areas that remain, particularly the sleeve and cuff areas.

3. Now select the Sharpen tool (R) and set the Intensity to 25 with a Size of 25 (use default Edge of 100). Click (don't drag) over the control knobs to bring them out. If you go too far, you'll see white showing through, but you can always undo (CTRL/CMD+Z). Click over the eyes and hand edges and basically anywhere you want a bit more detail. We clicked in the hair a few times but it's easy to over-sharpen, so be careful.

Adjusting the image border

You can add a simple border by drawing a rectangle over the canvas with no fill and a thick stroke. You can also use the rectangle as a mask, cut out the edges, and then use the Reshape Area tool to reshape them. But, for this image, let's use another Alien Skin plugin—the Skin Splat! Edges that ships with Fireworks MX 2004.

1. Select the image and choose Filters ➤ Alien Skin Splat LE ➤ Edges….

2. Check out the different edges in the Edge Mode drop-down menu if you've never used it before, then move the sliders to experiment with the effect. When you're done playing, use these settings:

★ Edge Width: 15

★ Margin: 0

★ Feature Size: 25

★ Edge Mode: Torn Paper

3. Click OK to add the border to your image.

11

Changing the shirt's color

Nothing is actually wrong with the color of the shirt in this image, but let's change it anyway for fun. Fireworks isn't designed to be a full image-editing program, but when you need to do a bit of image repair, it really does have an amazing array of tools.

You can use the following method to replace color or you can use the Replace Color tool (detailed in Chapter 2). For this exercise, we prefer this method because it doesn't accidentally alter any of the shadow areas.

1. Use the Polygon Lasso tool to make a selection around the green shirt.

2. Choose Filters ➤ Adjust Color ➤ Levels…. In the Levels dialog box, choose Green from the Channel drop-down menu. Now you can make adjustments to just the green channel. Because the shirt is green, you'll get a good color replacement. If you didn't make a selection, the entire image's green channel would be affected.

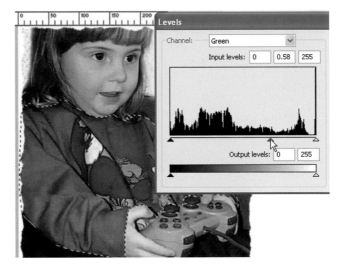

3. Move the center slider to the right until you get a nice blue. Experiment by moving the sliders to see what effects you can achieve and click OK when you have a color you like.

And there you go—here is a pair of "before" and "after" pictures to be proud of!

before   after

Image composition

In this final example, you're going to bring together some of the techniques you've learned in this chapter to compose images from many different modified images, colors, and shapes. In the process, you'll do some masking, apply some effects, and use blending modes.

Background

1. Open texture.jpg from the download files.

2. Choose Modify ➤ Canvas ➤ Canvas Color... and change the canvas color to #FF9900 (orange).

3. Select the image and choose Adjust Color ➤ Color Fill from the Effects menu using these values:

   ★ Color: #FF9900

   ★ Opacity: 55%

   ★ Blend mode: Multiply

4. In the Property inspector, change the image's opacity to 55%.

texture.jpg   after steps 2, 3, and 4

5. Open `flowers.jpg` from the download files.

6. Using the Pen tool, make a rough outline around the main flower. It's okay
to make it a bit spiky, as this is the
desired effect. A copy of the selection
is saved as `flowerselection.png` in
case you want to skip this step.

7. Change the stroke to null and the fill to white. Select
Feather from the Edge drop-down menu and set it to 3.

8. *SHIFT*+select the filled object and the image, then
choose Modify ➤ Mask ➤ Group as Mask.

9. Use the Subselection tool to rearrange any points where there are still unwanted background areas visible.

10. Select the flower layer and copy and paste it into your texture document, choosing Don't resample in the pop-up. (You can now close the original flower image.)

11. Make the flower 353 pixels wide and 300 pixels high, and position the flower over your background, as shown here:

12. From the Effects menu, choose Shadow and Glow ➤ Glow using the following values:

   ★ Width: 3

   ★ Softness: 4

   ★ Color: yellow (#FFFF00)

   ★ Opacity: 100%

13. Rename the masked flower "mainflower" in the Layers panel.

14. Copy and paste it twice so that you now have three copies of the flower in your image. Rename the bottom copy "flowerdark" and the center copy "flowerlight".

15. Turn off both the mainflower and flowerdark layers' visibility. Select flowerlight and change both its width and height to 436, repositioning it as shown here:

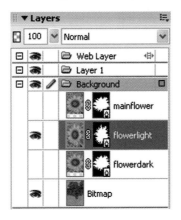 

11

16. Change the flowerlight layer's blend mode to Screen and its opacity to 55 percent.

17. Turn off flowerlight layer's visibility and make flowerdark visible again.

18. Select the Scale tool and stretch (drag down on the bottom control handle) the flower until the bottom is near the bottom edge of the document.

19. Change the blend mode to Multiply, then select the Eraser tool and set its properties to

★ Size: 70
★ Eraser opacity: 100%
★ Edge: 100
★ Shape: Round

20. Drag the Eraser tool over the top portion of the petals and part of the center until your flower looks like the one shown here:

21. Now, select the mainflower object and click the little i icon in the Effects list to access the Glow values. Change the opacity to 40%.

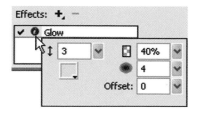

22. Finally, turn the visibility back on for all the flowers.

Adding texture and lines

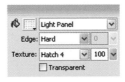

1. Draw a rectangle with a Hard Edge to cover the entire canvas.

2. Select Pattern ➤ Light Panel from the Fill category drop-down menu in the Property inspector. Change the Texture to Hatch 4 and 100 percent.

3. Change the opacity of the rectangle to 20 percent.

   To finish up this effect, let's install a command we made for you. You don't have to restart Fireworks in order to access commands that you add; they show up immediately.

4. Open the Fireworks application folder and locate the Commands ➤ Creative folder. Next, copy Square dashes.jsf (located in the download files) into this folder.

5. Back in Fireworks, choose Commands ➤ Creative ➤ Square dashes. Make sure the Edge size is 5 and the opacity is 20.

   > *A command was used here because we wanted a specific shape of square dash that isn't available in Fireworks. But a new feature of Fireworks MX 2004 makes a stroke with dashes. Draw your line, then in the Stroke category, select Dashes and the desired type of dashed line. You can adjust the size and edge just like any other stroke.*

6. Make three copies, and place them as shown here (or wherever you prefer). We also changed the opacity of the top and bottom line to 45 percent.

7. Next, add some dotted circles to the background with the Ellipse tool, using these values:

   ★ Width and height: 100

   ★ Fill: None

   ★ Stroke category: Dashed ➤ Basic Dash

   ★ Stroke size: 2

11

8. Make seven copies of the circle. Change the size of one circle to 160×160, its opacity to 45 percent, and place this one over the center of the flower. Arrange the other circles around it.

9. Save your file now to maintain all the objects' editability. Alternatively, a copy of the project up to this stage called background.png is available in the download files.

10. Choose Select ➤ Select All and then Modify ➤ Flatten Selection. This will make your file a bit more manageable. Rename the object "background".

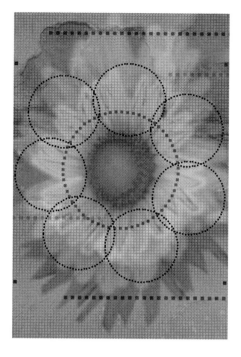

Adding buttons

Let's move on and add some buttons to the background image.

1. Add a new layer and name it "buttons".

2. Use the Ellipse tool to draw a circle with the following properties:

- ⭐ Width and height: 30
- ⭐ Stroke category: Dashed ➤ Dotted
- ⭐ Size: 4
- ⭐ Fill color: brown (#AB701A)
- ⭐ Stroke color: black
- ⭐ Blend mode: Tint

3. Make six copies of the small circle and arrange them on the perimeter of the larger circles, as shown here:

4. For the actual button, choose Edit ➤ Insert ➤ New Symbol..., choose Button, name it "button", and click OK.

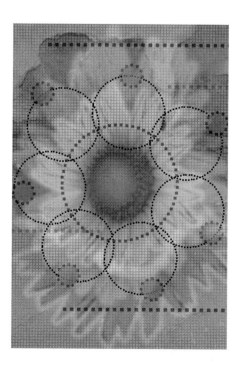

5. Choose File ➤ Import and locate glassbutton.png from the download files. Click to place it in the Button editor and center it over the crosshair.

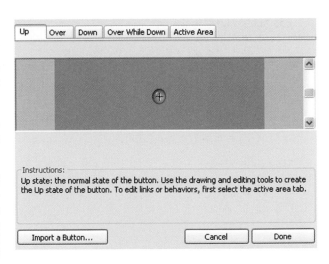

6. Select the Over tab and then click the Copy Up Graphic button.

7. Select the button and choose Adjust Color ➤ Color Fill from the Effects menu. Change the color to yellow (#FFFF00) and change the opacity to 35 percent. Click Done to finish editing the button.

8. Place the button in the center of a small circle. Drag a copy of the symbol from the Library panel, or press the *ALT/OPT* key and drag a copy out, and place it in another of the small circles. Repeat for each small circle until each of them has a button inside.

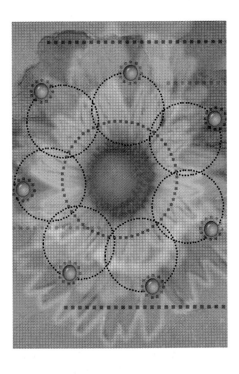

11

Adding text

1. Use the Text tool to type "Fireworks MX 2004" on the image. Choose your own font and size that fits the top of the image. (We used a Splash font, size 25, and colored it dark gray.)

2. Make a copy of the text, and this time, use a dark gray stroke and no fill.

3. Next, select the original filled text and change the blend mode to Screen.

4. Type the words "Zero to Hero" at the bottom of the image and then repeat steps 1 through 3, but make the font size smaller. The font size in this example is 24.

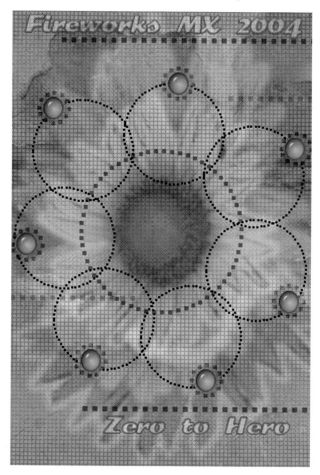

We're not crazy about mystery navigation, so let's add some text to indicate each button as well. The font used here is Silkscreen Expanded, with a point size of 8. This font is made for small text and, again, is dark gray.

Jason Kottke (www.kottke.org/plus/type/silkscreen/ index.html) allowed us to include the silkscreen font in the download files for both PC and Mac platforms. Install them and you're ready to go!

5. Type in the following labels and place them in each circle:

- ★ Buttons
- ★ Navigation
- ★ Animation
- ★ Vectors
- ★ Color Retouching
- ★ Special Effects
- ★ Text Effects

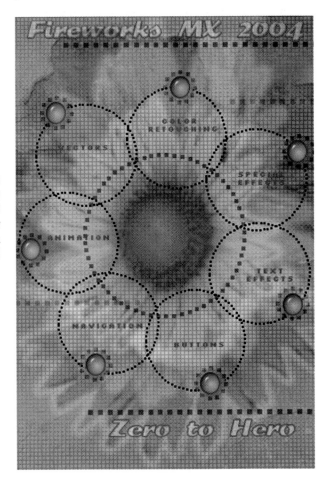

And there you have it! All you need to do now is add some interactivity to its buttons, and you have yourself a very funky and original looking interface. A copy is saved in the download files folder as `collage.png`.

Summary

This has been something of a whirlwind tour of the different things you can do with images and color. We started by looking at how to import images with a scanner and digital camera and then went on to look at how to retouch your images and make quick color changes. After this, we proceeded to the more complex areas of correcting colors, removing artifacts from scanned images and JPEG files, and building a composite image using blending modes and multiple layered images.

Although we've looked at some fairly specific examples, you should now be able to take the ideas underlying those examples and use them to work with your own color images—whether you created them yourself or brought them in from the outside world.

Web Page Layout with Fireworks and Dreamweaver

In this chapter

You can use Fireworks in many ways. You can export an entire design as a web page, or you can export portions as HTML files and separate images. But the capabilities go even further; you can export as CSS layers, Flash SWF files, and even Dreamweaver Library items. Fireworks is a wonderful tool for visually laying out a web page design. You can move things around, resize, edit color, and so on. If you're experienced at laying out web pages, you'll have an easier time exporting your design even during the layout and design process. This experience helps you visualize how you're going to get your design to display in a browser as you intend.

In this chapter, you'll get hands-on experience using many of the Export options in Fireworks. You'll export portions of the design with images and HTML, just images, and as a Dreamweaver Library item. You'll analyze the best way to reproduce the mockup you see here in a Dreamweaver layout. You'll see how to make a page that is "fixed" (where the size doesn't change with the browser window size) and how to make the design "stretch" to fit a browser window as it expands.

Export as a web page from Fireworks

Once you're satisfied with your design, the next decision is how you're going to present it to the world. If you don't own Dreamweaver (or another page layout editor) you could simply export your design from Fireworks as a completed web page. This method isn't recommended, as you'll see in this section.

This site design is copyrighted and provided here for learning along with this project, not for public use. Horse Adventures is a children's site where they have "sim" horses and is currently closed until a database is completed.

Start up Fireworks and open ha.png from the FW_DW/source folder in the download files.

Take a bit of time to look over the layout (you won't be making the graphics in this project). Here's a summary of what's been done up to this point:

★ The top banner was made by masking each horse to remove it from its background; then each horse was placed in the banner.

★ The title "Horse Adventures" was made using the rusted text technique from Chapter 8.

★ The smaller images are also masked images. I made a feathered selection of part of the main collage background and used it for the background of the small collages.

★ The red curve shape was made using the Pen tool.

★ The navigation bar at the right was made using the Button editor.

Take a look at the slices. The green areas have been defined for slices. All the areas outlined by the red lines are where Fireworks will slice the unsliced areas (if you choose that option).

Code the links

The navigation area in this design contains multiple symbols. To add links, simply select one of the buttons and type the URL into the Link field in the Property inspector. Don't forget to add your Alternative text too.

If you need to change any button names, double click to open the Button editor, make your edit, and then click Done.

Optimize the slices

1. Select the slice in the center of the page named `largetextbox.gif`. In the Property inspector, change the Type to HTML. Any text typed below this slice will be rendered as HTML and not as an image. You can add the text here in Fireworks or in Dreamweaver.

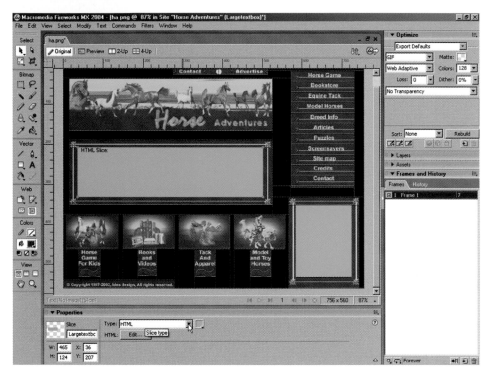

Prior to exporting you need to optimize your slices.

2. *SHIFT*+select the large top banner and each of the small collage images near the bottom of the page and then open the Optimize panel. Set the export file format to JPEG and set the Quality to 60. You just set the optimization settings for all the bitmap images.

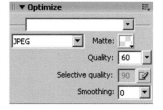

3. *SHIFT*+select all the links and border slices around the text boxes and set the export file format to GIF with 32 Colors and No Transparency.

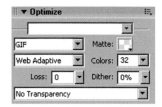

4. *SHIFT*+select the link images below the small collages and set them to GIF, 32 Colors, and Index Transparency.

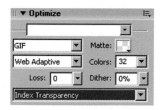

5. *SHIFT*+select the two HTML slices and change them to GIF, 2 Colors, and No Transparency. The bright green of the HTML slice will change color when you change the optimization to 2 colors.

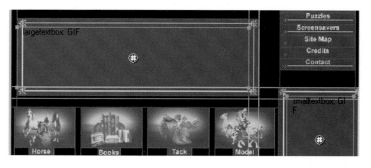

6. Select the Copyright slice at the bottom left and both the Contact and Advertise slices at the top of the page. Set these to GIF, 4 Colors, and No Transparency.

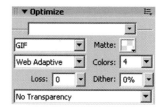

7. Save your file.

Export the file

Now that the images are all optimized, it's time to export the file.

1. Decide where you want to export the images to and choose File ➤ Export. Name the file ha.htm. In the Save as type field, ensure that HTML and Images is selected in order to export the code needed to place the images into a table and make the rollovers work.

2. Select Export HTML file from the HTML drop-down menu; then select Export Slices from the Slices drop-down menu and check Include areas without slices. This will slice the areas between the red lines. Also check Put images in subfolder and click Save.

Open the folder you just exported to. You'll see an images folder and the ha.htm file.

3. Double click the `ha.htm` file in your browser. Notice all the broken images? These are the areas without slices. The first thing we check is the images folder to be sure that the spacer.gif image is present—it is—the problem lies in one of the optimization settings.

4. Back in Fireworks, click in one of the black areas and look in the Optimize panel. It's set to TIF. Make sure that you're aware that this change is why the images are broken. The unsliced areas are solid colors, so change the export file format to GIF. (If you had gradients present, you'd choose JPEG.)

5. Export your file again and click OK to overwrite the existing files with the same names. Preview the file again in a browser.

Open your images folder in Windows Explorer or Finder. The images total 85KB. The `ha.htm` file is 21KB, which is actually larger than we normally have for a web page. The audience loves pictures of horses, though, and are willing to wait, but we'll explore other options in this project.

Export for layout in Dreamweaver

In this section, you'll learn how to export certain parts of the design in different ways. You'll export the navigation area as a Dreamweaver Library item. In addition, you'll export just images and also one area with HTML and images to use as a nested table.

Export the navigation area

1. *SHIFT*+select all the navigation button symbols at the right side of the page.

2. Choose File ➤ Export.

3. Select the Dreamweaver Library (.lbi) option from the Save as type drop-down menu. Check Selected slices only and click Save.

A warning opens saying you need to create or navigate to a Library folder. Click OK and you're presented with the Select Library dialog box. Add a folder, name it "Library", open the folder, and click Save.

Export the bottom images and rollovers

When evaluating the design to determine how to best lay it out in Dreamweaver, we decided that the bottom area with the small collages and images below it will be nearly the same as in Fireworks. We'll need spacers between the images and the link images, however. Because we've already coded the rollovers and links, it'll save time if we export the entire area including the HTML code.

> *Note: The only better way would be to export just the images and add space around the images using CSS styles (in Dreamweaver), which is beyond the scope of this book.*

1. Select the Export Area tool (on the Crop tool flyout menu).

2. Drag out the area you want to export—start at the top-left corner of the first image and drag to enclose both rows of images as seen here:

3. Double click in the export area to open the Export Preview window. Set it to GIF and 2 colors. Don't worry about the preview. Because you've made slices and optimized them, this setting will only affect the unsliced black areas.

4. Click the Export button. A warning of slice objects being ignored opens, but still click OK.

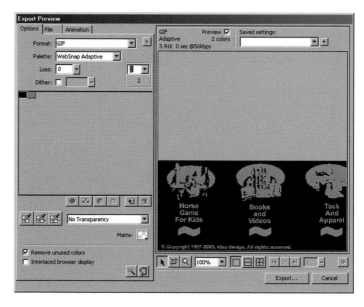

5. In the Export dialog box, navigate to the folder where you want to save. We made a new folder named btm_navigation because a lot of images will be generated and we want to keep them separate. Select HTML and Images, select Export Slices from the Slice drop-down menu, rename the file if you prefer, and then export.

6. Test out the newly exported file to see the fully functional rollovers. A copy is in the FW_DW/btm_navigation folder named ha.htm.

New slices for stretchy table

Because you're going to lay out this page in Dreamweaver, you'll use the borders around the content area in a stretchy table. This will require the four corner images and then a small slice of the horizontal and vertical lines to use as a repeating background.

1. Delete all the slices around the large content box area.

2. Zoom in to the top-right corner. Make your rulers visible (View ➤ Rulers) and drag four guides to completely enclose the little burst design, as shown here:

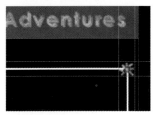

3. Select the Slice tool and drag a slice over the burst design.

4. Name the slice "tbl_tright". Repeat for all four corner starbursts (the slice size is 18×16).

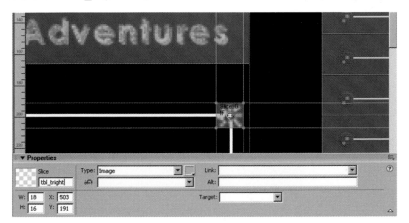

5. Draw a thin slice over the top horizontal white line. The slice is 16 pixels high matching the corner image. We made ours 5 pixels wide. Name the slice "tbl_thorz".

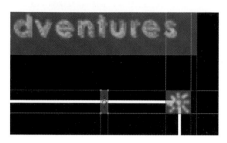

> Note we use tbl in front of each image name so that images for the table will be easy to find in the Assets panel in Dreamweaver, which lists the images alphabetically.

6. Repeat for the remaining three sides. The vertical sides need to be 18 pixels wide.

7. Optimize the lines as GIFs using 2 colors. Make the corner bursts GIF and 32 colors.

Export images only

When you want to have total control over placing your images in a Dreamweaver layout, you'll need to export each slice. For this example, we'll only export the slices that we haven't already exported. In your site, be sure you export every image—one way or the other.

1. Select the large banner.

2. *SHIFT*+select the Contact and Advertise slices.

3. Zoom in to the table slices. If they're too small, you won't be able to select them. Press *SHIFT* and select each corner and each vertical and horizontal line slice.

4. *SHIFT*+select the Copyright slice.

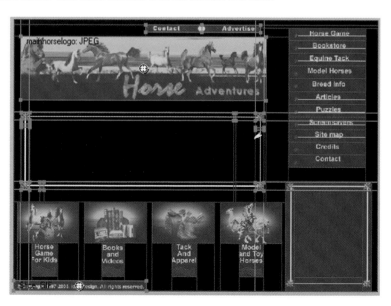

5. Right/*Ctrl*+click and select Export Selected Slice.

6. In the Export dialog box select Images Only from the Save as type drop-down menu.

The Selected slices only option is checked. You can right click selected slices because this option is automatically selected. If you choose File ➤ Export, the option is not selected and if you are like us, you inevitably forget to select it. As you can see, we added a new folder named images_dw, because we want to keep it separate from the first images folder that was exported.

7. Click Save to export.

8. Save your ha.png file and close Fireworks.

Layout in Dreamweaver

A new feature of Dreamweaver MX 2004 is that you can work on a page without it being part of a defined site. But this isn't the best way to develop a site. Because the Horse Adventure layout is part of a site being developed, you'll want to put everything into one folder, which you'll set up in Dreamweaver as the site folder. At the end of this session, we'll show you how that will work with the new **Site Management** feature in Fireworks. If you're going to have any dynamic data (data pulled from a database), you'll need a testing server. The local testing servers for Windows users are IIS and ColdFusion. Put a copy of the site folder into the www.root folder of the testing server, or use a remote server for testing.

Define the local and remote site

1. Open Dreamweaver and define the **Local** and the **Remote** server. Choose Site ➤ Manage Sites ➤ New ➤ Site and name your site. This name can have spaces, as it has nothing to do with folder names, only your site list.

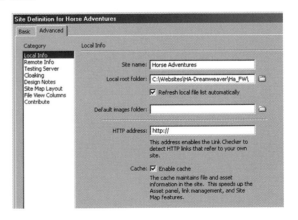

2. Click the yellow folder next to the Local root folder field and navigate to the folder that contains your site. Open the folder and click Select. Don't worry about the other fields.

3. Click the Remote Info category. In the Access field select FTP if you have a server. If you're developing locally and using IIS or ColdFusion, select Local/Network.

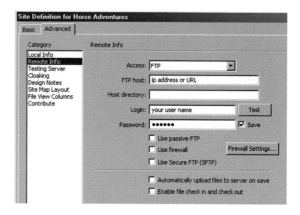

4. For FTP, fill in your host info, username, and password. For the Local Info, browse to the local folder.

5. Click OK to finish the local and remote site definitions.

6. Click the Done button and the site cache will be created. The cache will make it so your pages and images load and view in Dreamweaver more quickly.

Upload the site

All you have to do at this point is define the local portion of the website. The remote and testing servers are optional unless you want to use the Site Management features in Fireworks. These features allow you to check files in and out from Fireworks and upload and download images only or the original PNG file for sharing. The Site Management tools are most beneficial if you're working in a team. When working in such an environment, more than one person may need to use and edit the same file. The Check In and Out feature makes sure that one person doesn't overwrite another's work.

1. If you're using a Remote server, you'll need to upload your site. Open the Files panel (*F8*) and select the site folder.

2. Click the Put icon (indicated in the illustration). Because you told Dreamweaver where to connect and what your username and password are, it will automatically upload. Click OK when you see the Are you sure you want to upload the entire site? message.

3. To test locally, copy your site folder and paste it into the IIS or ColdFusion www.root folder.

If you now open Fireworks and your ha.png file, you should see the Site Management icon (the blue/green arrows) activate at the top right of your document.

Open the site generated by Fireworks

If you plan on using Fireworks to export your entire design, then be prepared to use it pretty much as is. If you start editing it in Dreamweaver, it will pretty much fall apart.

Open the ha.htm file you exported from Fireworks. We exported to different folders in the first section of this project. The Fireworks-generated page was exported to our Ha_FW folder, part of our root folder, so it's visible in the Files panel in Dreamweaver. Expand the site folder, then the Ha_FW folder, and double click the ha.htm file to open it.

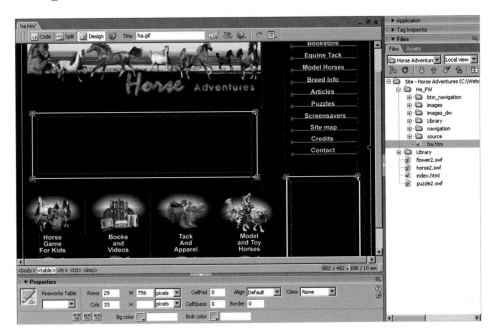

It's difficult to see what's really going on in this layout, so click the <table> tag in the status bar (bottom left of your document window). In the Property inspector, check out how many rows and columns there are—29 rows and 33 columns! Outrageous! This site will take forever to load. Also note the download statistics on the right side of the status bar: 65K. This isn't actually that bad for this many images, but you can't always believe this number. In Windows Explorer, I can see that the HTM file is 21K and the images are 82K, which doesn't equal 65K. The best way to try out the download is always to test the site in your target browser using the target connection. Once developers get high-speed access, it can sometimes become easy for them to forget to test for the many modem users.

You can close the page. You'll see a far superior way of building this page in the next section.

Laying out a web page in Dreamweaver

You'll need Dreamweaver MX 2004 (or MX) for this portion of the exercise. You can get a free 30-day trial at www.macromedia.com/downloads. You'll need to register first, but it's free and easy. Install it once you've downloaded it.

Now you'll see how you can rebuild the Horse Adventures page yourself in Dreamweaver. You'll have much more control over how the page is viewed and how it loads.

The first thing to do is a bit of house cleaning. You've exported into different folders but don't need the Fireworks ones. If you leave them, it'll mess you up later when you're using the Assets panel, which will show all images in the site—including those you don't want to use. So, make a backup of the site if you want, then delete the ha.htm file and the images folder. You should be left with the following:

★ Images_dw

★ Library

★ Btn_navigation

★ navigation

> *If you've never used Dreamweaver before, this part could be quite challenging. Dreamweaver is a complex program and teaching you the ins and outs of using Dreamweaver is beyond the scope of this book. If you want to learn how to use Fireworks and Dreamweaver to build an entire site, check out* Web Design Complete Course, *or* Dreamweaver MX 2004 Complete Course, *both by Joyce Evans (John Wiley & Sons, 2002).*

1. Now you need a new HTML page. Choose File ➤ New and select Basic page in the category. Highlight the Title field and type in "Horse Adventures sim horse game for kids". Choose File ➤ Save As and name it index.htm or default.htm depending on what your server requires.

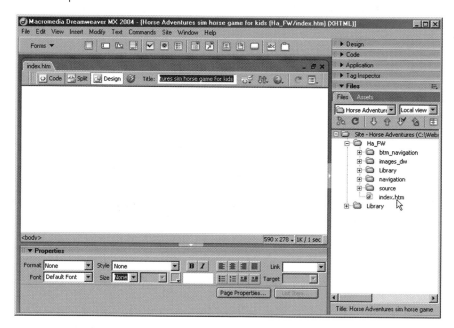

The Horse Adventures design is better suited to a "fixed" table. This means that you design the table so it's the same size no matter what the browser window size is. So, you need to decide on the size you want. Today, the lowest standard is typically 800×600 pixels, so if you make your tables about 760 pixels wide, most of you audience won't have to scroll, but the users with a larger resolution will have a lot of dead space.

> *Note that the default HTML file extension for Windows users is .htm and for Mac users it's .HTML.*

A stretchy or "fluid" table is where a portion of the design stretches to fill up the available space in a browser. We typically design a table that has both fixed and fluid columns. For instance, if the navigation is on the left side of the page, we'd set that column to a fixed width—it wouldn't change. But, the column with the content would be set to 100 percent. You can do this with the Horse Adventures design, and we'll show you how. The trade off in the current design is that the banner and images will be centered. The other option is to redesign it a bit and move the navigation around.

To layout the Horse Adventures page using the current design, you'll use two different tables. You could use one with multiple rows, but the modular table design makes loading faster and editing easier. The browser loads one table at a time.

2. Choose Insert ➤ Table. In the Insert Table dialog box, set it to 2 Rows, 2 Columns, 100 percent Table width, and zero for the other fields. Type "Layout table" into the Summary field at the bottom (this is for accessibility).

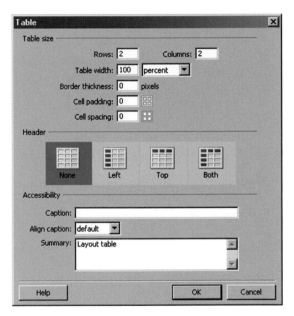

3. Click in the left side of the first row. In the Property inspector, set the Horz to Right so that anything you put in this cell will align to the right.

4. Open the Assets panel (*F11*). If you don't see a list of images, click the image icon at the top of the right column. Scroll to find `contact.gif` and then click the Insert button.

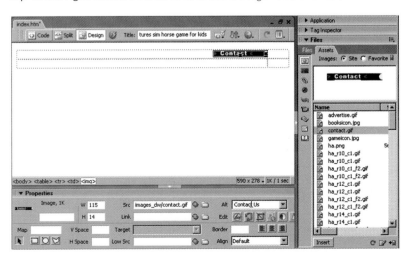

5. In the Property inspector, add your Alt text. We used "Contact Us".

6. Select `advertise.gif` in the Assets panel, click Insert, and add the Alt text.

7. Click in the left column of the second row. Locate `mainhorselogo.jpg` in the Assets panel and click Insert. Type in the Alt text.

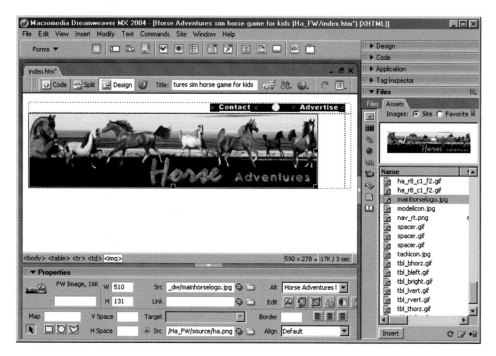

Now you'll change the vertical alignment for the entire second row. You want the images to go to the top of the cells.

8. Select the `<tr>` tag in the Tag Selector. In the Property inspector set the Vert field to Top.

9. Click in the right column of the second row. If your columns have collapsed and you can't get your cursor into it, you can select the image and press the *TAB* key.

Now you're going to quickly add the entire navigation area. This is one of the neat shortcuts you get to utilize by designing your navigation in Fireworks. If you recall, you exported this area as a Dreamweaver Library item.

A new feature in Dreamweaver MX 2004 is the Expanded Table view, which helps you select columns. Choose View ➤ Table ➤ Expanded Table Mode. *The additional space doesn't view in a browser, but it does mess up your visual design.*

10. Open the Assets panel and click the Library icon at the bottom of the icon list on the left.

11. Select the ha library item and click the Insert button. Pretty cool? Instant navigation! The best part of this is that if you want to edit this menu, you edit the Library item and the change filters through to every single page that uses the same Library item.

There's no background color yet—you'll add that using a CSS stylesheet.

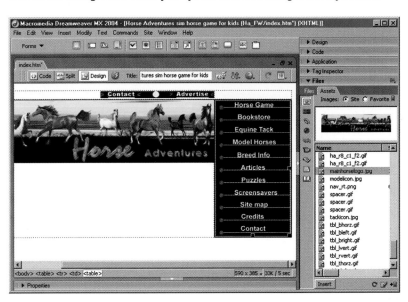

12. Preview in a browser and mouse over the links. If you had pages made for the link names, they would be fully functional.

Adding the table with corner images

The table we're going to show you how to make uses the same method as a rounded corner table, but instead of the burst images, you use rounded corner images. This table is going to be a "stretchy" or "fluid" table.

1. Select the logo image, click the right arrow key to get into the cell, and press *ENTER* to add a paragraph space.

2. Choose Insert ➤ Table. Enter 3 Rows, 3 Columns, 80 percent, and click OK.

3. Now you're going to align the table. Don't be tempted to simply center the table because doing so would add align=center tags and that code is deprecated. Select the table (select the <table> tag in the Tag Selector).

4. Choose Insert ➤ Layout Objects ➤ Div Tag. Skip Class because you don't have any styles set up yet, but give the table the ID name "content". Select Wrap around selection from the Insert drop-down menu and click OK.

5. In the Property inspector, click the align center icon. Click Split view and you'll see <div align=center>.

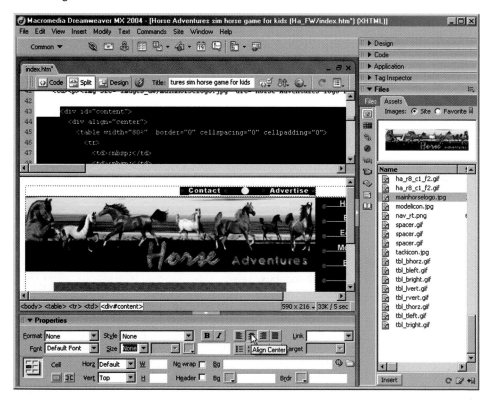

6. Click in the top-left cell and insert the `tbl_tleft.gif` image.

7. Click into the last cell of the top row and insert `tbl_tright.gif` image. Now you see why you named all the table images with the `tbl` prefix: this makes it much easier to locate them in the Assets panel.

8. Repeat for the corners of the bottom row using the bottom images.

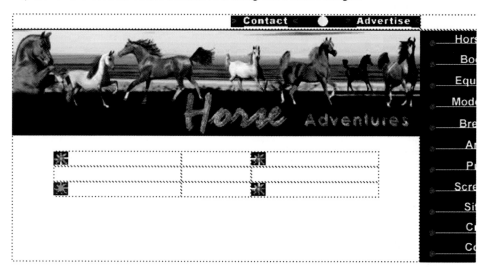

9. Select the top left image and note its width in the Property inspector (18). Press the right arrow key to place your cursor in the cell and type "18" into the width field. This will collapse the column around the images for the entire column.

10. Select the top-right image and repeat step 9.

11. Save your file.

Using CSS to style the content table

Now you need to add the lines. They're going to be done as background images. You could do it using the Property inspector but that would embed CSS code into the head of the document. A better method is to use an external stylesheet, which you'll do in this section.

1. Open the Design panel group and select CSS Styles. Click the Add New Style icon (+).

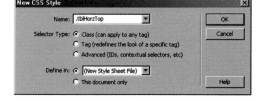

2. In the New CSS Style dialog box, select the Selector Type of Class (can apply to any tag).

3. In the Name field, type a name for the class starting with a period. You're going to use this class to set the background image of the top row. I named it `.tblHorzTop`. In the Define in field, be sure that (New Style Sheet File) is selected and click OK.

4. Your site folder should open. Name the file ha and save.

5. In the CSS Style Definition dialog box, select the Background category. Set the Background color to black.

6. Click the Browse button, navigate to the images_dw folder, select tbl_thorz.gif, and open it.

7. In the Repeat field select repeat-x. This will allow the small image to only tile horizontally. Click OK.

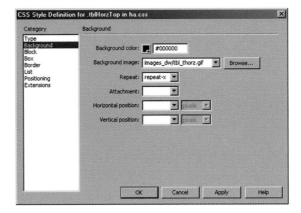

8. Click inside the top-center cell and select the <td> tag from the Tag Selector. Right/*CTRL*+click, select Set Class, and select the .tblHorzTop class. You'll see the line added to your document.

There's one more thing you need to do to ensure that the background is seen correctly in Netscape. The background image isn't considered content, and without some kind of real content in the cell, it may not preview.

9. Place your cursor in the top-center cell and insert a spacer.gif from the Assets panel. Leave the default size of 1×1 and preview the site.

10. Repeat for the bottom and two sides using the appropriate images. Use class names of

- ★ .tblHorzBottom
- ★ .tblVertLeft
- ★ .tblVertRight

11. Set the repeat for the vertical images to repeat-y.

After you set the class and add the spacers, preview it again. It probably doesn't look too good yet. Your lines may not line up with the corner images; this will be fixed next. Also note that the image in the left-bottom corner is wrong; this will also be fixed later on.

12. Click in the top-center cell and select the `<tr>` tag. Set the Vert field in the Property inspector to Top and repeat for the other two rows. Now save and preview.

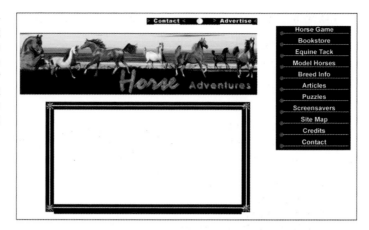

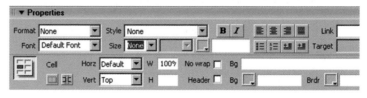

13. Now, to make the table expand or contract depending on the available space, click inside the center column. In the Property inspector set the width to 100%. You must type the percent character.

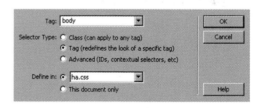

14. To change the background color of the entire page, you need to make another style. Click the New Style icon in the CSS Styles panel.

15. Select Tag (redefines the look of a specific tag) and choose body (or type it in) from the Tag drop-down menu.

16. Be sure Define in ha.css is selected and click OK.

17. Select the Background category in the CSS Style Definition dialog box and set the color to black. Click OK. Notice that you didn't have to apply the tag; it's automatically applied to the `<body>` tag.

18. Now check the site in a browser. Make the window smaller and larger and watch the table expand.

Add the bottom table

Now let's add the bottom table for the image links and small side table.

1. Click to the right of your main table. If you can't get your cursor there, then select the main `<table>` tag and press the right arrow key, or place the cursor in last right cell and press the *TAB* key.

2. Choose Insert ➤ Table. In the Insert Table dialog box, set Rows to 2, Columns to 2, 100 percent, and all zeros for the other fields.

3. Now align the table. Select the `<table>` tag in the Tag Selector.

4. Choose Insert ➤ Layout Objects ➤ Div Tag. Skip Class because you don't have any styles set up yet, but give the table the ID name "btmNav". Select Wrap around Selection and click OK.

5. In the Property inspector, click the align center icon. Click Split view and you'll see div align=center.

6. Place your cursor in the top-left cell and choose Insert ➤ Image Objects ➤ Fireworks HTML. Browse to the btm_navigation folder, select the ha.htm file, and click OK.

   Now you have to get into the code a bit but it's pretty painless.

7. Click the Split view icon and, in your document, click inside your stretchy table with the corner images and select the nearest `<table>` tag from the Tag Selector. Look in the code. It's selected but the div tags didn't get included. Press *SHIFT* and select in front of `<div id="content">`, scroll down until you see `</table>  </div>`, and *SHIFT*+click. Now copy (*CTRL/CMD+C*).

8. In the document, click in the right cell, go back to Split view, and you'll see the cursor in the `<td> </td>` tag. Highlight the ` ` code (non-breaking spacer) and paste. This pastes the table into the bottom-right cell.

9. Switch back to Design view. The table is pretty small but you'll fix that.

   You want this column to be the same size as the column in the table we just discussed that holds the navigation area.

10. Click one of the navigation buttons, then select the `<table>` tag. It's 159 pixels wide. Press the right arrow key. In the Property inspector, type "159" into the width (W) field.

11. Select your table in the bottom-right cell, then press the right arrow key. Type "159" into the width field.

12. Just to make your table view better, let's add a spacer image to hold open the center of the table until you put in real content. Click in the center of the table and insert a `spacer.gif` from the Assets panel. In the Property inspector change the height to 50.

13. Add a spacer image to the large table and make its height 100.

14. Click to place your cursor into the bottom-left cell. In the Assets panel, select ha_r20_c1 (a slice we forgot to name, so it got named by Fireworks) and click the Insert button.

15. Save your site and preview it. This is what it looks like in Netscape, full screen, on a 15-inch wide-screen monitor.

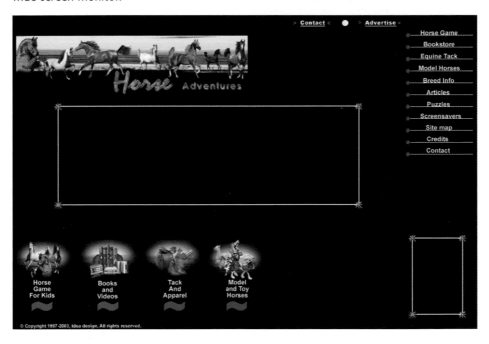

Expansion decisions

The way the design is now, if you expand the browser window, the left columns stretch to fill the space. It doesn't look good because the logo banner stays at the left side, the Contact and Advertise links move, and the content table is centered. Next, you'll see two different choices— both look better.

First, to maintain the original layout design, you need to make the main layout tables fixed so that they won't expand.

1. Click in the cell containing the Contact link and set the width to 550. The width was determined by looking at the design. The largest image content was the bottom table with the images in it. It's 550. You'll want to keep this column the same in both tables so that it looks like one seamless table. No one will ever know (unless they read your code!).

   Because the top row is the same table as the logo image and the content table, it receives the same width setting automatically.

2. Click to the right of the bottom navigation images. Be sure the cursor is in the cell and set the width to 550.

3. The table's total width will now be 709 (550 plus 159). Click inside the top table and select the `<table>` tag. Change the width to 709 pixels.

4. Repeat for the bottom table.

5. The bottom table image is larger than the logo image and you want the two top links to line up with the logo image. Click to the right of the Advertise image and insert a `spacer.gif`. Make it 40 pixels wide.

6. Save and preview the file. Now, even when the browser window is expanded, the design is maintained.

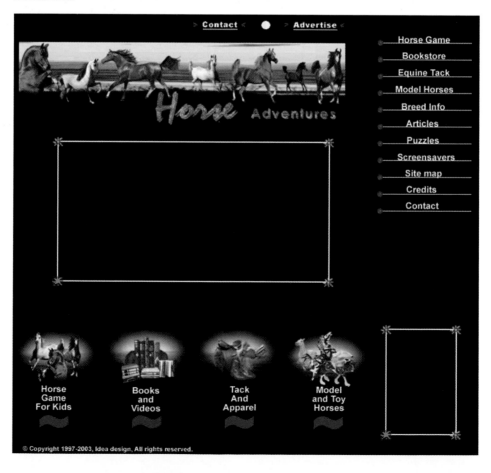

7. However, if you want the left column where the content goes to be flexible, you can do that too. The first step is to return the two tables' widths back to 100 percent. Select each table and make the change.

8. You can delete the spacer to the right of the Advertise image. Set the width of this cell to 100 percent and the Horz field to Center.

9. Repeat for the logo cell, the bottom navigation cell, and the copyright cell.

10. Click in the bottom-right cell (the Copyright row), insert a `spacer.gif`, and make the width 159.

11. Save the file as `index2.htm` and preview it. Expand and contract the browser window.

expanded view

contracted view

Editing images

In this section, you'll see how to use the Fireworks Site Management feature and how to edit an image directly in Dreamweaver. We'll start within Dreamweaver.

1. Select the Advertise image. It wasn't optimized properly and the colors aren't accurate.

2. Click the Edit button in the Property inspector. A dialog opens asking if you want to edit the GIF or use a source PNG file. We saved the image as a PNG to show you how this feature works.

> *If the image you want to edit the PNG file in isn't separate, you can't use the `ha.png` because the table structure isn't the same.*

3. Select use PNG. Navigate to the source folder and select advertise.png.

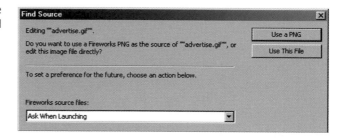

4. In Fireworks, change the number of colors in the Optimize panel to 8 and then click the Done button. The image will be exported and updated automatically in Dreamweaver.

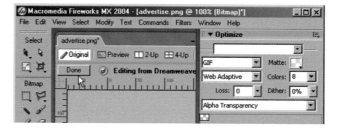

5. Close Dreamweaver and open Fireworks. Navigate to the sites\images_dw folder and open tbl_bleft.gif.

Notice that the Site Management icon is active. This is because you opened a file from a defined site with a remote server. You can change this image and then put it to the server, but in this case, that isn't much help because it's an optimization problem. You really need to edit the source. We don't see a lot of use for this feature because we always have our source available and it's the better way to edit. However, in this case, this feature is useful to you, so we wanted to show you how to use it.

6. If you get a corrupted file or a colleague uploaded a new version, you can download a file from the remote server by clicking the Site Management button and selecting Get.

7. Close the file.

8. Open the ha2.png file from the source folder. Zoom in to the bottom-left corner table image. Select it (with slice view turned on) and, in the Optimize panel, change the number of Colors to 32.

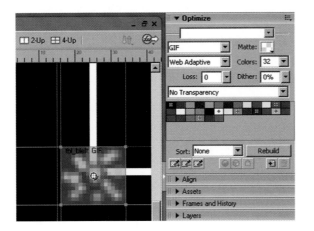

You may notice when you change the GIF color setting that it's already set properly. We noticed that when a group of images were selected and exported, one didn't optimize properly. We think it's a Fireworks glitch. Just reexport the image.

9. Right/*CTRL*+click and select Export selected slice. Be sure to save it in the images_dw folder and click OK to overwrite it.

Check in/out site management

Now let's take a quick look at the **check in / out** features of Site Management. Remember the following things you need to do if you want to use this feature:

★ Define a site in Dreamweaver.

★ Set up the Remote Info.

★ Export your files into the site root folder.

★ Save your Fireworks source file somewhere within the site folder.

Get will copy the version on the remote server to your local root folder. This will overwrite your local version.

Put will copy your version of the file to the remote server. This will overwrite the remote version.

Check Out only works if you've set the Dreamweaver preferences to use check in and out. If you have, the option will be available. It will overwrite the local version with the remote version. You make this selection in the Remote Info category of the Site Definition dialog box. You'll also see additional options where you can enter a checkout name and an email address so that others know how to contact you if you have an image.

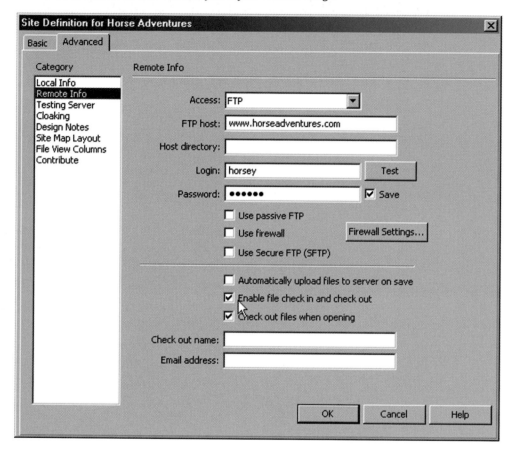

Check In will check the local file in, which will overwrite the remote version. This also has to be enabled in Dreamweaver in the Remote Info category.

Summary

You sure covered a lot of ground in this chapter. You saw how to optimize a layout made in Fireworks and export it as a complete, fully functional web page. However, you saw that you could export every image to use in a layout editor such as Dreamweaver. The best of both worlds was to export parts of the layout as images only, then to export a portion as a Dreamweaver Library item, and still another portion as a table with images that you simply inserted into the Dreamweaver layout. By placing the pieces into Dreamweaver yourself, you gain a lot of control over your page. You're able to add stylesheets, and then you can easily edit the structure to resize when the browser window resized.

Media Player Interface

In this chapter

You'll make a futuristic interface to display movies that will be added using Flash and limber up your vector skills along the way. The design used here was supplied by Eyeland Studio Inc. (www.eyelandstudio.com), which specializes in Flash interfaces. It's part of their Photoshop Foundry collection. Of course, you won't need Photoshop for this design because we're going to show you how to do it in Fireworks. The starting image is a flattened bitmap that you'll use as a guide only.

Making the center ellipse

1. Start a new 450×350 canvas with a white background.

2. Draw a 320×165 ellipse with no stroke and a Gradient ➤ Cone fill. Work from left to right across the gradient bar, using the following colors:

★ #568FC5

★ #65BACA

★ #B5BCE5

★ #C77273

3. Select the ellipse and adjust the gradient handle to a color position you like.

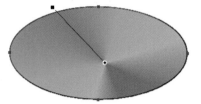

4. Go to Edit ➤ Clone (*CTRL/COMMAND+SHIFT+D*) twice. Select the bottom image and choose Modify ➤ Alter Paths ➤ Expand Stroke. Select the options shown here and click OK.

5. Change the fill category to Solid and a dark gray color (#333333).

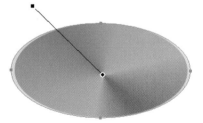

6. In the Layers panel, select the top oval and choose Modify ➤ Transform ➤ Numeric Transform. Choose Scale and reduce it to 80%.

7. Fill this oval with a solid color of #B5BCE5.

8. Change the Edge to Feather with a value of 5.

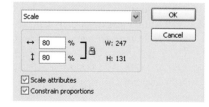

9. Select the center oval and choose Bevel and Emboss ➤ Inner Bevel from the Effects menu with the following values:

* ★ Bevel edge shape: Smooth
* ★ Width: 20
* ★ Everything else: default

10. To the oval on top, add Shadow and Glow ➤ Inner Shadow from the Effects menu with the following values:

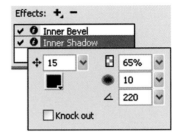

* ★ Distance: 15
* ★ Softness: 10
* ★ Angle: 220
* ★ Opacity: 65% (default)

11. Now add another Inner Shadow with these values:

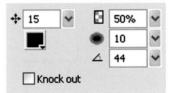

* ★ Distance: 15
* ★ Opacity: 50%
* ★ Softness: 10
* ★ Angle: 44

This is how your interface should look so far.

12. Save your document and leave it open; you'll be coming back to it shortly. A copy is saved in the download folder as oval.png.

Center screen

Next you'll make the center burgundy colored screen as seen in the starting image. This will be the default screen the user sees before a movie plays.

1. Open screen_bk.png from the download files.

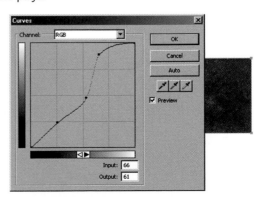

2. Choose Adjust Color ➤ Curves from the Effects menu and make a curve similar to this one. Look closely at the green background and you'll see white spots that have become more predominate and could resemble stars.

3. Choose Adjust Color ➤ Hue/ Saturation from the Effects menu, and use the settings shown here:

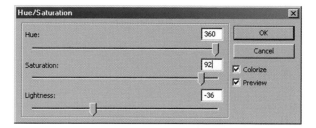

4. Choose Adjust Color ➤ Levels from the Effects menu. Select the midtone color eyedropper and sample from the darker areas on the image. You're darkening the dark spots.

Your background should be similar to this one.

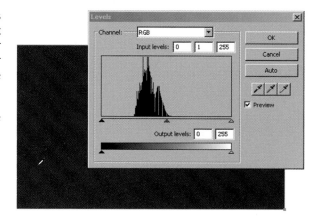

5. Save this file as screen.png and close it.

6. Go back into the document you were working on previously (oval.png), draw another oval, and make it 225×113 pixels. Position it in the center of the main shape.

7. Select this new oval, click the Fill category drop-down menu, and choose a fill type of Pattern ➤ Other.

8. Navigate to the screen.png file you just made (or use the download file) and click Open. You should now have the burgundy star pattern filling the oval.

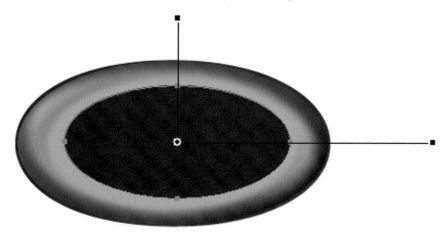

Curve support

You're now going to draw a shape that goes around the screen and curve edges.

1. With your oval file open, choose File ➤ Import and navigate to the download files for this chapter. Open tracing1.jpg and click in the document to place it. Lower the opacity to 50% and position the imported file over your oval.

2. Select the Pen tool with a 2-pixel-wide black stroke and no fill. Click the bottom of the left curve, click again at the peak, and drag up and to the right, adjusting the drag until it fits the curve.

3. Click to place a point at each of the locations shown here but with one exception. When you reach number 6, click and drag to fit the curve, and then click 7.

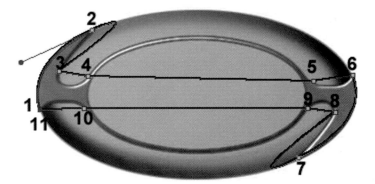

4. Select the Subselection tool. At point 2, click and drag the top Bezier handle toward the point to tighten the inner curve.

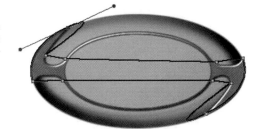

5. Click point 3. Press the *ALT/OPTION* key and drag down to turn this straight line into a Bezier curve. Drag until it fits the contour of the shape of the left side of the large curve only.

6. Click point 4. Press the *ALT/OPTION* key and drag up to turn this straight line into a Bezier curve. Drag until it fits the contour of the shape of the left side of the large curve only.

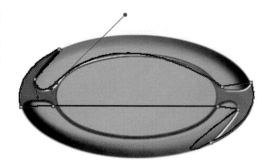

7. Click point 5 and move it up a bit higher on the large curve. You may need to adjust the Bezier handle of point 4 again, but now you'll get a better fit.

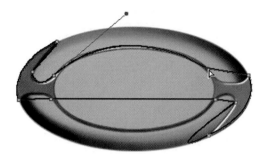

8. Select point 5. Press the *ALT/OPTION* key and drag down, dragging until the curve fits.

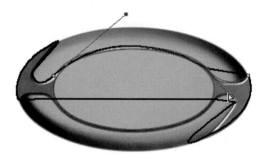

9. Click point 7. Click and drag the lower handle on the left toward the point to fit the inside curve.

10. Click point 8, then press *ALT/OPTION* and drag up until the curve fits.

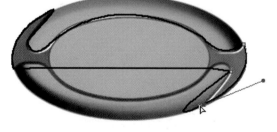

11. Click point 9, then press *ALT/OPTION* and drag down to fit the right side. Move point 10 as shown here and adjust the handle for point 9 if you need to.

12. Click point 11, press *ALT/OPTION*, and drag up until the curve fits.

It takes practice to get good with the Pen tool but it's very versatile once you learn how to use it well.

13. Save your file. A copy is saved as `oval2.png` in the download file.

Shading the shape

Next you're going to give the support shape you made some color and depth.

1. Select the support shape and set the stroke to null and the fill to the solid color #808080.

2. Select the Pen tool and click in the center of the curve on the left side, click again, and drag to form the curve. Click again, as shown here, and drag to follow the curve.

3. Change the stroke to Air Brush ➤ Basic, make the stroke width 4, and change the Edge to 50.

4. Add two more shading lines using the same techniques and same stroke settings.

5. Select the first highlight line you just made and choose the Path Scrubber Subtractive tool (in the Freeform tool flyout).

6. Zoom in to the right edge, click near the point once, move to the left a bit, and click again. Do this until the edge appears as if the highlight is fading into the shape. Repeat for the left edge at the first point.

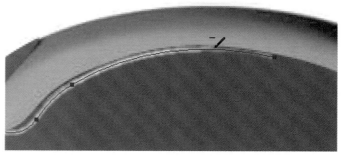

7. Select the large gray shape and choose Bevel and Emboss ➤ Inner Bevel from the Effects menu with the following values:

- ★ Bevel edge shape: Smooth
- ★ Width: 5
- ★ Everything else: default settings

8. *SHIFT*+select the shape and the three highlights from the Layers panel. Group them together (*CTRL/CMD*+G) and change the object name to "support".

9. Delete the tracing image object and drag the support object below the burgundy screen.

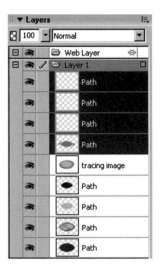

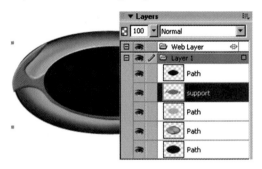

10. Draw a new oval shape with the following properties:

- ★ Fill: none
- ★ Stroke: Basic ➤ Soft Rounded
- ★ Stroke width: 8 pixels
- ★ Edge: 30
- ★ Stroke color: #808080
- ★ Oval dimensions: 208×114

Position the shape over the burgundy center. Adjust your width if any burgundy shows through.

11. Choose Bevel and Emboss ➤ Inner Bevel from the Effects menu, with the following settings:

- ★ Bevel edge shape: Smooth
- ★ Width: 8
- ★ Softness: 2
- ★ Default opacity and angle

12. Use your keyboard arrow keys to place this new shape just under the white highlight that's part of the support group. Move it so the white can just be seen.

13. Select the burgundy screen shape and change its size to 205×113, positioning it under the bevel you just added. You may need to use different settings depending on the shape you ended up with.

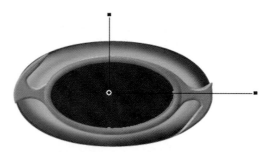

14. Select the support shape and ungroup it. Using the Subselection tool, make any changes necessary to smooth out the curves or to fit the center bevel. When you look at the following figure, you can see that we need to bring in the curve a bit at the top right.

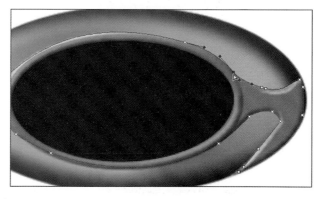

And here's the finished main shape:

15. Save the file. (A copy is saved as oval3.png in the download files.)

Outside curve shapes

Now you'll make the funky curved shapes that go on either side of the interface.

1. Open `tracing2.jpg` from the download files.

2. Trace this shape using the Pen tool with a stroke size of 1, color black, and no fill.

3. Move the new shape off the tracing shape so that you can see what you are doing. Change the stroke to null, the Fill category to Gradient ➤ Cone, and place gradient color boxes as shown here. The color codes from left to right are

   ★ #5799C4

   ★ #6EBECD

   ★ #C5C1E9

   ★ #B8747B

Original

Cone Gradient

Contour Gradient

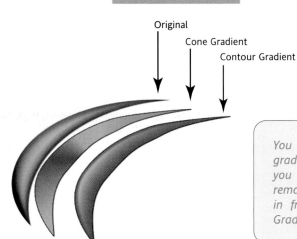

> You may want to try the Contour gradient as well to see which one you prefer. For the contour, we removed the light blue color marker in front of the pink one in the Gradient editor.

We weren't able to match the gradient perfectly to the original. We prefer the cone gradient so that's the one we're going to use.

4. Choose Bevel and Emboss ➤ Inner Bevel from the Effects menu using these values:

   ★ Bevel edge shape: Smooth

   ★ Size: 5

   ★ Softness: 3

5. Now choose Shadow and Glow ➤ Inner Shadow from the Effects menu with these settings:

   ★ Distance: 10

   ★ Softness: 10

   ★ Angle: 21

6. Clone the shape and change the fill of the bottom copy to black, remove the effects, and lower the opacity to 40 percent.

7. Increase the height and width of this shape by 2 pixels and press the up and left arrow keys once each.

8. *SHIFT*+select the two new shapes, group them, and add a 1-pixel-wide black stroke. Copy and paste this group into your working document. Make a second copy and choose Transform ➤ Rotate 180, using this image as a guide for placement.

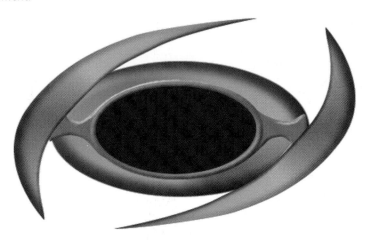

9. Save the file. (A copy is saved as oval4.png in the download folder.)

10. Using the Pen tool with no fill and a 1-pixel black stroke, draw the shape shown here and fill it with a linear gradient. For the color boxes in the gradient, use black, dark gray, white, dark gray, and black. Adjust the gradient handles until it looks like this image.

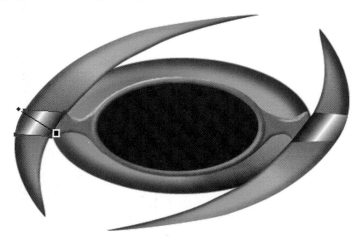

11. Repeat step 10 to create a similar shape at the opposite side.

12. Use the Pen tool with a light gray stroke, Basic ➤ Soft Line, a stroke size of 2, and an Edge of 50. Draw a line right along the top edge of the left gradient shape you just made.

13. Edit ➤ Clone this line and press the up arrow key twice. Change the stroke color to dark gray. Repeat this for the bottom of the shape, but this time, make the line against the edge black and the lower line light gray.

14. Repeat the previous two steps for the right side of the shape.

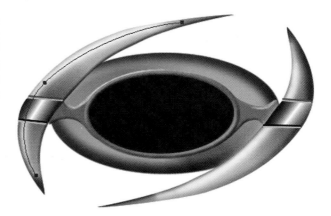

15. To add highlights to the curved shapes, use the Pen tool to draw the contour of the top-left side. Use a white Air Brush ➤ Basic stroke at size 20 with an Edge of 100.

16. Move this path to just above the shape in the Layers panel so that it's below the gray gradient you added. Use the Subselection tool to refine any of the paths points to fit the contour nicely.

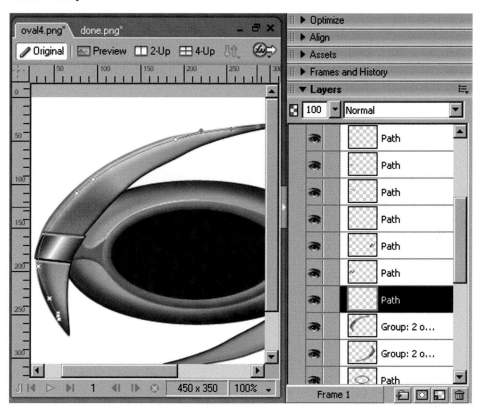

17. Use the Path Scrubber Subtractive tool on each end to taper it.

18. Make a clone, change the stroke size to 10, and move it down by 2 pixels. Make any adjustments to the edges to taper them.

19. Repeat the previous four steps for the inside curve on the right side.

20. Save the file. (A copy is saved as oval5.png in the download folder.)

Side buttons

Now you'll add the neat little buttons that go on top of the gray gradient overlays you made. They're decorative only—not real buttons.

1. Draw a 22×22 oval with no stroke and filled dark gray.

2. In the Effects menu, choose Bevel and Emboss ➤ Inner Bevel with the following settings:

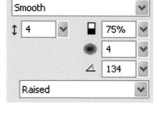

   ★ Bevel edge shape: Smooth
   ★ Width: 4
   ★ Softness: 4
   ★ Angle: 134

3. Now add a Shadow and Glow ➤ Inner Shadow with these settings:

   ★ Distance: 4
   ★ Softness: 3
   ★ Angle: 145

4. Use the Pen tool to add a small highlight at the top left of the oval. Use a white Air Brush ➤ Basic stroke with size of 2.

5. Use the Path Scrubber Subtractive tool and click once on each end of the highlight to taper it.

6. *SHIFT*+select the button and highlight and group them. Clone and position each button above the gradient shapes at either side of the interface.

7. To make the buttons more realistic, add an inner sphere. Draw a 13×13 oval with a black Basic ➤ Soft Rounded stroke, at size 2 and Edge 50.

8. Fill the oval with a radial gradient using white to black. Zoom in close, select the object with the Pointer tool, and move the white portion to the top-left area.

9. With the Pen tool, draw a line using a Basic ➤ Soft Rounded, white, size 3 stroke. Make the line's width 1 and place it at the bottom of the sphere.

10. Clone the little line and change the stroke to 1 pixel and Basic ➤ Hard Rounded. Make a clone and move it up to the top highlight area.

11. In the Layers panel, select the sphere and all the highlights and group them. Clone this group and repeat for the other side.

12. Make a copy of this button group and position it at the right side of the interface.

Here's the interface so far with a background added (screen_bk.png). The next step is to resize the interface to use in Flash and then add the buttons that will be used to load the movies.

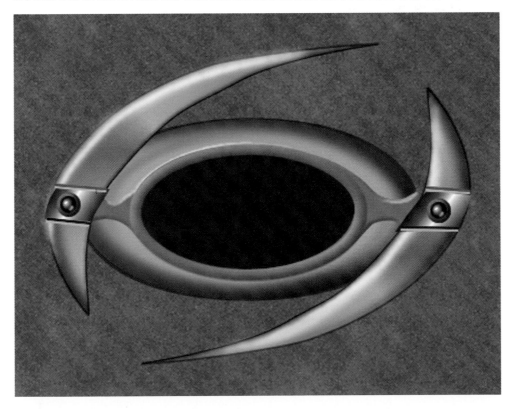

Resizing the interface

Remember we told you that by drawing this interface using vector tools it would remain editable and scalable? Well now you get to experience just that. When this design was originally made, it wasn't intended for a Flash interface so it's too small to show any movies in. Now you'll see how to resize the interface without losing any image quality.

1. Open the `interface_png` file from the download files. This is the same as the previous example, but without the background.

2. Select everything on the canvas (*CTRL/CMD+A*) and group (*CTRL/CMD+G*) the shape.

3. In the Property inspector, change the width to 604 and the height to 388.

4. Choose Modify ➤ Canvas ➤ Canvas Color. **Select** Transparent and click OK.

5. Choose Modify ➤ Canvas ➤ Fit Canvas.

6. Notice that the image still looks as good as it did at the small size. Save the file as `interface2.png`.

Making the shape for the buttons

Now you'll make the navigation buttons. They will follow the contour of the main oval, so you'll use the oval as a punch to get the right angles.

1. Open `button.png` from the download files. This file contains two of the oval shapes from the original design. You'll be using the colored one as a cookie cutter.

2. Select the gray oval, lower the opacity to about 50 percent, and move the shape down below the multicolored one. This new shape is going to be used for buttons that will go below the interface shape.

3. Change the fill to the Bars gradient and use a dark gray and white color.

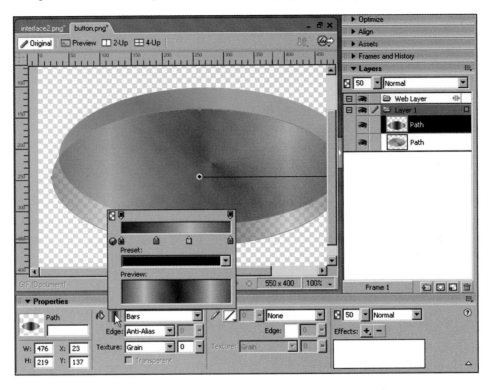

4. Select the gray shape and change the opacity back to 100 percent.

5. Adjust the gradient keeping in mind that only the bottom portion will be seen once the shape is punched.

The colorful shape will be used to punch the shape for the buttons.

6. In the Layers panel, click and drag the colored shape to the top of the stack. *SHIFT*+select both shapes on the canvas.

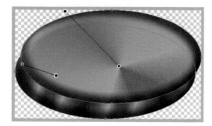 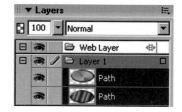

7. Choose Modify ➤ Combine Paths ➤ Punch.

8. Notice that the fill is now too dark. In the Effects menu of the Properties inspector, click the check mark to the left of both inner shadow effects to turn them off. Click the little i next to the Inner Bevel and change the width to 10.

 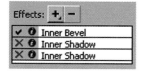

Making the buttons

Now that you have the shape made for the buttons, you need to cut it up so it can function as individual buttons.

1. Select the new shape and choose Modify ➤ Flatten Selection. You're going to use the Marquee selection tool next and it won't work on the vector shape.

2. Select the Marquee tool and draw a marquee around the button end. Copy and paste (the marquee will snap to the shape).

3. Be sure you have rulers visible (View ➤ Rulers) and drag out a guide to the right side of the marquee as a marker, then deselect all (*CTRL/CMD*+D).

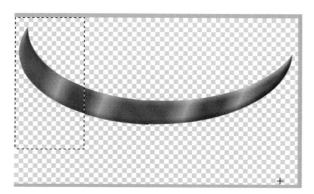

4. Select the large shape in the Layers panel (not the pasted new shape) and make a selection next to the ruler as shown below. Drag out another guide, copy, paste, and deselect.

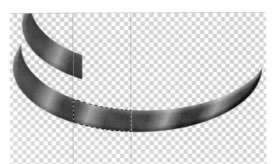
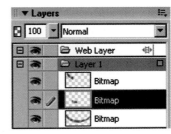

5. Select the large shape again and make another selection to include the rest of the shape. Copy, paste, and deselect.

6. Select the large shape in the Layers panel and delete it.

7. Separate your three new shapes. Select them one at a time, right/*CTRL*-click, and select Add Slice. Name each slice in Property inspector. (We named ours "button1", "button2", and "button3".)

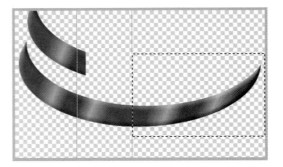

8. In the Optimize panel, use GIF as the export file format (it's important for the background of this interface to be transparent), change the number of Colors to 256 and set the Matte to none.

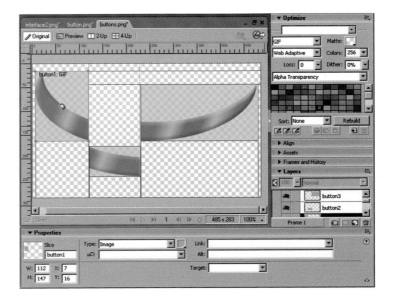

9. *SHIFT*+select all 3 slices, right/*CTRL*-click, and select Export Select Slice. In the Export dialog box notice that the Selected slices only option is checked. Because your slices are already named, don't worry about the File name field. Navigate to your sites folder and click Save to export.

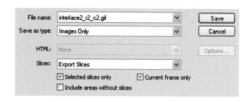

10. Save your file as buttons.png and close it.

Import into Flash MX 2004

You'll need Flash MX 2004 for the next part of this tutorial (Flash MX Professional 2004 is fine too). Nothing in this exercise uses features that aren't in both programs. If you don't have Flash, you can pick up a 30-day trial version from Macromedia at www.macromedia.com/downloads. You'll need to register if you haven't already, but it's free.

You'll be using the interface you just made in Flash; you'll make the burgundy screen area ready for a movie to play in it, and you'll add the button you'll need to use for the code that will make your movie play.

1. Open Flash. Click Flash Document in the Create New column of the Flash MX 2004 start page.

2. Click the Settings button in the Property inspector. Change the stage width to 620 pixels, its height to 440, and the background color to black.

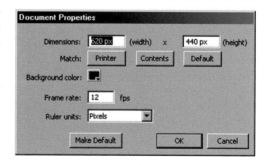

3. Choose File ➤ Import ➤ Import to Stage and navigate to the folder where you saved interface2.png (or use the download file). Select and open it.

4. The Import Fireworks PNG Import Settings dialog box opens. Check Import as a single flattened bitmap and click OK.

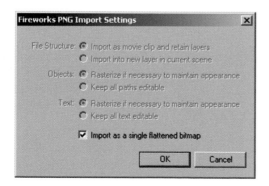

Note that Fireworks paths and vectors can be maintained in Flash, but for this design, because of the gradients, this would have imported horribly. This is why you flattened the image in Fireworks prior to importing it into Flash.

5. Double click the layer name in the timeline and rename it "interface".

6. To position the image, open the Align panel (Window ➤ Align) and center both horizontally and vertically to the stage.

7. Save the file (File ➤ Save as) as interface.fla.

Creating the movie mask

Let's make a mask that will allow a movie to display through just the center burgundy portion of the interface.

1. Add a new layer in the timeline by clicking the Add new layer (+) icon. Double click the layer name and rename it "buttons".

2. Choose File ➤ Import ➤ Import to Library. Navigate to your site folder, select all three button GIF files you exported earlier in the project, and click Open.

3. If you press *F11*, you'll see your bitmap image and three buttons stored in the Library. (These buttons are also included in the download files.)

4. Click and drag button1 from the Library onto the stage. Position the button as shown here.

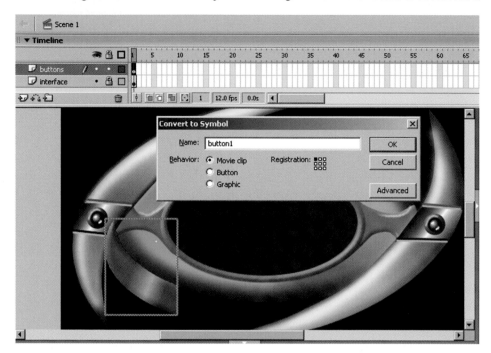

5. Go to Modify ➤ Convert to Symbol. Name it "button1" and select the Movie clip behavior.

6. Click and drag both button2 and button3 out of the Library and onto the stage. Repeat step 5 and name the buttons appropriately, referring to the image here for placement. Don't worry about the buttons covering part of the interface. We left a small space between button1 and button2, but you don't need to if you'd prefer to have a seamless shape.

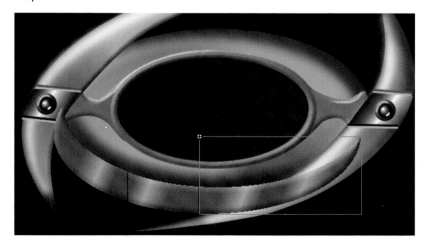

7. Drag the buttons layer to the bottom of the timeline.

8. Select the interface layer and add a new layer called "movieHolder".

9. Go to Insert ➤ New Symbol and create a new symbol called "movieHolder" with a Movie clip behavior.

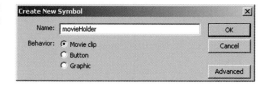

10. Click Scene 1 and switch on the guides' visibility (View ➤ Guides ➤ Show Guides) and rulers (View ➤ Rulers). Drag out four guides to form a frame around the burgundy "screen" in the center of your interface.

11. Select frame 1 of the movieHolder layer and drag out a copy of movieHolder from the Library. Place it at the top left intersection of your guides.

12. Add a new layer at the top of your timeline and call it "mask".

13. Select frame 1 of the mask layer and ensure that guide snapping is on (View ➤ Snapping ➤ Snap to Guides). Select the Oval tool and draw an ellipse that completely covers your burgundy screen, dragging from the top left intersection of the guides to the bottom right corner. The fill or stroke colors don't matter, as they'll be invisible when you convert it to a mask. It's just important that the ellipse is exactly the same shape as the burgundy screen.

14. Right/CTRL-click the mask layer and choose Mask from the context menu. Notice the layer icons have now changed, indicating that the mask layer is masking the movieHolder layer.

Button editing in Fireworks

The buttons you imported from Fireworks need text added to them. You can add text in Flash but Fireworks has a nice Text on Path feature so you can get a contoured shaped text.

1. Open the Library and double click the button1 symbol to open the Symbol Editor.

2. With the button selected on the stage, right/*CTRL*-click the button and choose Edit with Fireworks. In the pop-up, choose Use this file and Fireworks will open.

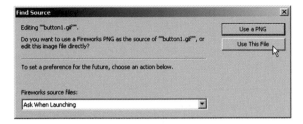

3. Select the Pen tool with a 1-pixel black stroke and click near the top left of the button. Drag to near the end of the button, forming a slight curve to follow the curve of the button.

4. Type in some text for the movie. We used 25-point Verdana, bold, with a black color.

5. *SHIFT*+select the text and the line.

6. Choose Text ➤ Attach to Path. Move the text if you need to.

7. Once you've finished editing your button, click the Done button at the top left of the document. The file will be automatically saved and the symbol updated in the Flash Library.

8. Back in Flash the text has been added to the button.

Loading an external movie

You're now going to make an external SWF movie load into the movieHolder movie clip when the user clicks button1. Because this movie clip is masked, only the area behind the elliptical mask shows through. This provides the illusion that the external movie is playing on the elliptical screen.

1. Exit the Symbol Editor and go back to the main timeline by clicking the Scene 1 button at the top left of the document.

2. Select button1 on the stage and give it the instance name button1_mc. Do this by clicking in the field that currently says <Instance Name> (in the Property inspector) and then typing "button1_mc" into the field.

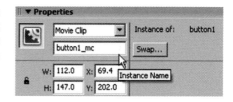

3. Insert a new layer at the top of your timeline and name it "actions".

4. Make sure frame 1 of the actions layer is selected in your timeline and open the Actions panel (F9). Click in the right pane and type in the following ActionScript code:

It can be difficult to select the button because the interface covers it. Try hiding the interface layer in the timeline, selecting the button, naming it, and then turning the interface visibility back on.

```
this.button1_mc.onRelease = function() {
  loadMovie("video1.swf", movieHolder_mc);
};
```

The onRelease function executes the loadMovie action when you click and release button1_mc When this happens, Flash loads a movie called video1.swf into movieHolder_mc, the instance of the masked movie clip on the stage.

5. Grab video1.swf from the download files and save it in the same folder as your interface.fla.

6. Save your file and choose Control ➤ Test Movie.

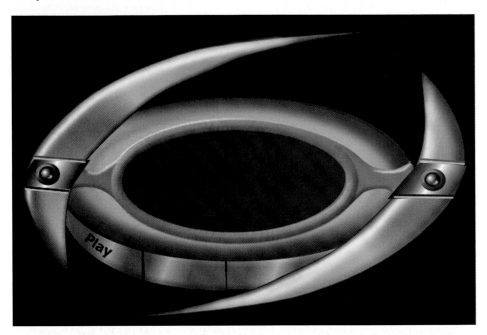

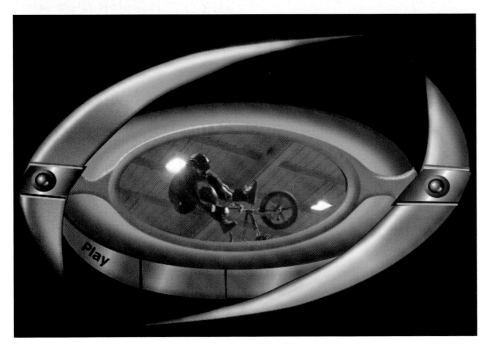

Index

Index

Index

Index